MEN ♂ PAUSE AND PONDER ...

STEVE McEWEN

BALBOA.PRESS
A DIVISION OF HAY HOUSE

Balboa Press books may be ordered through booksellers or by contacting:

Balboa Press
A Division of Hay House
1663 Liberty Drive
Bloomington, IN 47403
www.balboapress.co.uk
UK TFN: 0800 0148647 (Toll Free inside the UK)
UK Local: 02036 956325 (+44 20 3695 6325 from outside the UK)

Print information available on the last page.

ISBN: 978-1-9822-8338-4 (sc)
ISBN: 978-1-9822-8339-1 (e)

Balboa Press rev. date: 04/26/2021

Dedicated to 'Penny Poo'

– my long suffering wife ... and all my family ...

.... along with all the amazing Nursing
teams at Russell's Hall and Queen
Elizabeth hospitals

CONTENTS

PREFACE

This book is not a scientific or a medically researched piece of work, deliberately not so! It tells the stories of four modern day men in a humorous, fictional context, to promote discussion and to raise awareness and acceptance of the Male Menopause condition. This condition is referred to in a few serious medical journals but is otherwise subordinated to many other issues that affect our modern day lives. It's time to raise the flag and develop awareness of the Male Menopause in our society to ensure it becomes increasingly understood, accepted, and supported!

The behaviour of the Male members of the human species is based on three founding instincts, all beginning with the letter 'P'. They are Provision, Protection and Procreation. Going back to the origins of the human species, our male forefathers were active hunters and latterly farmers, ensuring food was provided for their families. They also developed weapons and built homes to protect their families and were driven by sexual urges to procreate with their female counterparts.

So how do these founding instincts translate into the behaviours of modern man?

The stories in this book are based on the lives of four fictional males - John, Tony, Paul and Steve. They follow the development and experiences of these males from children to young men, through to adulthood and into old age. These stories suggest that adult male behaviour is determined at an early stage in child development, that these formative years are all important in helping us understand why certain issues are important to us in our adult lives.

This is particularly relevant in boys, to understand and debate their intriguing journey through into manhood and then those twilight years.

This edition is referred to as MM1. Further editions (MM2, MM3 etc) are anticipated from other authors, all contributing to understand and debate the Male Menopause condition. The Female Menopause is evident largely by emotional and physical changes whereas by contrast, the Male Menopause is evident largely by behavioural changes, often humorous but to date quietly accommodated in our modern, busy lives.

MM1 considers the male cycle of life through six phases -Development, Discovery, Desire, Demand, Delight and Detachment.

The characters in this book are entirely fictional and any resemblance to actual human males is entirely coincidental (honestly!). This book is for Men and Women; for Men to reflect and review their own behaviours and for Women to gain an insight to the mystery of Men, what they think about and why they behave in such entertaining ways!!

So, just what is the 'Male Menopause?' Read, enjoy (& discuss please!)

**The Male Cycle of Life
Development / Discovery / Desire /
Demand / Delight / Detachment**

INTRODUCTION

The rain was falling, it was cold. John was wearing a large blue overcoat. He was standing beside his lifelong friends, Tony and Steve who were both feeling cold too, and sad. All three men were standing in the church graveyard beside the freshly dug grave of their lifelong friend Paul.

The service had been good; the vicar had not rushed the proceedings. The chapel had been packed with Paul's family and friends. Tony had given an excellent eulogy; it had caused John to think a lot about Paul and how much they would miss him.

There were just so many memories; they had first met at Primary School. Paul had always advocated you should live life to the full and, 'Make the most of every day' was something he was renowned for saying. John hadn't agreed with everything Paul had said, but that's what good friends are for, the ability to discuss and argue things that we believe in is so important in any good friendship.

John smiled as he reflected further and thought more about Paul; he particularly recalled Paul's interest in the 'Male Menopause', all four friends had discussed and debated the issue so often. It was not medically recognised, yet it was a condition that so obviously needed to be acknowledged. 'There is no such thing as the Male Menopause,' was one of the main things Paul often said jokingly and he would certainly be remembered for; they knew and understood so much more now than when they had all been younger.

John smiled to himself as he recalled those early years and everything that had happened since to all four of them.

CHAPTER 1

DEVELOPMENT PHASE
John's reflections, the early days

JOHN'S EARLIEST MEMORY was his first day at school. Mum had packed him his favourite egg sandwiches and a chocolate biscuit in case he got hungry. The school provided milk during morning break, also a cooked lunch, but Mum still felt the need to pack John off with more to eat; John felt embarrassed by this.

The uniform felt strange too, the school colours were green and yellow. The cap didn't fit properly but what was worse, John found it was only the 'new' boys that wore them. John had an elder sister who teased him at breakfast and on arrival at school some bigger boys teased him also. Mum didn't seem to notice this as she walked John across the playground to the main entrance. John felt uncomfortable in the new shirt; it had a stiff collar and tying that yellow and green stripped tie was a complete mystery. The jumper was also too big, and the trousers were loose on his waist.

When John got home that night, his Mum and Dad made eager enquiries but were then very disappointed when John said he didn't like it. He hadn't told them about his biggest concern though as his teacher, Mrs Collier, was really strict and had kept shouting at the class telling them to keep quiet and listen. She had shouted several times and each time she'd gone red in the face and the exertion caused her to spit too! John didn't really like Mrs Collier. That night, after a warm bath, John's Dad read him a story in bed. Mum came in to say 'goodnight' and they both reassured him things at school would get better. John wasn't so sure; he didn't go to sleep easily.

The following morning John felt tired; he had slept wistfully with lots of strange dreams. His Mum and Dad's eager calls 'Come on John, hurry up!' just didn't help. He had to ask his Mum not to give him any extra lunch, school meals are 'just great' he explained and told her about the mid-morning milk break too. Coat on and with that big cap on his head, John set off with his Mum. They walked to school and John thought through the day ahead, wondering whether Mrs Collier would be shouting at them again.

Arriving at school, John had no idea what was in store for him. Walking across the playground again with his Mum, he heard those older boys laughing at his oversized cap but took no notice. Hanging up his coat and satchel, he was embarrassed as his Mum kissed and hugged him goodbye, in case anyone noticed. He watched her going back across the playground and then turning back, saw another boy he recognised from his class, equally awkward in new uniform as his Mum said goodbye with a kiss and a hug. 'Work hard and behave Tony,' she said. Tony looked embarrassed also and glanced at John to see if he'd noticed. John smiled and then looked away.

The large, handheld school bell was rung by the head teacher, signalling the start of school. All the classes had to line up in the playground in their class groups. John's class were all new starters; the boys and girls were evident by those bright, clean green and yellow ill-fitting uniforms. Silence was called, Mrs Collier appeared and indicated to the boy at the front that they could proceed into the classroom but remain silent!

Entering the classroom, John was shown to his seat and was really pleased he was sitting beside Tony. They didn't talk at first, but listened to Mrs Collier marking the attendance register (you had to say 'yes Miss' in a loud, clear voice when your name was called). Mrs Collier then set out the plans for the day, which included early morning school assembly in the main hall with children from all the other classes too. When she'd finished, the children were asked to stand up and walk to the main hall in pairs, to hold hands and remain in silence.

John walked with Tony following the other children in a straight line and they didn't say a word. It felt strange to hold Tony's hand, Tony's grip was strong. It was a short walk to the main hall where Mrs Collier was at the door and directed them to sit down at the front and remain silent. The hall was full, all the bigger children from the other classes were there. They were all silent, but there was a strange feeling of anticipation in the room. John had never felt this before.

Mrs Collier then appeared at the front of the hall. She took a deep breath and said, 'All rise for your headmistress Miss Seath,' at which point all the children stood and a lady appeared through a side door. She wasn't very tall and walked with a slight limp to the front. She paused, turned to face the whole school and said, 'Good Morning children,' and the whole school responded, 'Good Morning Miss Seath,' in loud voices.

Miss Seath paused, looked around the room and then announced in a quiet voice that everyone was to sing a song called 'All things bright and beautiful'. A lady John had not seen before was playing an upright piano in the corner; she wore half rim glasses and was concentrating on the sheet music in front of her. John didn't know the song and neither did Tony, but they both mouthed and hummed as best they could. The older children seemed to enjoy it and sang with loud voices.

At the end of the song Miss Seath asked everyone to sit down again and still talking in her quiet voice, she welcomed everyone back into school. In particular, she welcomed all the new children in Mrs Collier's class and at this point the whole school clapped! John looked around him; there were lots of new faces and some of the children were really big.

Miss Seath made several other announcements that John didn't really understand. One of the girls from the top class read the story of Goldilocks, but not the same one that John's parents read to him. Finally, they all had to stand again for another song and a prayer after which Mrs Collier returned to the front of the assembly, asking everyone to dismiss in silence and return to their classrooms in their pairs.

On the way back to the classroom, John and Tony didn't talk. They sat down at their desks and then Mrs Collier announced their first lesson would be art. She passed around some large workbooks with blank sheets of paper and explained they were to share coloured wax crayons and draw something to remind them of a holiday. She also said the children could now talk amongst themselves, provided they spoke quietly.

Tony was the first to talk, rather it was a barrage of questions as if he'd been pent up by Mrs Collier's strict regime. He looked at John and asked, 'What do you like best, planes or trains?' and then many more questions about football teams, cars, colours, food and family. Initially, John was quite taken aback, but found he liked Tony's energy and inquisitiveness, so he happily answered whilst also asking Tony similar questions.

They quickly became engrossed and unwittingly their voices raised, causing Mrs Collier to come over. She was cross, her face was red again (but thankfully she didn't spit). She told them they'd not started their drawings and reminded them they could only talk quietly. 'Yes miss!' they both answered in unison, but they were embarrassed to see other children around them had noticed they'd been told off! A few minutes later the hand bell was rung again, indicating the start of mid-morning break. Mrs Collier shouted, 'Walk quietly into the playground, don't run!'

Once out in the playground John chased Tony, dodging the elder children until they were out of breath, laughing and screaming like a lot of the other children with relief at being released from the strict classroom environment. Then they noticed a lot of the children were gathered by a table under a side porch. John went first and Tony followed. They walked nearer to the table and one of the older girls beckoned them nearer and asked, 'Have you had your free milk yet?' John said, 'No,' and a small bottle (a third of a pint) was passed to him and similarly to Tony. They took the tops off and drank both, exclaiming 'WOW' as it was so cold but equally refreshing.

John and Tony stood drinking and enjoying the milk together. They then started talking about the school and progressed quickly to talking about Mrs Collier. 'Oh, she is even stricter than my Mum.' Tony said and John added, 'Have you seen how red she goes in the face and seems to shake and spit too?!' Tony smiled, nodding his head in agreement and added, 'Maybe we should call her 'Mrs Collywobbles' rather than Mrs Collier?!' John shrieked with laughter at this. Tony and John were becoming firm friends and united in adversity which they would reflect on later in their lives.

At this point the hand bell rang again and all the children lined up in their class groups. Mrs Collier appeared and invited them into their classroom but emphasised that they must remain silent. John and Tony returned to their work desks and became absorbed in developing their wax pictures; John was trying to draw his Dad's car, but it didn't look right. Equally Tony was concerned that the picture of his house didn't have the right shape and number of windows. A few minutes went by and John looked up at Tony and said, 'Tony, rather than 'Collywobbles' we could call her 'Wobblycolly?'

Tony was caught unawares by this as he'd been so absorbed in his poor drawing. He laughed out uncontrollably at John's comment and said, 'Ha! Collywobbles, Wobblycolly' in a loud voice. In that moment, he realised his error as Mrs Collier was within hearing distance and moving rapidly towards them.

The rest of the classroom fell noticeably silent as Mrs Collier raised her voice to them. 'How dare you!' she screeched, 'How very rude', and then, taking them both firmly by their arms, she escorted them over to the blackboard in the corner of the classroom. She told them to stand behind the blackboard and remain in complete silence until lunchtime. Both Tony and John felt upset and close to tears; their first week in school and they were in trouble. They were aware the other children had seen the whole thing and were whispering. John and Tony felt awkward and embarrassed, but even worse their thoughts turned to what might happen at lunchtime?

At lunchtime they heard the hand bell ring again. They heard Mrs Collier address the class to explain they could now go to the main hall for lunch in their pairs and to walk slowly. Then Mrs Collier appeared at the side of the blackboard and stared down at the two boys. Her face was stern as she said to them, 'Come here you two, follow me', and walked across to the other side of the classroom to her desk and sat down.

John and Tony felt anxious; they stood awkwardly in front of Mrs Collier's desk. She inhaled deeply and said, 'Never in my thirty five years of teaching Primary School children have I known such misbehaviour as yours in the first week. Calling out my name in such a disrespectful way will not be allowed again. I can see I need to keep a close eye on both of you and will be moving you to a table nearer to this desk, is that understood?' The two anxious boys readily replied, 'Yes miss,' at which Mrs Collier raised her eyebrows and told them to go to the main hall and that she would reorganise the classroom that very afternoon.

Once John and Tony got out of the classroom, they looked at each other, 'Phew!' said John, 'I can't believe that happened, she was so cross with us'. Tony was upset as well and said, 'I wonder where we will be moved to and who we will be sitting with?' and added, 'Will she be telling our parents?' 'Oh NO!' John said, 'that would be terrible; it was bad enough that the rest of the class saw what happened!' Both boys made their way to the main hall, in deep thought and wondering what lay in store for them later that day.

A boy from one of the top classes was standing at the door of the main hall. Apparently, he was a dinner monitor and asked which class they were from so that he could show them to their table. As they sat down, one of the girls from their class asked if they were alright. She also explained they were about to be called up to the dinner queue to collect their lunch from the kitchen hatch. At that moment the dinner monitor called them up and they collected their meals.

During lunch, several other children commented and wished John and Tony 'good luck' which was well intended, but only served to heighten the anxieties they both felt. After lunch, they were dismissed from the main hall by the dinner monitors and allowed to play in the playground. Neither John nor Tony felt like playing and wandered aimlessly around the playing area, contemplating what might happen. They discussed the likely reaction of their parents if they were to hear of the morning's incidents and imagined the shame and consequences. In Tony's case, he was an only child and explained he had never been in any sort of trouble before wanting to make his parents feel proud of him. In John's case, he explained he had an older sister and imagined the reprimands his parents would impose to make an example to his sibling. Both felt uncomfortable.

The handheld bell rang, playtime was over. John and Tony joined their class group and lined up in silence. Mrs Collier appeared and beckoned the class group into the classroom. On entering the room, Mrs Collier asked John and Tony to stand to one side. Once all the children were seated, she led them towards her desk and the nearest table. There were two other boys sat at the table that John and Tony recognised. Mrs Collier told them to sit down at the table and to remain silent.

Neither John nor Tony were aware of the notion of 'anti-climax', but that is just what happened through that afternoon; a period of calm and orderliness ensued in stark contrast to the morning's events. Mrs Collier led the class through wall chart chanting routines to learn the alphabet, number recognition and then copy writing some key words in their workbooks. Mid-afternoon and the hand bell rang; Mrs Collier dismissed the class asking them to go quietly out into the playground. John and Tony followed the two other boys from their table with a feeling of relief; the afternoon had not been as they had feared, so far!

Out in the playground the four boys stayed together and started a game of tag, chasing each other around in which one boy had the 'lurgy' and by touching any of the other boys he could pass it on. It was really great fun, there was lots of laughter.

They were all soon quite exhausted and gathered under the porch area. 'I can't believe what happened to you two this morning', said one of the boys to John and Tony. 'What's it like being told to stand in silence behind the blackboard?' and then added, 'But we thought 'Collywobbles' was a better name than 'Wollycobbles!' They all laughed out loud together but then quickly glanced around in case they'd been heard. Thankfully the noise of the other children playing had drowned them out and relieved, they carried on talking. 'What are your names?' asked Tony. 'I'm Steve,' answered one and the other, 'I'm Paul and what are your names?' Thus, the four young men met and unbeknown to them, it was the start of lifelong friendships. The school hand bell rang. They lined up in silence and returned to the classroom.

The afternoon passed without mishap; the four boys worked studiously together but in relative silence, aware they were not far from Mrs Collier's desk and may be overheard. At one point all the boys were called up, one by one, to Mrs Collier's desk and had to take their workbooks for assessment. Throughout the afternoon no further reference was made to the morning's antics.

Before long the hand bell rang to indicate the end of school. All the desks had to be cleared and work tidied away. Then the children had to stand quietly by their desks with their coats on. Mrs Collier paused and looked around the room, then she announced in a quiet voice that class was dismissed and, 'See you tomorrow'. It was in fact quite a cheery end to the day!

John's mother was waiting for him at the school gate; he ran up to her and held her hand as they walked away and back to their home. Whilst walking, John's mother asked about his day and John responded by asking what was for their evening meal (or 'tea' as it was called) and to explain he felt really tired. His mother smiled wryly.

They chatted on the way home, but there were no further references to school.

That evening, and once John's elder sister and father were home, they chatted happily together over 'tea'. John explained that at school he had done some artwork, spelling and maths and that he had three new friends, Tony, Steve and Paul. John didn't talk about Mrs Collier or the incident that had taken place; he hoped he would never have to.

John's Mum and Dad reflected later that evening, once John was asleep in bed. They were pleased to see how happy and settled John now seemed in his new school, his new friends and what a good teacher Mrs Collier must be.

The next few days quickly turned into weeks and then months. In fact, time flew by and increasingly the friendship between the four boys grew stronger and stronger but within the confines of a strict school regime. Mrs Collier retained her strict disciplines within the classroom, expecting her class to obey periods of silence and to work diligently on the learning tasks she set.

Miss Seath, the headmistress, remained softly spoken, but oversaw all the school's activities with regular routines and encouraged the development of her pupils in all respects. She ran a happy school and was often heard to say she hoped the children were, 'fulfilling their potential.' In asking this question of her staff, parents and also the Governors she remained relatively satisfied, retaining a professional air of diligence. It was good that she was never fully relaxed.

The four boys settled and developed in this environment during their first year, developing plenty of new abilities in the classroom, but also in the non curricular activities. They particularly developed a passion for games on the school playing fields. The debate on whether they preferred 'Collywobbles' or 'Wobblycolly' was to remain with them for years, always raising a smile when recollected.

This overall environment steadily increased their confidence. It was during the ensuing years they were to become more competitive. Also, alongside this, their interests were rapidly developing in various subject areas. However, would all this progress smoothly or were there challenges ahead?

At this stage of their lives there was no awareness of the Male Menopause. Yet, in years to come, they would reflect on their years at Primary School and would realise the strict learning environment had been such an important foundation, a foundation that determined their values and the lives they would lead.

CHAPTER 2

DEVELOPMENT PHASE
Primary School years

JOHN, TONY, PAUL and Steve were never far apart during their years at Primary School. They enjoyed each other's company at school and out of school they often visited each other's homes or went on short excursions to the local parks and even sometimes to the seaside. It was surprising they got on so well as they came from very different backgrounds.

Steve was the eldest child in his family. He had three sisters and a brother; they lived on a busy fruit farm requiring a disciplined home environment. Meals needed to be at set times, the whole family met for breakfast, lunch and the evening meal, and woe betide anyone who caused disruption to this routine!

Unfortunately, Steve was mischievous and took great pleasure in teasing his siblings often testing his parents' patience. On one particular occasion his Grandparents were expected for Sunday lunch. The house was cleaned and tidied, the lawns were mown, the garden tidied, a new bottle of sherry purchased. A three course lunch was prepared and finally, the children were changed into their

Sunday best and told to behave and only speak when spoken to!

So, the scene was set, and all was ready for a perfect family occasion, well nearly. As the preparations were being made, Steve had been asked to lay the table and prepare the dining room. In the dining room there was a long table surrounded by ten wooden chairs; each chair had a loose cushion on the seat secured to the back of the chair with a couple of ties.

Steve, who was nearly seven years old at the time, was busily preparing the room when he was struck by an idea. He had recently bought a 'Whoopee' cushion from a friend at school; these cushions were basically a flat rubber bag, circular in shape, with a sealed flat tube on one edge through which the bag was inflated and then the flat tube was closed. When the bag was compressed, the air exhaled through the flat tube causing it to vibrate and sound like a large bout of flatulence! Fetching the bag, Steve inflated it and set it under the cushion his Grandmother was to sit on.

The grandparents arrived; it was a warm sunny day. They came in a large car and were greeted outside the house by all the family. Wandering through the garden, they admired the flowers and borders, chatting and catching up with all sorts of family news. Finally, they entered the house and went into the lounge for a pre lunch sherry. The children stood by attentively. Listening to the grown-up conversation, they could all smell the lunch and felt hungry. At long last, with a break in the conversation, it was agreed to go through to the dining room. Steve's father led the way, escorting his mother to her seat. With everyone in the room standing in front of their seats, Grandmother was asked to sit down first.

Well, what happened next is hard to relate; an enormous sound of flatulence boomed around the room taking everyone by surprise. They were all quite shocked. There was a moment of silence which was suddenly broken by Steve's uncontrollable laughter. This proved to be his undoing and horrified glances swung in his direction, particularly from his parents. It was then that the unexpected really happened, as Steve's Grandmother also broke into a fit of uncontrollable laughter and such was the tension in the room, that everyone joined in. The laughter was finally broken by Steve's father, explaining to him that they would need to talk later.

A happy lunch and afternoon was had by all. Later that afternoon the Grandparents were waved off in their car and when everyone returned into the house, Steve's father called him back into the lounge for what he called a 'father and son chat'. The 'chat' was short. Steve's father could see the funny side of the events that had taken place but feeling protective towards his son wanted to explain he was very lucky and that the event could so easily have caused many problems. Steve readily agreed and undertook to behave more in future.

The next day at school, Steve told the story of his Grandparents' visit to Paul, Tony and John who were all amazed at the turn of events and how lucky Steve had been that everything had turned out well in the end. They were also keen to borrow the 'Whoopee' cushion themselves, but this proved to be impossible as when Steve returned home that evening the cushion had disappeared. His mother surmised it may have been put out with the rubbish after the Grandparents visit, suggesting that it was probably a good thing. Steve never saw the cushion again.

Paul's family background was different to Steve's. His father was an engineer and his mother worked in a local factory. Both parents were in full time work. Paul had two elder brothers with whom he went to school each morning. In the evening they all returned home to carry out domestic chores before Mum and Dad arrived back.

Paul inevitably drew the short straw when the chores were assigned, his brothers always imposing the worst jobs to him. Although the youngest, Paul had a fighting spirit and was determined to show his brothers he could manage or cope. It was quite a different domestic situation to Steve's. Paul's instinct 'to cope' though was to serve him well in adult life.

All three brothers were keen on sport, particularly football. One day, when Paul was eight years old, the three brothers decided to play football on the local recreation ground. Mum and Dad were at work and Paul had invited his friends, he was pleased that John and Steve could play with them. Tony's Mum had insisted that he went shopping with her; Tony was upset by this.

The pitch was full size, it was a windy day and they played in one goal area. Paul was in goal and they decided to divide into two teams, with Paul's brothers splitting up as they were older, one playing with John and one with Steve.

Behind the goal area there was a slow moving stream with reed beds either side. The match was in full swing and evenly matched. There was lots of laughter and many goals scored with regular disputes and calls for penalties or fouls on minor technicalities. They were fully absorbed. After around an hour, the boys were getting tired when John took a long shot at goal. However, he mistimed his kick, and the ball went high in the air, flying above the goal. At that moment a strong gust of wind caught the ball and much to everyone's horror, they saw it carried into the stream behind the goal.

The boys ran over to the water's edge and watched as the ball drifted slowly down the far side of the stream and then became lodged in a group of reeds. John started to throw stones from the riverbank in an attempt to dislodge it and the others followed suit. It wasn't easy as, although the distance was only a few feet, their aim was not good. After a few minutes, one of Paul's brothers suddenly shrieked in surprise. He turned and thrust his 'stone' into Paul's hand. Paul looked down into his hand and was, in that moment so shocked, he froze on the spot. He realised he was holding a rusty World War 2 hand grenade!

The other boys all gathered around and then stood back. Paul was still frozen in shock and couldn't move. 'What shall we do?' they asked and, 'Do you think it'll go off?' Then one of Paul's brothers said, 'The best thing is to take this over to the Police Station, they'll know what to do. You take it over there Paul and we'll get the ball back.' Paul, being used to doing what his elder brothers asked, started to walk off carefully with the hand grenade at arm's length. John and Steve decided to follow Paul, but at a distance.

The Police Station was only a short distance away. It was a rural station. Two Constables were based there with their families living in houses either side of the station. Paul walked slowly. 'Don't worry,' said Steve reassuringly, 'the grenade is rusty, I'm sure it won't go off,' to which Paul grimaced.

They reached the station. Paul was still being followed, but at a distance by John and Steve. Holding the grenade at arm's length, Paul pressed the external bell when he reached the front doorsteps of the station and waited. After a few minutes the door opened with a cheery, 'Good morning, how can I help you?' from one of the constables. His cheeriness rapidly disappeared as he focussed on the grenade in Paul's outstretched hand. Despite all his experience and years of training to remain calm in situations, the way he asked, 'What on earth are you doing with that?' displayed a good deal of concern, not least because he was thinking of the wives and families in the two houses either side of the station!

The constable quickly recovered his composure and professional demeanour as he realised the potential danger, they might all be in. His first thought was that Paul was only young, his intentions were probably good and that if he were to alarm him it may have resulted in a dangerous outcome. He noticed Paul and Steve a few steps away and, in that instance, he also noticed a pile of grass turf stacked to one side of the drive. His years of training were paying off as he came up with a plan.

He calmly thanked Paul for bringing the grenade and asked him to keep holding it. Speaking to Paul and Steve, he asked them both to move back and away to the other side of the station. He then led Paul quietly over to the stack of turf clods and asked him to lay the grenade on top of the stack and then wait with his two friends. Paul did this and was relieved to release the heavy grenade as his arm ached. However, he was not nearly as pleased as the constable who proceeded to lay other turf clods either side and on top of the grenade and then stepped away over to the three boys.

The constable's first instinct was to move the three boys into the station where they were safe. He then asked them to wait for a few minutes whilst he alerted his family and his colleague's family of the situation. The boys were asked to wait and to remain indoors. Returning to the station, the constable then called the Army Bomb disposal unit and was relieved to receive confirmation they could attend immediately, though they were a couple of hours away. The constable's next priority was to get the three boys away from the area and, taking their names and addresses, he escorted them down the drive and asked them to return to their homes.

It was two evenings later when Paul's father opened the front door of their house to let the constable in and showed him into the front room. Paul was called down from his room and his brothers and Mum also joined them to hear what the constable had to say. The constable was friendly and quickly confirmed no one had been hurt, that the Bomb Disposal team had arrived and safely removed the grenade in a bomb proof case.

He went on to thank Paul for his well-intended actions but said that in future, in the unlikely event of another grenade being found, they were to leave it where it was found and just report it. Paul's brother, the one who had handed Paul the grenade, looked embarrassed. The constable went on to explain he needed to complete a statement to close the matter. He also explained he would be visiting John and Steve's parents to inform them of the situation.

When the constable left, a family discussion took place. Paul's parents were really concerned the elder brother had passed the grenade to Paul thinking of all the potential dangers that the boy's actions might have caused. There was an air of relief in the conversation and Paul's parents took time to stress the need to protect each other more and others around them too!

The next day at school and in the playground before school started, Tony was amazed to hear what had happened. 'Thank goodness my Mum wanted me to go shopping,' he said, and laughed. John and Steve explained that the constable had visited their houses too and that they'd been reprimanded by their parents for the potential and unnecessary risks and to be more careful in future. The school bell rang. All four boys smiled as they reflected on the grenade event and how lucky they had been. The story went quickly around the school.

School was a good environment for the four boys, not only the structured learning environment but also the social development, learning how to make new friends and develop relationships. There were also the sports activities through which they gradually built skills and confidence that would be useful later in their lives. But overall, the priority of the school, as a Primary School, was to prepare them for secondary education and at the end of their time at the Primary School, they were all to participate in an assessment exam which would determine which type of Secondary School they should attend. In some cases, it would be an academic school environment and in others a more vocational education.

The four boys were fully aware that this exam was to be taken when they were in their final year at Primary School, at eleven years of age. In Tony's case, he was an only child and with no brothers or sisters and was often left to entertain himself at home. He became naturally intrigued by things that moved and how they worked as his parents were to discover. Tony was only seven years old when he became interested in the plastic salt and pepper pots at home. They were lime green in colour, with a black screw in base you removed when refilling the pots. The salt pot had a single hole through which the salt was poured onto the meal, whereas the pepper pot had several holes.

One afternoon when Tony had been left to his own devices, he was idly playing with the two lime green pots when he was struck by an idea; why not swap the salt and pepper pots over by removing the salt from the salt pot and then pouring the pepper from the pepper pot in. Then putting the salt in the pepper pot. Easily done, Tony was intrigued to see if both pots worked, and they did! However, Tony's attention was then distracted by something else, and he forgot to switch the salt and pepper pots back. In fact, he forgot about them completely and this was his undoing!

Tony's parents were both 'in retail' they used to say. Tony's Dad worked in a major clothing store. He often told people he was a tailor, and his Mum worked in a local small newsagent restacking the shelves and working the cash tills. Their hours varied a lot from week to week and often Tony had to go to and from school on his own, which he didn't mind. Tony's Dad's retail shop was particularly busy during what was known as the 'January sales' and it was on one of these days when he had to work an evening overtime that he returned home quite late and was really pleased to find his wife had prepared his favourite meal, a simple cheese and onion omelette. He was tired and hungry and looking forward to the meal. As his wife placed it in front of him, he leant forward and reached for the lime green salt pot, he always liked some salt on his omelette.

It was midevening; Tony was in a deep sleep when he vaguely heard the words 'Tony!' in a loud piercing voice coming up the stairs. He sat bolt upright in surprise and then heard his father's voice calling, 'Tony' again followed by a deep spluttering cough! Tony quickly woke up. What could it be, was the house on fire? He jumped out of bed and opening his bedroom door he ran across the landing to hear his Dad coughing again and calling his name angrily. Tony looked over the banister and saw his Dad at the bottom of the stairs in deep distress but there was no sign of smoke or fire so what could it be? His Mum also appeared at the bottom of the stairs anxiously patting her husband on his back as he called out to Tony to come downstairs immediately.

They sat in the dining room together. Tony saw the table was set for a meal and there was an uneaten omelette on a plate. His Dad coughed and spluttered again and then, in that moment, Tony recalled the salt and pepper swapping experiment and what must have happened to his Dad. He let out an involuntary, 'Oh no!' to which his Dad said, 'Did you do this?' but the question was unnecessary as the look on Tony's face of guilt and despair told its own story; they just could not believe it had happened!

Tony's parents were not normally strict, in fact, as Tony was an only child, they doted on his every deed, well usually! Tony's Dad was upset and tired explaining to Tony that he and his Mum worked really hard to earn money to provide food and clothing, to pay the bills, to pay for holidays and that this had made him upset. Tony felt bad, his parents worked so hard to give him a good home and a good life, he hadn't wanted to upset them but unbeknown to him a far worse incident was to occur in Tony's final year at Primary School.

John was different again to the other three. Whereas Tony was a little shy and lacking confidence, John was outgoing and engaging. He had a similar mischievous streak to Steve and like Paul, he worked hard at home and was expected to carry out domestic chores. The biggest influence on John's life was his one older sister. In fact, she was ten years older than John and adored her little brother, but also teased him as his reactions made her and her friends laugh. John's parents were easy going and not strict, regarding the banter between John and his sister as fairly harmless.

John admired and loved his elder sister; she was so cool, dressed well, and spoke of things John didn't really understand. She had a large group of girlfriends who were frequently calling round to their house, talking animatedly and with lots of laughter. However, one big problem emerged as John was growing up. When he had just had his seventh birthday she started to smoke. Initially, John became aware of the smell, but over the weeks she openly brought packets of cigarettes home leaving them around the kitchen and living rooms. She shared them with her friends when they came around. John's parents didn't seem to mind, though they insisted she should not smoke in the kitchen.

John wished his parents could have been stricter, as not only was the smell just horrible but also the ash was dirty and seemed to get everywhere around the house. Shelves were dusty, clothing smelt and there were cigarette ash trays around the house that were often full of used cigarette butts. When he told his big sister that he didn't like her smoking she rebuffed him explaining he couldn't possibly understand. Smoking was just so cool, and all her friends did it and John should take no notice.

This response frustrated and upset John but then one day he had an idea. He found an opened packet of his sister's cigarettes in the lounge. It was a packet of twenty and had been recently opened. There were around fifteen cigarettes left in the packet. The house was quiet, his parents were out, and his sister was asleep upstairs. John took the packet of cigarettes into the kitchen and carefully removed one of the cigarettes. He also found a box of wooden matches. With a dining fork, John carefully removed some of the tobacco from the cigarette end. He then took three matches and cut off just the match heads with a sharp kitchen knife. John then inserted the match heads into the cigarette and pushed back some of the tobacco he'd removed. Looking at the cigarette, John was satisfied there was no outward sign it had been tampered with and he carefully put the cigarette back in the box. He then tidied up the kitchen and returned the cigarettes where he'd found them in the lounge.

John then left the house to play football with Tony and Paul, returning at lunch time to find his parents were back. They explained his sister had gone out to the local town and was not expected back until teatime. They enjoyed a quiet lunch and John spent the afternoon helping his Dad with chores in the garden; it was a nice, peaceful afternoon.

It was late afternoon when the tranquillity of the garden was broken by the sound of the front door being slammed. John and his Dad looked at each other in puzzlement as they heard John's sister's raised voice talking to her Mum. They couldn't quite hear what she was saying so decided to go and find out.

They found them both in the kitchen, John's sister was delirious. She was laughing excitedly yet almost in tears as she attempted to explain what had happened to her. Apparently, she'd gone into town and met her friends. They'd gone into a coffee bar and John's sister had generously shared her cigarettes around. They were all happily chatting when suddenly, 'You won't believe this,' Johns sister said, one of the cigarettes exploded in her friend's face! It was 'just terrible,' she went onto say, a loud 'woof' sound and then the cigarette was on fire! John's parents were keen to ask if the friend had been hurt and relieved to hear not, but that she was in a state of shock and the friends had taken her home.

John's sister was amused on one hand about the whole incident (so glad her friend had not been hurt), but on the other hand felt she must do something to warn the cigarette company that their cigarettes were dangerous. She was so upset she needed help from her parents to calm down and then eventually she decided to write a letter to the cigarette company and post it that very day.

John was quite taken aback by the strong reaction his idea had caused and felt too embarrassed to confess it was he who had caused the incident. He decided to keep quiet. The letter was written and posted that day. Later John was interested to hear his sister say that she was worried other cigarettes might be dangerous and that she might give up smoking. 'Hurray!' thought John but deep down he remained embarrassed and felt that he should have confessed to his mischief!

And so, with a few mishaps along the way, the four boys passed through their Primary School years. They were fulfilling years, making plenty of friends, enjoying the lessons, a lot of sport and school excursions to see castles and museums. In fact, the years rolled by all too quickly and before they knew it, they were in their final year and being prepared for their final year's exam to determine which senior school they would move on to.

The boys often discussed this and shared conversations they had had with their families. Their parents were anxious to indicate the importance of good education to help their 'successful' career development, yet none of the boys really had a clear idea on the careers they might pursue. There were discussions around becoming famous footballers, policemen, brain surgeons, farmers, train drivers and these ideas changed and developed constantly with no real conclusion or clarity; they were just too young.

As the weeks rolled by in their final year, these conversations occurred more frequently, particularly as the 'exam week' was anticipated. All the boys were encouraged by their families to read often. Tony's parents were happy that he had an inquisitive mind and would do well. John's parents and sister were encouraging him to make the most of his opportunities. He was often 'tested' at family mealtimes with questions and discussions in a relaxed but purposeful environment. Steve and Paul's parents took matters a stage further. In Paul's case he had some external tuition arranged with a retired teacher. Paul explained he was taken to this teacher's house two evenings a week after school to look at old exam papers and discuss the best way of answering them. In Steve's case his father helped him with some maths tuition at least two evenings a week after he got back from the farm and after the family tea. Steve found he quite enjoyed these and suggested to his Dad that he should have been a teacher, to which his Dad raised his eyebrows and urged his son to 'just concentrate and check your answers, talk less!'

Finally, 'exam week' arrived; in fact, it was only three short written exams on separate mornings in comprehension, maths and writing. In the exam room, the school hall, the children were asked to be silent, and the papers were distributed face down on their desks. Miss Seath supervised the exams, and it was only when she said, 'Turn over and start,' (having checked they all had sharpened pencils), that they could begin. Apart from a few involuntary 'gasps and grunts' as the papers were turned over, the silence was only broken by the occasional cough or when Miss Seath announced the time they had left.

None of the children had experienced this type of tension before and it was therefore a huge relief when the final exam finished, and the papers were collected (ensuring each student's name was clearly written on the top of the front page). The children ran out of the exam room when dismissed and were allowed an extended playtime in which they all expressed relief. There was plenty of laughter but oddly they felt a little aimless, a sense of post exam relief they supposed, and it was this relaxed post exam feeling that led to an unexpected situation for Steve and Tony.

It was lunchtime and exams had finished that morning. The four friends had enjoyed their post exam playtime and were now at lunch. They were fatigued, relieved but most of all they were hungry or 'famished' as they liked to say. Lunch was two courses, a meat dish with potatoes and vegetables followed by a pudding. On this day the pudding was one of Tony's absolute favourites, sponge pudding and custard! Tony was so enthused explaining to the dinner ladies at the serving hatch that it was his favourite, that one of the dinner ladies gave him an extra helping which he proudly showed the other boys on returning to the table.

The boys finished their sponge and custard quickly and then looked at Tony's extra portion, asking Tony if he would eat it all himself, surely not?! Tony was thinking how the sponge might be shared and then came up with a novel idea. He placed the extra sponge and custard portion on the handle of his fork in the middle of the table and explained to the others that when he banged down on the fork prongs, the fork would act as a catapult and send the sponge up in the air and whoever caught it could eat the sponge! All the boys readily agreed and thought it would be a great idea. They started a countdown from ten and the excitement grew with every reducing number approaching zero, when Tony would bang down on the prongs.

However, Steve just couldn't contain his excitement. Maybe it was the build-up of all the exams (he thought later), but for some reason, as the count was going down from four to three his mischievous tendency kicked in and he just couldn't wait. He leaned forward and hit the fork prongs with all the strength he could muster.

Years later, when the boys reflected on the situation, they agreed it was as if time had stood still. Unfortunately Steve hit down on the prongs with a lot more strength than was required to send the sponge to only to the boys on their table. The sponge leapt up in the air, slowly rotating as it was launched high up into the beams of the hall and seemed to slowly drift across the room. Then, much to the horror of the boys they realised it was heading in the direction of Mrs Collier, who was in deep conversation with other staff members at their table, happily reflecting on what had seemed to be a successful 'exam week'.

In fact, as the sponge and custard slowly fell, they realised it was heading straight for her. In that instant there were 'Oh NO!' feelings amongst the boys, which worsened as they saw the sponge was going to hit her on the side of the head, and then it did. It landed on the side of her head, the sticky custard and sponge mix penetrating her buffoon type hair style making a terrible mess.

Time stood still. Initially Mrs Collier was in a state of complete shock, having been deeply involved in a friendly, happy conversation with her colleagues. She then felt the fairly solid impact of the sponge and looking at her hand realised what it was, but was ignorant of where it had come from and how on earth had it got there? She whirled round. Her colleagues were in a state of complete shock too. The children on tables close by were dumbstruck, not believing what they had seen, and the room then fell completely silent as Mrs Collier rose to her feet and shouted out, 'Who did this?' Walking across the hall she noticed various children looking over to the table where the four boys were sitting.

Mrs Collier approached the four boys. Her face was red, and she spat uncontrollably as she demanded, 'Who did this?' again. The sideways glances were clearly directed at Steve but it was at this moment that the Headmistress Miss Seath appeared at Mrs Collier's side and in her quiet but penetrating voice said 'Mrs Collier, Mrs Collier, I'll handle this'. Mrs Collier was embarrassed by the mess in her hair and slipped off to the ladies' room, feeling angry and humiliated. The other children in the hall were whispering excitedly, not believing what they had seen and discussing the distressed state of Mrs Collier. Meanwhile Miss Seath stayed with the four boys and asked what had happened. She could see the guilt and uneasy expressions on their faces. Perhaps it was her calm demeanour that relaxed the boys who opened up to her to explain it was an accident, that it wasn't intended and how sorry they were for what had happened.

Miss Seath deduced it was principally Tony and Steve who were the culprits and during the afternoon staff meeting it was decided that examples needed to be made, to show the other children that the school would not, under any circumstances, even though it may have been an accident, tolerate this type of behaviour. It was decided that during the following morning's assembly that Miss Seath would summon Tony and Steve to the front of the hall to be caned. Also, that a letter would be sent to their parents explaining the punishment and that furthermore, Steve and Tony would be banned from school lunches for one week starting the following Monday.

The following morning assembly was held in the main hall as usual. After the reading Miss Seath stood up to make the announcements and there was a feeling of anticipation amongst the children. They still couldn't believe what had happened at lunch the previous day and they were not to be disappointed. Miss Seath spoke in her usual quiet voice; the hall was hushed, and the children and staff listened intently whilst Miss Seath recounted the custard sponge incident during the previous day's lunch and that it was just not acceptable behaviour. She went on to explain the main culprits were Steve and Tony who were to be made an example of. They were to be excluded from school lunches all next week and furthermore they were now to step forward to be caned. There was a noticeable hushed gasp amongst the children; they had never seen this before!

Tony and Steve were to say in later years how shocked they were too. It all seemed to happen in a daze. They stepped forward as requested and held out their opened right hands to Miss Seath who was holding a small twelve inch ruler. She struck it across each of the boy's hands three times and then told them to return to their places. Miss Seath hadn't stuck the boys with any force at all, however the shame and indignity of being punished in this way, in front of the whole school, was something the boys never forgot and neither did all the other children in the school.

The situation was to get worse for Steve and Tony though, as that evening, when they returned to their homes, they each found their parents awaiting them and holding a letter from Miss Seath. The letter set out the incident, for which the boys were responsible and explained that the school found it completely unacceptable, that the boys had been caned and were also expelled from school lunches all next week.

Steve's parents were initially lost for words and asked him what had happened. Appalled to hear of his involvement, they expressed their complete disappointment and referred to the bad example he had set his younger sisters and brother. They also highlighted the shame he had brought to their family. Just what on earth had he been playing at? Tony's parents were similarly dismayed. Tony's Dad was particularly upset as many of the school's parents were regular customers in his shop and he was really anxious as to how he might be required to explain and discuss the incident with them.

Both boys felt ashamed; they realised the seriousness of the situation and how much they had upset their parents. They wished there was something they could do but, despairingly, realised there was nothing to be done. On that note there was something they'd not considered.

Monday lunchtime Steve and Tony were dismissed from school. When the lunchtime bell rang, they walked off to their separate homes to be greeted solemnly by their parents. They both ate a quick lunch in shameful silence, and then walked back to school. The same routine took place on Tuesday; the atmosphere in both their houses was at best sombre, and at worst they felt total humiliation and shame.

Wednesday lunchtime the routine was completely, surprisingly, incredibly different!

Both boys arrived home to be greeted by smiling parents who gave them a great hug saying, 'Well done, we're so happy!' Steve was dumbfounded and said later that he felt in a daze. He couldn't understand what was happening. He was ushered into the lounge and a pre-lunch, small sherry was thrust in his hand with his Father saying how proud and pleased they were with the letter they'd received that morning to explain Steve had passed his exams and secured a place at Grammar School!

Lunch was a joyful, chatty occasion with eager talk about the Grammar School, what a good education they gave and the great career opportunities that would emerge. Steve was still in state of happy shock as he was waved off by his proud parents. He arrived outside the school gates just as Tony arrived, also with a huge grin on his face. He'd passed as well and had also been treated like a complete hero!

It was a total turnaround. The shame and humiliation had gone, their parents had now retuned to being proud and happy. The boys felt so relieved and there was a real skip in their steps as they ran back into the playground to find Paul and John, who then became anxious wondering what news awaited them when they got home? However, their anxieties were thankfully misplaced. The following morning, both John and Paul confirmed they'd passed too with Paul gaining a place at the Technical School and John at the same Grammar School as Steve and Tony. There was initial concern that they were to be separated with Paul going to a different school, but relaxed as they discussed how close the schools were and how they would continue to see a lot of each other.

The boys' final days at Primary School were happy. The school sports day was great fun. Paul won the boys sixty yards sprint, John won the sack race, Tony came second in the egg and spoon race while Steve and John came third in the three legged race. Parents were allowed to attend, and this was a good opportunity for the boys' parents to meet and catch up. They reflected on the custard sponge incident, the exam results and speculated on the boys' futures.

A few days later, the school fete took place on a Saturday afternoon to raise money for some new sports equipment and the following Friday it was the 'leaving service' at the local church. Again, parents could attend, the school choir performed, and prayers were recited wishing all the leavers the very best of luck in their new schools. At the end of the Service, those children leaving had to file past the staff members to shake hands. The boys later commented that they thought Mrs Collier had a smile of relief, whereas Miss Seath was as stony faced as ever, true to form they thought and smiled!

And so Primary School days were at an end. There were mixed feelings, happy memories overall but also some wry reflections on the various incidents and stories that had happened in and out of school as the boys had developed, with memories they would certainly never forget.

John often recalled the cigarette issue with his older sister and could never bring himself to reveal the full story to his family. He satisfied himself that his intentions had been good, that he really wanted to protect her and help her give up that smoking habit and it had worked! Steve's reflections were numerous, and he recognised he would need to contain his mischievous nature in future. He'd been lucky with the 'Whoopee' cushion (though he often reflected on his father's protective caution) and the outcome of the custard sponge incident. He realised how fortunate he'd been that the exam results had come out soon afterwards and thank goodness he'd passed!

Tony had similar reflections to Steve about the custard sponge but also every time he saw a salt and pepper pot, he was reminded to contain his curiosity! Paul often thought about the grenade issue. What on earth had he been thinking in taking it along to the Police Station, blindly following the instructions of his elder brother. He knew his intentions had been good to protect others but thank goodness no one had been hurt or injured!

Of all the stories they were to reflect upon, the one that cropped up most was the incident with Mrs Collier in the first few days of school. Her angry reactions, the blackboard, the red face, the involuntary spitting and the debate on which name was best, 'Collywobbles' or 'Wobblycolly' were to remain with the boys forever!

In years to come the boys would reflect in their discussions about the Male Menopause and realise it was during this period, the latter days at Primary School, that subconsciously the three P's were emerging. In the case of 'Provision' they had become aware how hard their parents worked and how important exams were to ensure they did well in their own careers and be similarly able to provide for their families.

In the case of 'Protection' they had learned about working together, playing sports and how important teamwork was, that working together achieved results. On the converse they'd become aware that misbehaviour could cause serious problems and the stories about Whoopee cushions, hand grenades, green salt and pepper pots and flying custard sponge would remain with them forever as a reminder. In the case of 'Procreation' this wasn't fully understood yet, though there was the occasional thought that some girls sometimes looked quite pretty, but that's as far as it went at this stage!

And so, the boys' characters and behaviours were changing as they progressed through boyhood at Primary School. Signs of manhood were soon to emerge as they started at the Grammar and Technical schools, however, their early experiences were to continue to influence their lives in ways they could not imagine.

CHAPTER 3

DISCOVERY PHASE
Secondary School years

♂ **JOHN AND PAUL** were first to realise there was something about girls that they had not appreciated when they were younger. In John's case he often heard stories from his older sister, particularly when her friends came around. In Paul's case he heard his two elder brothers often discussing girls in their local area.

Awareness of this 'girl thing' (as it became known) emerged towards the end of their time at Primary School and increased significantly as they started senior school. Often when they met to play football or visiting each other's houses the subject of 'girls' would crop up with John or Paul and bit by bit, Tony and Steve also latched onto this 'girl thing'.

Tony had a naturally curious mind and was always keen to know how things worked. One summer's afternoon, the four boys were sitting happily together beside the local football field; they had just been kicking a ball around and needed a rest and a drink. It was Tony who started the conversation saying, 'I just thought Mums had babies naturally,' to which there were sideways glances and smirks from the other three. 'Don't you know about sex?' asked Paul and went on to say how he'd heard his elder bothers discussing a girl at school and how one of the brothers was planning to take her out on a date and 'give her one', being the expression Paul had heard. John added he'd heard this type of conversation also when hearing his older sister and her friends talk and initially some strange words. 'None of these words meant anything to me at first,' said John, but then he went to explain how surprised he was to hear one his sister's friends explaining how a boy and girl make babies.

Tony and Steve were surprised to hear this and the boys became more confused as the conversation progressed. They were relieved when John changed the conversation, asking if anyone wanted to play football again later that week?

Many years later the four friends would recall these conversations and, smiling, would realise just how naïve they had been!

Alongside increased awareness of this 'girl thing', the boys were starting at their new schools. It was like stepping back in time with new, ill-fitting uniforms. There were plenty of new experiences such as travelling to school in the local town on a bus, having to do homework and return it on time and making lots of new friends. A whole new way of life was opening up to them.

It was in Steve's third year of Secondary school that he really became aware of girls. The French teacher was keen for the pupils to participate in the 'language exchange scheme' as it was called. English students were paired up with French students, then sent to live with the French student's family home for three weeks. A few weeks later the French student would come to live in the English student's family home for three weeks.

A letter arrived at Steve's home from the exchange scheme announcing he had been assigned to a French student called 'Maurice' and his family in Avignon. Tickets and travel information were enclosed, and he was due to go in a months' time! Steve was shocked, the letter seemed to bring home the reality of the scheme which had otherwise just been talked about in class but now it was really going to happen!

There were excited discussions at school the following day. Other students had also received their letters. Many were going to Paris and some were only going across the English Channel to Calais. Steve had no idea where Avignon was, he'd not even heard of it before. In class they looked at a map of France to find it was way down in the south, south of Lyon, and on the River Rhone. Also, it was apparently famous for something called the 'Palais des Papes'.

The more he found out, the more daunted Steve felt. How would he get there, what were Maurice's family like, what was Maurice like, how much money would he need? Steve's parents were very supportive and explained it was 'good education' and would be 'a great experience'. His younger sisters and brother teased him saying, they were looking forward to three weeks peace and quiet whilst he was away!

The month passed by quickly. Steve had packed and said his goodbyes to his siblings and his Mum. His Dad gave him a lift to the railway station to meet his school friends and they were off! The train journey first to London (where many other students joined them from other schools) and then down to Dover was great fun. There were lots of excited conversations as they then boarded the ferry across the Channel to Calais and then onto a French SNCF train to Paris. Each student had been given an identity tag to tie onto their coat collar, providing information on their name, school, destination address and contact information.

On arrival at Paris 'Garde de Nord', the students were divided into groups on the platform by destination; Steve suddenly found himself separated from his friends (there was no time to even say goodbye) and amongst other students he'd not met before. There was a new 'Group Leader', a teacher from another school, who explained they were to follow him. The new group set off and the excited chat and atmosphere transformed to a mood of anxiety as they boarded the French underground, the Metro train, to 'Gare de Lyon' where they boarded the Lyon train. They were told it would take four hours to get to Lyon and then a further two hours for those travelling onto Avignon. The teacher advised them to get some rest and that he would be providing drinks and sandwiches later.

The students were tired; their limited conversations were guarded and cautious as no one knew each other. All the students were apprehensive about the unknown experiences that lay ahead. They thought about families they were to live with, what would the French student they had been assigned to be like, how would their limited ability at speaking French stand up, would their attempts to speak the language be ridiculed and in fact, it made them question just why had they agreed to participate in this exchange programme?

On arrival in Lyon, the students were broken up again; those being assigned to Lyon based families were introduced by the Group Leader to their families. Steve and the rest on the 'onward journey' group waited and watched. There was clearly some awkwardness as students shook hands and attempted their language. There were puzzled frowns and smiles from the French families as they tried to understand, followed by a lot of eager nodding of heads to indicate they had understood. It was really amusing to realise both the students and families were thinking 'three weeks of this?' It helped Steve and his new smaller group to anticipate what lay ahead in Avignon.

Maurice greeted Steve at the platform gate in Avignon Station appearing outgoing and confident. Steve was shattered from the journey and wary, trying to take everything in. Maurice took Steve's small suitcase and walked outside the station where they met his Mum and set off in her car to their home in the old part of Avignon, a short distance from the railway station. Their house was old, on three levels with a courtyard with plenty of character, however being a town house, it was in stark contrast to the farmhouse Steve lived in back in England.

Steve learned that Maurice was the youngest of four children and that he would be meeting all the family at dinner that evening. Although it was early afternoon, Maurice's Mum suggested Steve might like to nap? Steve readily agreed and was shown to a room on the upper third floor adjoining Maurice's room and alongside a bathroom too.

Maurice woke Steve at six to explain it was nearly time for evening dinner, that his sister and one brother were downstairs and that his Dad had just got home. Steve quickly doused his face to freshen up, combed his hair and followed Maurice down the large stairs and into a room with high ceilings. Maurice introduced Steve to his Dad, his sister and one brother, explaining the eldest brother was away at University.

The family were very welcoming. Maurice's Dad in particular made a great show of offering Steve a small glass of wine. 'Don't tell your Mother,' he said and then carefully corrected Steve on his attempts at French, correcting vocabulary, advising on pronunciation and breaking into English when Steve was in difficulty, which was often. Maurice's Mum stepped in to advise dinner was ready and looked at her husband to suggest he should give Steve a bit of a rest.

The dinner was superb, homely French cuisine at its very best. The family asked Steve a lot of questions about

England and Steve's family but as the conversation progressed Steve found he became increasingly enchanted by Maurice's sister. There was just something about her, the way she spoke, the way she laughed, her hair, her looks and all in all she seemed really nice. In later years Steve would laugh and reflect on that dinner and realised this was the first time he'd really 'noticed' a girl and that he'd really 'fancied' her!

As Steve went to bed that night, he felt strangely happy. Certainly not homesick as he'd anticipated. He looked forward to seeing Maurice's sister again the following day and felt he might quite enjoy his time in Avignon. However, Steve was to be disappointed; in conversation with Maurice the following day he learned that his sister actually didn't live at her parents' home, but with her boyfriend! This surprised Steve, he'd not realised this and, in his dreams, had thought he might be able to get to know her better. He had not for one moment imagined she might be in a relationship. How stupid he thought he'd been, to even imagine she might be interested in him as she was so much older than him. Yes, a feeling of disappointment he'd not experienced before, and it made him feel quite down.

However, as the days progressed in Avignon, Steve grew to enjoy living in a big town; it was such a contrast to his home life being marooned on a remote farm and having to suffer his younger sisters and brother! Furthermore, he was impressed by Maurice as he had such a large circle of friends. They met regularly in the town's cafes, discussing music, sport, politics and so many other interesting subjects. Steve could not initially participate as his French language was far from fluent, but he was learning quickly, and he was eager to improve. He liked the way Maurice had a large circle of friends including some good looking girls and after his experience and feelings for Maurice's sister he found he was taking more interest, in fact girls were quite nice he thought!

Mopeds were another interest for Steve. Nearly all of Maurice's friends had one, and French laws were relaxed allowing fourteen year olds to ride one. Maurice had a black Mobylette with pedals and a small engine. Maurice let Steve ride it around the town square a few times and experience the thrill of the power and speed, well, relative to the old push bike Steve had back in England!

Steve found he was spending more time in the bathroom in the mornings. He was certainly paying more attention to his appearance. He didn't own the trendy 'towny' clothes that Maurice and his friends had but at least he could wash more thoroughly and comb his hair. Then, one morning, whilst looking in the mirror he got a real surprise as he spotted a small black hair growing on his chin, his first ever black hair! 'Wow!' he thought, would he soon be able to grow a beard? So, here he was, just fourteen years old, girls were interesting, motorbikes were great, and he was starting to grow a beard! What next?

No one noticed Steve's small black hair, he didn't own a razor and decided to let it grow a bit and wondered if more would appear? He continued to enjoy his time in Avignon with Maurice visiting the town's cafes, talking to his friends, particularly his girlfriends (!) and riding the mopeds.

At the end of the second week, Steve started to go to Maurice's French school and joined his classes. Maurice explained it was called a college and that the following year he wanted to move onto a 'Lycee' and study for his 'baccalaureate' qualification. Steve didn't really understand this system; it seemed quite different to the system he was used to in England. He was impressed by Maurice and his friends as he could see they were eager to learn, they enjoyed school and were enthusiastic about many issues that Steve had just not thought about in his relative rural life back in England. It made him think.

The following weekend, the final one before Steve was due to return to the UK, Maurice told Steve that his parents were going to take them on a long drive to a town just outside Nice to visit his Dad's sister and her family and that they were going to stay overnight. Steve didn't think about it too much and enjoyed the journey through the French countryside. It was a warm day. Maurice's parents commented on Steve's French to say it had improved and asked him if he'd enjoyed his time in France. Steve readily told them how much he'd enjoyed it, not just learning the language but the whole way of life was just so different to his life back in England. Maurice and his parents were pleased to hear Steve's appreciation and the car journey went by quickly.

On arrival at a really large house outside Nice, Maurice's Dad blew the car horn as he pulled to a stop on the drive. His sister appeared at the door and with a shriek ran across the drive to greet them. She flung her arms around her brother and kissed him, then kissed Maurice's Mum on both cheeks, then Maurice on both cheeks (he called her Aunty or 'Tante') and then, much to Steve's embarrassment, she also kissed him on both cheeks. Maurice's father laughed at the obvious awkwardness Steve felt, explaining this was the custom in France; Steve laughed with them and said he didn't mind at all.

Walking into the house Maurice's Uncle appeared from the back garden and also warmly greeted them hugging Maurice and his parents and giving Steve a warm, firm handshake. It was at this time that Steve noticed two girls coming down the stairs. He realised they must be Maurice's cousins, though no one had told him about them. One of the cousins was young but the other one was the same age as Maurice and Steve. Her name was Camille, and she had brown eyes, long brown hair and a radiant smile. Steve thought she looked beautiful. He shook her hand and tried to appear cool as he spoke in his best French to say 'hello'. She smiled again and said, 'Nice to meet you,' in broken English. Steve was enthralled; he'd not really felt like this before. He felt a slight blush and hoped no one had noticed.

A happy weekend ensued. Meals were fun with plenty of laughter, the home cooking was superb, traditional French cuisine at its best. Some ball games were played on the back lawns in the afternoon, board and card games played in the evening. Steve was asked a lot of questions about England and everyone helped him as he tried to answer in his best French, correcting word orders and adding new vocabulary. Steve was learning fast; his language was improving markedly but also he was really enjoying his time in France. He wondered if anyone noticed that he was trying to talk to Camille as much as he could. He was pleased that she seemed keen to talk to him also!

After breakfast on the second day Camille's father suggested they should all go for a walk in the country. It was a lovely sunny warm morning, ideal conditions and there was a good path from the back garden. Camille's father set the pace and led the way. Steve was talking earnestly with Camille, and they were so absorbed in the conversation, that it wasn't long before they fell some way behind the others. Camille described her friends at school, her teachers, her interest in music, and her hopes for the future. Steve listened carefully responding with his thoughts and became entranced with Camille; she was just so nice and very good looking too.

They arrived at a closed gate and could see the others walking apace, ahead in the distance. Steve jumped over the gate first and then turned back and offered his hand to help Camille over the gate. Camille smiled, took his hand and jumped down and then they carried on holding hands as they walked along the path. Steve had never held a girl's hand before. He really liked it and hoped he'd never have to let go. He wondered if Camille felt the same.

It was then that the others walking ahead of them turned around and shouted back to them to hurry up and it was at this point that Camille's younger sister called out, 'Look, Camille is holding Steve's hand!' Everyone turned back again and laughed and shouted to them again to hurry up. Steve and Camille glanced at each other and smiled. The walk was nearly over, but a short distance from the house, the path went through a small wood and going through this Steve realised they had lost sight of the others ahead. He stopped and with his heart racing he turned and looked down at Camille. She looked up to him and smiled with those lovely brown eyes. Steve leaned forward to kiss Camille. She responded eagerly but the moment was then broken by the others ahead calling out, 'Come on you two, where are you?!' Steve and Camille looked at each other and smiled, nothing needed to be said. They then ran through the coppice still holding hands but let go as they got back to the house.

The rest of the afternoon passed by too quickly for Steve and before long Maurice's father said it was time to go. It had been a great weekend, and everyone was sorry it had to end, none more so than Camille and Steve. Kisses were exchanged, handshakes were firm, and gushing (but deserved) tributes to Camille's family were made for their hospitality and cuisine. When Steve came to say goodbye to Camille, they were aware others were watching and so he just kissed her on both cheeks saying how nice it was to meet. He felt a response from Camille as she gripped his arms firmly as he kissed her and then she smiled with those lovely brown eyes.

The car journey back to Avignon seemed a long one, tedious after the weekend they'd all enjoyed, and they were all tired. Maurice reflected with his Mum and Dad on all the things that had happened whilst Steve fell into a more sombre mood reflecting on Camille; he wondered what she was doing, and would they ever meet again? He recalled the feeling of holding hands and then that kiss, it was the first time he'd ever held a girl's hand or kissed, and it felt good! He remembered the way she'd looked, her perfume and the way she'd felt too. It was all a new experience, and he was aware again of his heart racing as he recollected the weekend's events!

The following week sped by quickly, Steve often thought of Camille and wondered if she thought of him. School was very interesting, so different to school in England. As the end of the week approached Steve found he was going with Maurice to all his old haunts around Avignon. It was hard saying goodbye but on the other hand, after three weeks away he was starting to look forward to meeting his own family and friends back in England and wondered how they were getting on.

Maurice and his Mum took Steve back to Avignon railway station and on arrival Steve recognised some of the other English students who'd travelled out with him. Maurice unloaded Steve's suitcase from his Mum's car and then gave him a big farewell hug saying he was looking forward to meeting him again and all his family back in England in a few weeks' time. Steve explained he was looking forward to it too and kissed Maurice's Mum on both cheeks; he thanked her and Maurice profusely for all their hospitality and said he'd really enjoyed it.

The journey back from Avignon started off quietly but quickly escalated into a noisy exchange, as all the children recounted their experiences, excitedly describing their exchange students, the families they'd met and the places they'd been to. This mood escalated further as they met students at Lyon to board the Paris bound train and again when they returned to 'Gare de Nord' where Steve finally caught up with all his school friends.

The journey back to Calais, the ferry crossing to Dover and then back to their hometown seemed to pass by so quickly, there were so many stories to share. Steve was met at the station in his hometown by his Mother and one of his sisters. They both greeted him warmly and said he'd been missed. Steve smiled and asked what was for tea when they got home.

Steve was shattered, totally exhausted, hungry too. On returning to his home, he greeted his Father, sisters and brother briefly and after eating his tea asked if he could go to bed? Wry smiles were exchanged between his parents, they could tell their son had had a good time, that he was happy and safe. Also, there was something different about him, but they weren't sure what.

Waking early the following morning Steve blinked to take in the familiar surroundings of his bedroom and then it all came flooding back to him; three great weeks in France and Camille. He thought about her and wondered what she might be doing, was she thinking of him, should he contact her, those brown eyes, that laugh, holding hands and that first kiss. He smiled in recollection and then his Mum knocked the door with a cup of tea.

It was a Saturday morning. Steve always met Tony, John and Paul for a kick around in the local park on Saturday mornings and with that thought he got up, washed and dressed. He then went downstairs for breakfast to find all his family there already and eager to hear more about his trip. There were loads of questions; what was Maurice like, what were his family like, did Steve learn any French, and what did he eat and so on. Steve was happy to tell them all his stories including the trip to Nice but didn't tell them about Camille. He didn't want his Mother and Father or siblings to know about that yet.

With breakfast and chores finished, Steve explained he was off to the park to see his friends and play some football. Arriving at the park it was as if he had never been away. Paul, Tony and John were already there and greeted Steve, asking how he'd got on. They were the same sort of questions Steve's family had asked though this time Steve told them all about Camille, how beautiful she was, holding hands and that first kiss. The other boys all laughed. Paul then told Steve he thought he was going 'soft' and calmly added that actually, something had happened to him this last week and he hadn't had to go all the way to France!

The focus of the conversation quickly switched from Steve to Paul and they eagerly demanded to know more. What was Paul talking about, what had happened? Paul smiled and said, 'Well, you won't believe this but,' and went on to explain he had been doing chores in the kitchen earlier in the week, his elder brothers were out and there was a knock at the back door. Paul expected it to be the post man and was surprised when he opened it to find one of their neighbours, Trudy, standing at the back door. Paul knew Trudy; she was about Paul's age and the younger sister of one of his brother's friends living just around the corner from them.

'Hello,' said Paul as he noticed Trudy was holding a polythene bag. She then asked, 'Would you like to come with me to collect some dock leaves for my rabbit?' Paul was surprised, he'd never really looked at Trudy before, but he noticed she had dark brown eyes and long hair just like Camille. He then added how good looking he thought she was and also, that he felt his heart race just like Steve had described! 'What happened next?!' they all asked.

Paul went on to explain that he walked with Trudy through the small copse behind their house and then out into the large grass field where there were lots of dock leaves and grass. Paul said later that he'd often seen Trudy getting on and off buses to school but that he'd never really spoken to her before. Whilst they were picking the leaves and grass Trudy talked a lot about school and her life at home and being an only child. These were all just casual 'getting to know you' items but as they were about to walk back,

Trudy asked if he had ever heard her and her friends at night in the copse? Paul was puzzled, what did she mean?

She responded to explain that about two months before a group of friends, (all of whom Paul would know as they get the school bus every day to school), decided for a dare to creep out of their houses in the early hours and meet in the copse! It was all harmless, but really great fun she explained and asked if Paul would like to come over that night? Paul said he definitely wanted to, but then wondered if his parents or brothers might hear him creeping out of the house in the middle of the night?

That night Paul couldn't get to sleep, he felt excited about the prospect of creeping out of the house unheard but also, if he went, what would it be like to meet all those girls in the woods? Trudy had said they went out at around one in the morning and crept back around three. 'Just a couple of hours,' she'd said and that some other local boys went as well. It was only a small group around ten in all and Paul had then recognised some of them as Trudy had told him more stories.

Paul looked at his watch again, it had now just gone past one o'clock, and it was dark and very, very quiet. Paul pulled on some clothes and carefully opened his bedroom door. You could hear every sound in the house at night. He crept across the landing and reached the top of the stairs. You could hear the floorboards creak and he could just hear his parents and brothers snoring. It all seemed peaceful, there were no indications of interrupted sleep. He carried on down the stairs. There were further creaks but still the sound of contented sleepers. Paul was relieved as his foot touched the carpeted hall floor. All the creaking sounds were over, yet the sound of the contented sleepers continued!

Paul crept through the lounge and then through the patio doors onto the patio. He'd thought through his exit route whilst lying in bed and had been concerned that if he'd used either the front or kitchen doors that his parents or brothers might have been disturbed. Paul was relieved to get out without disturbing anyone; he set off cautiously to the copse a short distance from the house.

There was an old oak tree in the middle of the copse that had blown over in a storm years ago. Trudy had explained they usually met there. As Paul approached though he couldn't hear anything; he became anxious but then suddenly he heard some muted laughter and within a few more steps he saw Trudy along with some other people. 'Hi,' whispered Paul and Trudy turned around with a big beaming smile, saying, 'Hi,' and proceeded to introduce Paul to everyone in a whisper. The next hour or so flew by as Paul got to meet everyone and realised that he'd met most of them before but fleetingly, on the morning bus, at school or in the local town centre.

After an hour the wind increased, blowing colder air through the copse. As Paul turned from a conversation, he found Trudy beside him saying she was feeling cold and would Paul hold her to make her warm. Paul readily agreed and leaning against the fallen oak tree he opened his coat and then wrapped it around Trudy as she leant against him. Trudy 'purred' with delight and whispered how nice and warm Paul was.

They remained locked in this position for some time; nothing was said. Paul had never held a girl like this before and it felt nice but strange, almost 'tingling' he thought. Her hair smelt so nice as her head nestled on his chest. Then Paul started to feel embarrassed as he felt other stirrings in his groin. He'd felt these stirrings on other occasions and wondered if Trudy was aware. It seemed not, as she remained nestled on his chest, in fact Paul wondered if she was asleep.

After half an hour though, Trudy lifted her head and looked up to Paul. He looked down and through the dark gloom he could see her smiling face. It all seemed so natural and felt so good. Paul leaned down to kiss Trudy and she responded eagerly. It was the first time Paul had kissed a girl and it really felt so good, in fact they carried on kissing for a good twenty minutes until they heard the muted coughs from some of their friends explaining they were going back. Paul and Trudy looked up and smiled; they both felt a little embarrassed but very happy.

Paul then walked Trudy back towards her house with a quick whispered, 'Goodnight,' a final kiss and a smile. Paul then walked back to his house and crept in through the patio doors. All seemed quiet. He carefully closed the door, then tiptoed through the lounge, across the hall and then waited at the bottom of the stairs and listened. He could still hear the soft sound of contented snoring, and just the faint sound of a clock ticking in the kitchen. Encouraged by this he crept up the stairs, anguishing at every creak but still all seemed quiet. Across the landing, more creaks and still all was quiet. Finally, into his bedroom, clothes off and Paul was asleep as soon as his head hit the pillow, but with a big smile. What a great night!

Steve, Tony and John were aghast to hear Paul's story. 'Wow!' said Steve. 'I travelled all the way to the south of France and you, you lucky so and so, get this experience on your doorstep!' They all laughed and went on to talk at length about girls. John explained that his older sister was always talking about boys with her friends when they came round to their house. By contrast Tony said that all he heard his Mum and Dad talk about was work, work and work and they all laughed again. Tony then added that his parents had booked a holiday for him and called it a 'sort of holiday', two weeks on the coast at a rescue training centre. They'd apparently thought this would be good for him!

The boys then realised they'd been sitting around talking for nearly two hours and hadn't yet played any football. 'It's this girl thing, takes up all our time!' said John and they all smiled and started to play.

Although laughing with each other about this 'girl thing' as John called it, the boys were getting increasingly aware of girls. One day Paul brought along some 'girly' magazines as he called them. He explained they belonged to one of his older brothers. The magazines caused delay to football again that day as they looked through the pictures of naked ladies exclaiming 'Wow!' and 'Look at that!' They spent more time though reading some of the stories and chatting about it amongst themselves. They did not understand everything, they were still in their early teenage years and they realised there was still a lot to find out.

At the same time other changes were happening in the boy's lives, from Steve's discovery of a single black hair at fourteen in Avignon he'd now grown a lot more. Still not enough for a beard or moustache, though enough that his Father had bought him a razor and his younger sisters and brother had been told not to touch, too sharp! The boys were all aware of each other's hair growth and used to tease and talk about it. John had none so far, Paul had some, but Tony was the first to actually grow a moustache and became nicknamed 'Adolf' as they were kicking the ball around.

The other big changes in their lives were at school. They increasingly realised that 'O' level exams were important for their future careers; the exams were looming and were to be taken at sixteen years old. Homework was a complete pain but had to be done. Paul was at a Technical School and enjoyed the practical elements saying he was going to be an engineer like his Dad. This often prompted Tony to say he didn't want to work in his Dad's shop but didn't like to tell his parents. He wasn't sure what he wanted to do.

Steve and John weren't sure either and used to discuss various ideas varying from top class footballers to policemen (recalling Paul's incident with the grenade), doctors, farmers (Steve would be interested in working with his Dad, he liked tractors), maybe a dentist. The ideas changed every week, and the discussion was endless. They knew that after their exams at sixteen they would be asked which subjects to choose for senior school and then University entry (did they want to go?), and so the conversations ran on without any serious conclusions in their early teenage years.

Although Tony, Steve and John were at the same school, they were in different class groups but often met each other at break times, at school sports events and on the bus journeys in the mornings and evenings. So the friendships developed as they progressed through their early teenage years.

It was sport though that inspired them all most, the desire to be the best, to beat all others, to be successful. They all enjoyed sport and tried many different ones at school and in local parks. Golf was enjoyable but difficult, tennis fun and swimming was exhausting (John said he got bored with it). Tony loved table tennis, snooker and often won at darts. Paul and Steve were keen on all sports but lacked good ball control. They had both started junior rugby and really enjoyed it.

The boy's development was taking place in several ways in their early teenage years. On the downside there had been examples of what are commonly known as 'Teenage Tantrums' but with boys this was often a case of a lack of food or sleep. They were all growing so quickly and developing with what were known as growth spurts. John used to laugh recalling how his Mum packed him off on his first day of school with extra sandwiches and fruit, how things had changed he laughed!

On the more positive side, it was the competitive instincts they were developing in sports though that would serve them well in future years, particularly in their working lives to achieve their best, but also to develop their confidences in coping with all the other challenges that adult life would bring.

In particular, though they weren't aware of this at the time, there were also links between their ability at sports and their attraction to girls. Going back to the three P's, sports skills enabled them to demonstrate their personal strength to 'Protect' and ability to 'Provide' but now, clearly emerging alongside these the 'Procreation' instinct was emerging with their evidently increasing interest in girls.

CHAPTER 4

DISCOVERY PHASE
(11 – 15 YEARS)
The 'Girl thing'

♂ **THE INCREASING AWARENESS** of girls continued in their early teens. Tony had forgotten about the course his parents had arranged at the coastal rescue centre until a large envelope arrived one day with all his travel information and joining instructions.

Tony was due to board a train the following week. His parents had arranged the course through Tony's school and another pupil, a classmate of Tony's, was due to go with him. However, at the last minute they heard the other boy was unwell and bedridden. Tony was relieved thinking that maybe he would not have to go but his parents quickly assured him he needn't worry, that they would take him to the train station locally and that he'd be collected at the destination by the course providers. Tony had no choice, he was going.

Tony's Mum took him to the station. She gave him a goodbye kiss and wished him good luck, but he was embarrassed by her affection and brushed it off with a wave and a glance over his shoulder as he boarded the train. The train journey was just three hours. Tony was not sure who to ask for on arrival but needn't have worried, as once through the ticket barrier he saw a small group of people with a large sign saying they were from the Centre. Tony went up and gave his name. They welcomed him and explained they were expecting him.

He was shown onto a minibus and within five minutes they were out of the town following a coastal road. There were magnificent views over the sea and twenty minutes later they arrived at the Centre. The boys on the bus were very friendly and welcoming, explaining that they worked at the centre, that it was a great place but run like a military facility with strict arrangements on punctuality and tidiness under the leadership of a Retired Naval Commander Thompson. 'He runs a tight ship,' they explained.

On arrival Tony was shown to his room. It was a long cabin with over twenty beds and there were showers and shared bathroom facilities at the end of the cabin. He was then given a quick tour of the Centre and shown the swimming pool, the canteen, the gymnasium and the external cabins along the quayside, where apparently all the maritime equipment was kept. It was only a short tour around and it was explained to Tony that they needed to be in the lecture room at half past four to meet the other students and there would be a welcoming address from Commander Thompson.

Tony was surprised as he walked into the lecture room. There was a group of very noisy boys, all older than Tony but talking animatedly. It seemed they all knew each other and there were two older men with them as well. When Tony was introduced, he quickly became aware they were all Police Cadets under the supervision of two Sergeants. Tony then realised he was the only private student and at that moment someone called out, 'Take to your seats and remain standing, Commander Thompson is due to arrive.'

Everyone stopped talking and quickly scrambled for their seats. Tony just took the nearest one to him and remained standing. The room hushed and fell silent. It wasn't long before approaching footsteps were heard and then the double doors were pushed open as Commander Thompson strode into the room. He was a giant of a man with an imposing, large white beard. He wore a weathered naval uniform and a polo necked white jumper underneath. He surveyed all the faces and with a smile said, 'Welcome, please be seated.'

Commander Thompson only spoke for around twenty minutes; Tony was spellbound. The Commander spoke quietly but with such an authoritative tone that held everyone's attention. He introduced the staff and then the programme for the next two weeks. All the health and safety issues were highlighted but the overall emphasis was on the development of personal fitness. He expected full commitment from all.

He asked if there were any questions at the end. There were none so he passed over to one of his support team and wished everyone 'good luck' as he strode back out of the room. It was then explained that the first exercise was to take place in the pool and that everyone needed to be changed and by the poolside in fifteen minutes.

When Tony got back to the Cabin, he found all the other boys, the Police Cadets, had moved in too. There was a flurry of activity as everyone tried to find their swimming gear, get changed and down to the pool within the fifteen minute deadline. Once on the poolside a crawl relay event was set up across the width of the pool.

The event was being monitored by the instructors to assess the relative abilities of the individuals. After fifteen minutes the groups were re arranged and the same event was held over the length of the pool. Tony was initially concerned as all the Police Cadets seemed at least two to three years older than him, yet he found he could keep up! However, he was really tired, in fact he felt exhausted and this was only the first exercise! The exercise lasted an hour, after which they showered, changed and were told they could go to the canteen for their evening meal. They had to be back in the lecture room again by six o'clock for a brief seminar.

The evening meal was a noisy affair with plenty of enthusiastic reflections from the cadets with a lot of laughter and leg pulling. Excited about the centre, they looked forward to the activities and challenges ahead of them.

However, Tony found it difficult to join in the conversations, he was clearly and understandably the outsider. They were older than him and had been working with each other for some months. The meal was really welcome after all the exercises in the pool, the cadets were ravenous and sought extra helpings. After what seemed only a short while though, a whistle was blown by one of the Instructors and he announced everyone needed to be in the Lecture Room in five minutes, no excuses for lateness!

The lecture was about 'mouth to mouth' resuscitation. The students were invited to consider several scenarios in which the mouth to mouth method could be used. It was explained how to check for vital signs and to ensure the head and particularly the neck were carefully aligned. Various diagrams were provided and then there was a practical element with dummy corpses to put into practice the theoretical information they had received. Tony found it all very interesting but quite straightforward. Little did he appreciate that he should have listened more attentively as he was to discover the following morning.

Tony was in a deep sleep at six thirty the following morning when the whistle was blown by an instructor asking them all to get up and be ready to go for a run on the beach in ten minutes. It took a moment or two to realise where he was and then, seeing the other boys leaping out of their beds and getting dressed he did likewise. He was soon ready in running shorts, T shirt and shoes though he felt weary and wished he was back at home with that traditional cup of tea his Mum always brought up in the morning.

His wistful reflections were soon forgotten though as they ran out of the centre and along the beach. The sun was bright, and a strong breeze greeted them; it was a glorious morning! They ran as a group onto the beach and along the soft sand in front of the breaking waves. The instructor had indicated they would jog but such was the competition amongst the cadets that they were quickly trying to outpace each other. They would quickly learn to conserve their energies however, as the next hour involved a lot of physical exercise including sprinting, press ups, relays and games of tag, all to develop their fitness and strength. Although Tony was younger, he found he could keep up, though the older boys seemed to have more physical strength than he did. The hour was soon over, and they returned to the centre at a markedly slower pace. They were really looking forward to a big breakfast but were alarmed to hear that before breakfast they were to get changed into their swimming trunks and to be poolside in five minutes.

Tony was aware of the quiet grumbling amongst the cadets. As Police Cadets they were being trained to follow orders and were outwardly responding positively, but there was a lot of muttering amongst them whilst getting changed and when running poolside. Their main concerns were wondering when breakfast would take place; food was certainly the priority for active, young men! Once poolside a whistle brought them all to attention. They were asked to jump into the shallow end and team up in pairs.

Tony jumped in along with the others who, knowing each other, quickly lined up in pairs, waist deep. Tony wasn't sure who he should pair with and was relieved when one of the large, bearded Police Sergeants saw his dilemma and beckoned him over. The instructor then explained they were to practise the mouth to mouth exercises they had discussed in the previous evening's lecture. They were to imagine they had rescued a person at sea, brought them into shallow water and that they needed to perform mouth to mouth in shallow water to revive the person or 'corpse' and keep them alive. They would need to work out how to support the body and carefully align the head and neck.

Tony turned to the bearded Police Sergeant who quickly said that he would be the corpse first and he fell back in the water lying horizontal with his eyes shut. Tony moved forward to support the corpse; he was a massive man, covered in hairs all over his upper body and was a lot larger than Tony who tried to ensure that the head and shoulders were supported as they had been shown. It was then, looking at the Police Sergeant's large beard and mouth that Tony became really alarmed at the prospect of applying his mouth to the Sergeant's. It seemed such a weird thing to do and yet the Sergeant was lying there in the water expectantly, behaving like the perfect corpse! Glancing around Tony saw, out of the corner of his eye, that all the other students were getting on with the exercise and therefore so should he!

What happened next is difficult to relate. On the one hand, Tony was about to suffer the most embarrassing experience of his life. On the other, it had the effect of Tony being accepted as a full colleague and comrade in the Police Cadets group. With hindsight Tony had missed a vital part on the previous evening's lecture, in which it had been explained that the rescuer doesn't apply mouth to mouth to a live body as this can be dangerous. The exercise was just to practise positioning and supporting the corpse. Once the rescuer had the body adequately supported, he was only to blow down the side of the corpse's neck!

Having missed this vital bit of information, Tony was feeling very uncomfortable looking down at the expectant Police Sergeant, with his bushy beard and big lips. Again, he glanced around at the others and realised he just had to do it also. Courageously, he leaned forward and firmly applied his lips to the Sergeant's.

In later discussions, the cadets described how there was what seemed like a massive eruption in the pool. The waters surged as the Police Sergeant leapt out of his composed corpse position to push Tony aside, letting out a loud shout saying, 'What the … ?' and then towered above him and demanded to know what he was up to! The Police Sergeant was to say later that it was the biggest shock of his career but also, in that moment as he glared down on Tony his shock turned to laughter as he saw that Tony was equally shocked.

In fact, it was bellowed laughter through which the Police Sergeant struggled to explain what had happened and that in all his years of public service, he'd never been kissed before. The rest of the group were initially puzzled and surprised to hear the commotion. As it became clear what had happened, they all laughed too.

The Instructor sought to remind everyone that the rescuer should never attempt mouth to mouth on live persons! Much to the delight of everyone, he closed the session and advised they could all go to breakfast. Tony meanwhile felt completely embarrassed and humiliated, though he had no idea that this 'incident' was to help him and his relationships with the rest of the group.

Tony continued to feel uncomfortable as he collected his breakfast in the canteen. Like the others he was ravenously hungry and collected as much as he could from the various dishes on the breakfast counter. He was painfully aware of the laughter and energetic discussions taking place around him and chose to sit on his own a little way from the main group, wishing that he wasn't there at all and that the ground would swallow him up!

But then, as is often the case in life, the unexpected happened. Three of the cadets got up from their table with their food trays and came over to sit with Tony. The ice was broken as one of the cadets explained he was jealous as he had fancied that Police Sergeant and all four of them broke into laughter. The conversation then flowed easily as Tony explained he had never carried out mouth to mouth before and his dilemma (and complete horror!) as he had stared down at the Sergeant's lips, believing he had to kiss them. The cadets laughed with Tony and went on to explain they were going for a walk that evening on the pier after the sessions were over and would Tony like to join them. No longer embarrassed, he started to feel accepted and part of the group at last.

The next few days flew by quickly with plenty of physical activities in the pool, at sea and the gymnasium, coupled with theoretical sessions in the lecture room to develop teamwork and understanding of the importance of good communication when rescuing people. Tony particularly enjoyed the sailing and the reel and line methods. He found he was being accepted by all the cadets who continued to make humorous references to the Sergeant kissing incident but laughed with him rather than at him.

Tony felt his physical strength and general confidence improve. This was particularly evident in the evenings when after the daily sessions were over, Tony and the three other cadets walked along the pier. The three cadets were nearly two years older than Tony and were interested in girls. As the walks progressed, they had met and got to know some of the local girls on the pier. The cadets spoke confidently to the girls discussing everything including sport, music, films and school, college and work issues.

After a few evenings there was some physical contact, just holding hands and arms around shoulders. Tony felt he should keep up with the others. The girl sitting next to him at the time seemed quite nice, so he moved his hand over to hold hers and was pleased she didn't withdraw. He glanced at her after a few minutes, and she smiled back at him! Over the next few evenings, the physical contact continued and progressed to kissing (or 'snogging' as it was called). The conversations subsided markedly as long bouts of snogging took place and Tony found he really enjoyed it!

All good things have to come to an end, or so the saying goes, and it was not long before Tony found himself back on the train and heading for home. There had been a course closing review in the lecture room the previous evening with an invigorating final address from Commander Thompson. The farewells to the girls on the pier afterwards had been particularly amorous and Tony smiled as he reflected on everything that had happened on and off the course. He was looking forward to visiting his sick friend when he returned home to tell him what had happened but also to tell John, Steve and Paul as well.

Tony was met by his Mum at the station. She explained his Dad was working on the shop, that the house had been extremely quiet and that they'd really missed him. Tony told his Mum he'd had a great time and described all the sporting events, the meals and the accommodation but avoided any mention of kissing either Police Sergeants or local girls!

Tony's Dad arrived home early evening and his Mum served up what she called a 'welcome home tea' with Tony's favourite eggy bread and tomato sauce. During the meal, Tony told his Dad the same stories he'd told his Mum earlier and again avoided any indication of kissing either Police Sergeants or local girls. His Dad was really interested and explained he wished he had gone on similar courses when he had been Tony's age.

At the end of the meal Tony explained he was going off to the recreation ground to play football with Steve, John and Paul. Tony's Dad wasn't happy about this and said they would like to talk more to him as they had not seen him for some time. There was an awkward atmosphere in the room which ended with Tony insisting he would go as he had not seen his friends for some time either. He thanked his Mum for the tea and left the house. Once he'd left, Tony's parents discussed the situation and although it had been a mild confrontation it was the first time they had experienced any assertion from Tony against their wishes. 'I suppose we'll just have to accept he is growing up,' concluded Tony's Dad with a grimace.

Tony ran to the recreation ground and was really pleased to see that John, Steve and Paul were already there. 'Who are you?!' Steve teased as Tony ran towards them. They sat down on the grass and started talking. Tony led the conversation with stories about his course at the coastal rescue centre but this time he included the time he kissed the Police Sergeant. This caused his friends' jaws to drop and then they rolled over in the grass laughing uncontrollably. They asked a flurry of questions to find out what the cadets had thought and were really interested when Tony explained how he had initially been really embarrassed and humiliated but then how the incident had broken the ice with the cadets, who accepted him into their group from there on.

It was when Tony went on to describe their walks on the pier in the evenings and how the cadets had helped him to meet the local girls that their attention was really gripped, particularly as Tony explained how he'd held a girl's hand and ended up having long 'snogging sessions'. 'Wow!' said Paul, 'That sounds like my sessions with Trudy!' but it was at this moment that the attention moved from Tony to John as he said quietly, 'It's great, I've been finding out about 'snogging' as well!'

John was smiling as they turned towards him but noticeably, he was a little flushed, 'You look embarrassed' said Steve, 'What's been going on John?!' John seemed hesitant at first as he explained his sister didn't know yet but that he'd recently met 'Susan'. He'd known her for some time as she was the younger sister of one of his sister's friends. 'All a bit complicated,' John said as he went on to emphasise that he'd like to keep it quiet for the time being in case his sister was upset by the liaison, though he couldn't think why she should be.

Apparently, John had recognised Susan only the week before at a local fete. 'Our eyes met, and she just smiled,' said John, 'I went up to her and we just chatted and recalled the last time we'd met over five years ago at a family party.' John described how much Susan had changed, that he remembered how she used to be a short girl but how she'd now grown taller and that she looked 'really nice' gesticulating to indicate she now had breasts and how taken he was with her. As they talked John said he had held her hand as well, 'Just like you with that girl you met Tony!' and they all laughed. On parting John said they had a brief kiss but agreed to meet again the following evening.

It was on the following evening that they had their first real kiss, John explained they had gone for a walk in the local park and as dusk went down, they had sat on a bench and kissed for a long time, 'Is that what you call snogging Tony?' asked John. It was then, when walking her home that she invited John around to her house to meet her parents the following week! 'Wow, things are happening quickly there John,' said Steve and they all laughed again.

The boys carried on chatting happily reflecting on recent events. 'We've been here over an hour and not kicked a ball yet again!' said Paul, 'Just as John said last time we were here!' and they all agreed things were changing. John said, 'Yeah, first it was Steve with that girl in France, then Paul helping Trudy collect rabbit food, then Tony kissing Police Sergeants (they all laughed) and now me with Susan. What's happening to us all?' They all laughed again, it was now too dark to play football, so they set off back to their homes.

The 'Procreation' instinct was now certainly established with all four friends and years later they would come to reflect fondly on these early experiences in their mid-teens.

CHAPTER 5

DESIRE PHASE
(15 – 18 YEARS)
Boys becoming Men

YES, THINGS WERE changing. In fact, they were changing a great deal and on a number of fronts as they moved from early to mid and then late teens. Perhaps the most noticeable changes were the physical ones; the boys had all quickly grown taller, become stronger with evident upper body strength along with increased facial and body hair. Tony was particularly proud of his moustache. They never told each other this, but each of them enjoyed strutting around in front of the mirror, privately admiring their evident progression into manhood.

Along with this spurt in growth there were marked changes in their appetites. The boys were always hungry, their parents noticed they had to make return trips to the supermarket each week to top up. There were emotional changes too, in part to develop their personal confidence perhaps due to the increased attraction to girls? It was no longer a case of 'this girl thing' but a strong sense of desire every time they saw a girl. They joked amongst themselves about what caused erections or 'Hard-ons' as they were called.

There were further changes, driven mainly by a sense of responsibility with growing up into manhood. What careers or jobs would they have, how might they earn a living and raise families as their fathers had done? Maybe they should work harder at school to get better exam results and eventually better jobs and greater earnings?

But they rarely discussed these matters amongst themselves. Their parents were always encouraging them to work harder and achieve more but there was still a lot they didn't understand and weren't ready for. Steve was still potentially interested in joining his Father on the family farm, he still liked tractors! Tony was certain he didn't want to join his Dad in the shop; he had no idea what he wanted to do. Paul still liked engineering; the Technical School he went to provided excellent practical assignments that he enjoyed, but he had no idea which area of engineering to work in. John was equally unsure and occasionally said he might go into teaching but was then teased by the others that he could never be another Mrs Collier! They all laughed at the 'Collywobbles' and 'Wobblycolly' memories.

The discussions around future career interests were to occur more frequently as they prepared for exams, but otherwise their main interests were sports and girls. All the boys were in various teams at their schools. There were excellent sporting facilities at the Grammar school and Tony, Steve and John all took an active interest in football in the winter months and cricket in the summer. There was a gymnasium for games of table tennis and badminton and an outdoor swimming pool as well. The sporting facilities at Paul's Technical School weren't quite as good as the Grammar school. Paul often reflected on this and realised more money had to be spent on the practical facilities the school offered and that these would then be much better than the Grammar School! Paul played in the cricket and football teams, but there was no swimming pool and only a small Gymnasium.

As far as girls were concerned, it was John who seemed to be making more progress than the others. His invitation to Susan's house had included afternoon tea and he found he got on well with her parents and was now often calling at their house. Susan and John both liked music. They often sat up in her bedroom listening to music whilst her parents were downstairs. It was getting serious, the privacy of her bedroom let them get on with plenty of snogging and a lot more besides. Susan said it was unlikely, but they were both anxious that her parents might walk in and find them in an amorous entanglement!

Steve was looking forward to Maurice's visit from France, to stay with him and his family. He was anxious though as his way of life was considerably different to Maurice's. Steve lived on a farm in a semi-rural location; he didn't have the network of friends and contacts that Maurice had in Avignon. Steve discussed this with his friends. They considered creeping out of the house in the middle of the night as Paul still did to join Trudy and her friends, but Steve felt this was just too risky. He felt they would be bound to wake up Steve's younger sisters and brother.

Instead, they arranged to meet Paul with Trudy and some of her friends in the woods in the daytime. Steve was looking forward to this. Maurice arrived the following week and spent the first few days settling in, meeting Steve's family and going around the farm. Steve was intrigued to see how Maurice coped with his English pronunciation and vocabulary. The roles were in reverse he thought and he smiled quietly as his Father often corrected Maurice in the same way that Maurice's Dad had corrected him!

Steve was surprised by one particular item though as when Maurice was describing his family, he made reference to his cousins living near Nice and specifically explained that his cousin 'Camille' was in love with a French boy of her age who lived near her. The news caused Steve to initially feel envious, perhaps jealous and certainly sad. He concealed his feelings as it was during a general family discussion but later asked Maurice who simply confirmed the news. When Steve then thought about it in his own privacy, he still felt sad, but resolved it was time to move on!

And so, the arranged meetings in the woods with Paul, Trudy and her friends took on an extra level of interest. Steve vaguely knew some of Trudy's friends and hoped they would turn up. It was mid-afternoon the following day that Steve took Maurice into the woods. He was surprised but pleased to see Trudy had brought several friends with her but then dismayed as Maurice quickly became the centre of attention. The girls were fascinated by Maurice's accent and overwhelmed him with questions about Avignon, his school, his family, his interests. The afternoon passed by happily and quickly and they arranged to meet again the following afternoon. At one point Paul glanced to Steve and muttered that he thought Trudy had forgotten him and grimaced. They both laughed.

The following afternoon started in much the same way. Maurice was the centre of attention. Talking with his French accent, he intrigued the girls again who implored him with more and more questions whilst Paul and Steve stood by. After half an hour though the situation changed. A girl with long straight blonde hair had been leaning on the tree alongside Maurice and everyone was surprised when he suddenly put his arm around her. The rest of the girls were aghast, realising he was interested in the blonde haired girl and not one of them. They tried to conceal their dismay. The blonde haired girl smiled.

It was Trudy who suggested they then went for a walk through the woods and as they set off, she put her arm eagerly through Paul's and smiled at him. Maurice was no longer the centre of attention, but he seemed very happy walking with his arm around the blonde girl. Meanwhile Steve found he was walking between two other girls, both good looking. The afternoon passed happily. At one point,

Steve looked ahead and saw Maurice was now kissing the blonde girl. He looked round to Paul who was also kissing Trudy. Steve felt left out but found he just enjoyed talking and laughing with the other two girls; he couldn't decide which one he preferred. 'Such a problem,' he thought to himself with a smile! The afternoon finished with Steve and Paul explaining they were taking Maurice to play football the following day, but they arranged to meet the girls again in the copse the day afterwards.

Football the following day was great fun, just a kick about but again, it was Maurice who was the centre of attention; he was enthusiastic but just so clumsy, the worst footballer the boys said, that they had ever seen. He tripped over, miskicked, ran into others but all the time there was great laughter with Maurice laughing with them and saying he obviously wasn't going to play football when he was older. The boys readily agreed.

After an hour or so, exhausted but still laughing, the boys sat down to rest. Steve and Paul told John and Tony what a complete hit Maurice had been with the local girls in the copse the last two days and how Maurice had ended up with the good looking blonde haired girl. Maurice's face coloured and he looked a little embarrassed but also smiled. John coughed and said that his situation had changed too. It was funny because as he said this his face coloured also and he too looked a little embarrassed. The other boys were really intrigued and implored John to tell them more!

John smiled. He then went on to explain he had been asked to go with Susan and her parents to an awards dinner at Susan's father's golf club where her father was the golf club President. John had to wear a jacket with a collar and tie. It was very 'posh' he said and went on to describe the amazing dress Susan had worn and how stunning she had looked. It had been a long night; the speeches were a little boring, but the food was great, and

Susan's father had kept buying them drinks all night. As he was the President, Susan's father had to stay until the very end and as they had been drinking a lot, they ordered a taxi to get home.

It was on the way home that Susan's mother realised it was late for John to get home and invited, or rather insisted he should stay overnight with them. She explained that she would call John's mother to let her know he was safe. John thanked her profusely and glanced at Susan who beamed back at him with a huge smile and hugged his arm. After a quick night cap, Susan's mother showed John to his room. It was a large house and the room was at the very back and next to a bathroom. Susan's parents slept at the front of the house. Susan's room was opposite John's and at the back of the house near the same bathroom.

John slept heavily; he'd drunk a lot. After a couple of hours though he was suddenly wide awake and needed the toilet, but where was he? It took a moment to recall and then he tiptoed out of bed and crept towards the bathroom. On his way back he noticed Susan's door was just ajar and decided to pop around the door to see if she was asleep. She wasn't.

She had heard John get up and, in a whisper, beckoned him towards her. John's heart was racing as he crept across her room. He sat on the edge of her bed and leaned over to kiss her. Susan's response was warm, she pulled open the bed covers, and he slipped in beside her, both their bodies trembling in anticipation. They spoke in the faintest of whispers, anxious that her parents should not be disturbed.

The sexual tension was so strong. John said how much he wanted to make love with Susan who said she felt the same way surprising John completely by saying she had a packet of condoms! John was amazed, but said he had never worn one before and they both supressed a laugh as she leant over to find the packet in her bedside draw whispering she had bought them 'just in case' and had felt and hoped this might happen. There was further supressed laughter as he opened the packet and fitted the condom, then they looked at each other through the darkened room and smiled. Susan said she had not made love before and asked John to be careful, they smiled again and kissed. They then made love quietly though thoroughly immersed in the pleasures of that first time experience of love making.

The following morning Susan's mother knocked on John's bedroom door and asked if he wanted a cup of tea. She then walked in and asked if he had slept well. John thanked her and said he had slept very well. Susan's mother asked if he could get down for breakfast in half an hour and closed the door as she left. John lay in bed with a huge, contented smile on his face; all the memories of the evening and night flooded back to him, he just couldn't believe all that had happened, and he felt so happy! He washed and dressed and then as he walked out of the room, he heard Susan talking to her mother downstairs in the kitchen. As he walked in Susan greeted him warmly with a smile and a kiss and asked if he'd slept well; it was so natural and almost as if nothing had happened! Susan's father then came into the kitchen complaining of a 'muzzy head' and getting no sympathy at all from his wife.

They had an enjoyable breakfast. John helped to wash up and then Susan came with him to the door to say goodbye. Their embrace was really strong and lingering. They then paused for breath, looked at each other with a beaming smile and then laughed, they were so happy. Susan whispered her love for John and that she couldn't bear to be apart from him. John hugged and kissed her more, saying he felt the same but had to go.

It was Steve who broke the moment. He and the others had been spellbound by John's story; 'Wow!' said Steve, 'That's amazing John, you're the first one of us to make love to a girl,' but at this point it was Tony who spoke up saying, 'Well actually he's not quite the first,' and all eyes swung in his direction. It was now Tony now whose face blushed, and he too looked a little embarrassed. Maurice was spellbound by all that he heard and found he was learning English much more quickly than he thought he would!

'What do you mean Tony?' asked Steve. Tony looked back and said, 'You won't believe this,' and then went on to describe a barbeque he'd been to, reluctantly, with his parents a week before John's golfing awards dinner. The barbeque was at friends of Tony's parents and they had been going to this party annually for what seemed like years. He'd not wanted to go at all and knew everyone there would be old and boring, or so he thought.

Tony followed his parents into the house, and they were warmly welcomed and introduced. There was someone there Tony had not met before, who was much younger than all the others. When they were introduced it was explained she was a cousin and had recently been divorced and moved back to the area. Her name was Celia. Tony thought she looked really nice. She asked him how old he was and when he said seventeen, she said, 'Wow! I thought you were much older than that!' and went on to make complimentary comments about his thick moustache.

Tony thought nothing more about it and enjoyed a couple of beers and a cheeseburger whilst listening to all the boring updates from his friends' parents. He found it particularly nauseating when they asked about his progress at school and then, perhaps well intentioned, but really patronising, they then said, 'If I were you ...' and went on to describe their careers, often forgetting they'd told the same stories last year.

A couple of hours had passed when there was suddenly a commotion. Celia was talking with the hosts in an anxious way and explained she thought she had not put her burglar alarm on properly in her new house. She looked over to Tony and asked if he would mind going back to her house with her to check everything was properly locked. Tony readily agreed; he was pleased to escape the barbeque and all those boring stories! He told his Mum he was off to help Celia and that he'd get back soon. Celia was waiting for him in the driveway of the house beside an open topped, red sports car. It was one Tony had always dreamed of, 'Wow!' he thought as he slid into the passenger seat and tried to look cool and calm.

Celia was a good driver; she knew how to handle a fast and powerful sports car. It took twenty minutes to drive back. The car purred as she sped along, the stereo system was at full blast and playing all the songs Tony liked. 'Are you ok?' she asked as they came around a sharp corner and Tony smiled back at her and said, 'Oh yes, this is like heaven.' He then threw his head back and laughed. Arriving at her house, Tony could not fail but to be impressed; she pulled up outside a gated entrance, the gate swung open with a remote control from the car and there was a short drive leading to a modern low level house set in immaculate gardens with a large swimming pool as well.

Celia let Tony in through the main entrance and they went to the security control panel which revealed everything was working, Celia need not have worried. She then showed him around the house, it was modern in décor and design, and Tony was impressed and said so. As the conversation developed it became clear that Celia had received a lot of money in her divorce settlement. References to 'her ex' were bitter. Celia offered Tony a drink and then explained she was going to check upstairs as well and to change her dress.

It was only a few minutes later that she called down the stairs and asked if Tony could come up as there was a window she couldn't close. Tony put his drink down and went up the stairs and heard Celia call out, 'I'm in here!' He pushed open a door leading into a large bedroom where he found Celia standing in a thin night gown and under a small dormer window that was ajar. He stepped forward and reached up to close the window and then looked down to see Celia beside him and looking up. She smiled. Tony felt aroused; he bent down and kissed her, it just seemed so natural. Celia responded strongly and as Tony's hands moved under her night gown, he realised she was wearing nothing underneath.

They made love twice in quick succession. Tony could not believe it had happened, he had not made love before and Celia was more than twice his age! It had felt amazing. He lay on her pillow with her head on his shoulder staring at the ceiling and reliving the last hour in his mind. He looked down to see her smiling at him on his chest. Yes, it was real! He found she was so easy to talk to and enjoyed being with her. Explaining he'd not made love before, Celia responded cheekily saying she could teach him a lot. He laughed with her but then they realised they should be getting back to the party as they'd been away nearly two hours. Travelling back in her car they chatted further. Celia asked if Tony would like to visit her again and smiled at his eager response, 'Yes please!'

It was John who chipped in first. 'Oh my God,' he said, 'that's a great story. I thought I was the first, but it was you, what an amazing experience! Have you seen her again?' There was a barrage of questions from all the others too who'd been entranced by Tony's story. They had thought John's experience was amazing too, but Tony's was 'something else' they said and smiled. Maurice remained incredulous and laughed saying that things just don't happen like this in France. He then asked Tony if he thought he should grow a moustache too, maybe that would that help him to find an older woman?

73

They all laughed at Maurice's question in his broken English but then John chipped in to say, 'You didn't answer my question Tony, are you seeing her again?' Tony looked reflective and said, 'I'm not sure, it's been over two weeks now and I've not heard from her, do you think I should call her?' There was no consensus; Steve and John said 'yes' but Paul said 'wait', Maurice didn't comment. There was no conclusion.

They carried on talking. John and Tony teased Steve and Paul about still being virgins and reckoned Paul would be next as he was getting on well with Trudy. However, Steve they said had no prospect in sight and in fact, Maurice stood a good chance with his blonde haired beauty or 'Blondie' as they now called her. The discussion was frivolous but fun. Tony was ridiculed when he said he'd read the posh word for sex was 'procreation', all agreeing that sex was a better word and 'easier to spell' someone said. It was late when they all decided to head home.

Although the four friends agreed 'sex' was easier to spell than 'Procreation' this was just a distraction. The truth was that they had all become focussed on sex becoming more important than their sporting or educational interests. It was like a great awakening, something they had not anticipated. They were surprised that it was something they just couldn't get out of their minds. They would reflect on these feelings later in their lives and smile.

CHAPTER 6

DESIRE PHASE
(15-18 YEARS OLD)
Boys become Men

PAUL WOKE UP early the following morning and reflected on the conversation with John and Tony. He wondered if they were correct in their prediction that he and Trudy would be the next to have sex or would he remain a virgin? He knew he fancied her, the snogging was great, and he felt they were becoming more physical, but he wondered when they could take it a stage further as there were always others around them. In Tony's situation with Celia, it had been in the privacy of her home, in John's case it was in Susan's parents' house.

He pondered further; it would be frustrating if Maurice managed to have sex with Blondie before he did with Trudy. Steve didn't seem to have any activity with any girls at the moment. In fact, it all seemed to be a bit of a race, the boys were trying to prove to each other that they were attractive to girls and if not, wondering if there be something wrong with them? Really? Paul thought on further. There were other things on his mind, and he suspected on the minds of his friends also: exams!

The boys were all in what was known as their 'O' level exam year and were taking up to nine subjects, two of which, Maths and English were compulsory. The other exams were across a broad spectrum of Arts and Science subjects. The boy's parents were eagerly encouraging them to work hard. They were talking to the boys, pointing out that the outcome of their 'O' level exams would help them choose which three 'A' level subjects they would specialise in and thereafter their choice of University and eventual careers.

These conversations with parents were often daunting and difficult. The boys all realised their parents were trying to help them but were frustrated as they really had no firm idea yet what they wanted to do in their careers. They didn't talk about this amongst themselves often, partly because it was a relief not to have to but also, they were much more interested in their conversations about girls and sport.

Paul was musing through these thoughts in his early morning slumber. He didn't think Tony would follow his Dad into retail. Tony had been quite open about this when they'd briefly talked about it saying it was long hours and often boring. Steve, on the other hand was a little more certain, saying that he might join his Father on the farm. But Paul was aware he was having second thoughts. Just what he was good at and would enjoy wasn't clear yet. John was openly despondent on his future career and prospects declaring he had 'absolutely no idea!'

Paul's thoughts then turned to his own circumstances. His Dad's engineering business seemed to be doing well and his two elder brothers were showing increasing interest in joining him once they finished senior school. Would Paul like to work with his two brothers? At home, it was always Paul who seemed to be landed with all the chores. Would it be like this also if he was working with his brothers? With this idle thought Paul became more awake. He realised he would not like the idea of working with his brothers but also, he was troubled to think that he just had no idea of what it was he wanted to do with his life!

As Paul got up, these thoughts faded, and he started to look forward to meeting Trudy in the copse with some of her friends along with Steve and Maurice. His brothers were in their usual mood during breakfast. There was plenty of teasing banter and then insistence that Paul should complete his chores. This helped Paul in his passing thoughts to realise again that he couldn't work with them when he was older, but just what would he do?!

He smiled as he walked into the copse as Trudy was already there with her friends. The sun was shining through the trees behind her and he thought she looked just great.

Steve and Maurice hadn't arrived. The girls were actively discussing Blondie and explaining she wouldn't be coming that morning, that in fact she didn't want to meet Maurice again as she didn't like him! How should they tell Maurice this when he arrived? They were still debating this actively, with no real conclusion when they noticed Steve and Maurice approaching and fell silent.

Steve noticed the fall off in conversation as they'd approached and with a cheery smile said, 'Morning all; is everything ok?' The girls remained silent, and Paul felt he should explain. He simply looked at Maurice and said, 'Your girlfriend is not here today and has asked us to tell you she is not interested to see you again.' Maurice's face was crestfallen; he was very upset and asked why. The girls now talked all at once, which served to confuse Maurice more. They could see he was upset and tried to explain.

The explanations were balanced with comments on what a nice person they all thought Maurice was but that Blondie had simply realised Maurice would be returning to France soon and that she could not see any future in their relationship and that she was also very upset. Steve added at this point that whilst he'd been in France, he had met a girl called Camille and really liked her. Explaining the background to the girls and added that they had kissed. He then looked forlorn as he explained she was now seeing a local French boy.

The conversation lightened as they talked more, Maurice was able to say how sorry he was and asked the girls to pass on his best wishes to Blondie. As he said this, he raised his voice and his arms in despair but with a smile too. Everyone smiled with him and said they would pass on his best wishes. They carried on talking as a group for an hour or so; there was a feeling of relief that a difficult situation had been dealt with. Towards the end Trudy leant forward to Paul and whispered, 'My Mum wants to know if you would like to come to our house for tea later this week?' Paul was surprised and initially taken back. 'Oh yes, I mean yes please,' he stuttered, and the following Friday evening was agreed.

They left the copse and Paul walked Trudy back to her house and kissed her. She responded readily and hugged him too. As Paul walked home, he smiled to himself and felt his relationship with Trudy was moving forward now, maybe they would become lovers. Steve meanwhile was aware Maurice was upset; he would be returning home to France that Friday evening. The visit had gone well, they had done a lot and Maurice's English had improved markedly. But had he been upset with the rejection by Blondie?'

Steve was relieved when later that evening Maurice spoke about it in a reflective mood to say that he had enjoyed meeting English girls but was now looking forward to seeing his French girls again back in his town. Steve laughed with him saying, 'There's plenty of fish in the sea you know,' and then had to explain this expression to Maurice. They both laughed.

Maurice left that Friday evening. Maurice thanked Steve's parents and family profusely for their hospitality, explaining he had really enjoyed his stay with them. Steve and Maurice would never speak again or have any further contact; they had both enjoyed the 'language exchange experience'. They had learned a lot from each other, and it was not all to do with just language! It was the same Friday evening that Paul went to tea with Trudy's parents.

Paul had made the mistake of telling his brothers and parents that he had been invited to Trudy's house to meet her parents. His brothers were merciless in teasing Paul and amongst many jokes they suggested he'd be married in six months. His parents anguished and asked the brothers to just relax and be quiet. They then explained Paul would need to look smart and take a present to thank Trudy's parents for their hospitality. Paul hadn't thought about all this fuss, he just felt he wanted to get closer to Trudy, he really liked her.

When he came downstairs to go to her house his brothers were waiting in the kitchen. Paul was wearing his best trousers and a shirt. The brothers wolf whistled as he walked into the kitchen and then smiled, clapped him on the back and wished him the very best of luck. Although they were teasing, it was good humoured and well intentioned. Paul went into the sitting room to say goodbye to his parents who also wished him well and his mum remarked that he looked 'very smart' reminding him there were some flowers by the door for Trudy's Mum.

Trudy answered the door with a big smile and stepped forward to give him a kiss. 'Wow you look smart,' she said. Paul noticed she had a really nice dress on as well and felt a stirring as he kissed and hugged her in their hallway, but Trudy stepped back saying, 'Come through and meet my parents.' Trudy's parents were sitting in their lounge, Paul stepped forward to shake Trudy's Dad's hand. It was a firm shake. They both looked each other in the eyes and smiled. As Paul turned towards Trudy's Mum, he bent down and kissed her on the cheek and passed the flowers to her. She seemed really impressed, saying how nice it was to receive flowers and looking to her husband as she said it. Paul noticed the glance and her husband's vexed look.

The conversation evolved; they discussed Paul's family and that he was one of three brothers. 'How nice, we'd have loved to have had more children' said Trudy's Mum with a wistful look. They weighed up the benefits of large and small families with Trudy's father commenting that she had all their time and attention. It transpired that this was the first time that Trudy had bought a boyfriend home to meet her parents. Paul felt flushed; he was encouraged and wondered whether this was going to become a more serious relationship soon?

Trudy's father asked him about his Dad's engineering business and Paul described the products they made. The conversation then moved onto sport and they discussed recent local and national events. It seemed to be going well. Trudy's Mum brought in plates of sandwiches with cake and biscuits and then poured the tea and passed it around.

A strange thing then happened. As they started to eat the sandwiches the conversation seemed to just dry up. Paul felt awkward, he wanted to make the right impression on Trudy's parents, but he didn't know what to say next. There was casual conversation as the sandwiches were passed around but also noticeable periods of silence. Paul racked his brains and then remembered a story his Dad had told him. Thinking it might amuse Trudy's parents he decided to tell it. This was a big mistake.

'Actually,' started Paul, 'I was talking to my Dad the other day about his early girlfriends, and he told me a very funny story.' Trudy's Mum smiled. 'Oh, do tell us Paul,' she said encouragingly. Paul smiled back and went on to explain his Dad had studied Mechanical Engineering at University; it had been a great course with a lively life on campus but was dominated by men. Apparently though, there was a Nurses' home attached to a hospital under a mile away and one night he met one of the nurses at the end of a disco on campus. They chatted and agreed to go out for a date the following Saturday evening.

During the afternoon of the following Saturday, Paul's Dad was working in his room in his hall when he suddenly realised that he only had one clean shirt left and that it didn't have many buttons on it. With that thought in mind he jumped up and checked in his wardrobe and sure enough, the shirt only had two buttons on the front. He didn't have any spare buttons, no needles and no cotton. He went out of his room and knocked on the doors of his fellow students to see if they could help but being a Saturday afternoon, they were all out. What should he do?

He checked his watch, there were still a couple of hours to go and he realised he had just enough time to walk up to the local Woolworth's store, buy the items, run back to the halls, sew on the buttons and then dash off to the nurses home. Yes, just enough time but it would be tight!

Paul glanced at this point and looked up to Trudy's parents; he could see they were fully absorbed in his Dad's dilemma. Paul carried on explaining his Dad dashed up to the store, but on arrival in the town realised that as it was just before Christmas, everywhere was very busy. He worked his way through the crowds in the Woolworths store to where they sold the linen and sewing items. He selected the cotton and buttons he needed and went towards the counter to pay but there was a long queue. Paul's Dad was starting to become anxious; time was ticking by. It was in the days before mobile phones, and he had no way of contacting the nurse. If he wasn't at the agreed rendezvous at the time they'd agreed, it was likely she would go. He checked his watch again; yes, it would be tight, and that queue seemed so, so slow! Paul glanced again at Trudy's parents feeling that they were becoming even more absorbed preventing any more awkward silences.

He carried on. When his Dad got to the till to pay, he was really running out of time (and patience too!). The items he wanted to buy didn't cost a lot; he was paying cash and had sorted out the exact amount of money to the penny. When he got to the till, he thrust the items and the exact cash into the cashier's hands. As she rang up the items, he picked them up and dashed off without waiting for his receipt or for the cashier to put the items in a bag. This was a big mistake.

As he worked his way through the crowded store and reached the exit door, he felt a hand close on his shoulder and turning around, saw it was a large man saying, 'Just a minute young man, I have reason to believe you are leaving the store with items you've not paid for?!' He then noticed an identity badge on the large man, he was a store detective! Paul's Dad started to explain, but it all seemed to happen in a blur. The exit area was busy, a large crowd gathered around and words such as 'thief' and 'serves him right' and 'blooming students' could be heard. Paul's Dad was relieved when the Detective explained they would go to the Manager's office; it was good to get away from the crowd. Paul's Dad thought he could explain the circumstances to the Manger and maybe ask the till girls to confirm he had paid? There was still just a chance he could get to meet the nurse on time, but only just a chance.

Paul glanced again at Trudy's parents, they were looking really concerned and Trudy looked anxious too. Paul carried on. The Detective took Paul's Dad across the store and indicated he should go up a flight of stairs to the first floor offices where the Manager was based. They knocked on the Manager's door and the Detective led Paul's Dad into the office and described what had happened. Paul's Dad was poised ready with his side of the story but was then completely taken aback by the Manager.

There was clearly no possibility of a reasonable discussion. In fact, far worse. The Manager banged on his desk exclaiming he was 'sick to death with you long haired young men who just think you can come into this store and take whatever you want and when you want without paying!' His face reddened as he stood up and thumping his desk again, he said, 'You will wait here in this office whilst we find a policeman to arrest you and hopefully get you locked up where you deserve to be!' With that he strode out of the office with the Detective and locked the door as they went out! Paul glanced again at Trudy and her parents, they seemed perplexed and concerned. Paul thought they were just 'gripped' by the story, so he carried on.

Paul's Dad was stunned; he just could not believe what had happened to him. The office was eerily quiet. He could just hear the hum and buzz of the shop below. He then started to think. Neither the Manager nor the Detective had taken his name or address details, he still had the needle and cotton. As his thinking developed, he walked over to the window and glanced down to the yard below noticing he was only one flight up. It wasn't far to jump. He could still get away to meet the nurse on time, but only just. He glanced around. The office windows were half glazed, no one could see into the office.

He looked through the window again. All was quiet below. He opened the window and sat on the ledge. He then put one leg out of the window and started to manoeuvre his body over the edge, it wasn't far to jump. It was at that moment that he glanced back to the office and was alarmed to see a Policeman's helmet above the glazed window and approaching the locked door!

Paul's Dad hesitated. This was a further mistake. Paul glanced again at Trudy and her parents; they were gripped! Paul carried on. The door was unlocked and as the Manager saw Paul's Dad sat on the windowsill with the window open and one leg hanging out, he called, 'Hey!' but in that moment the Policeman behind him rushed forward and he pulled Paul's Dad's leg!

Paul then added, 'Just like I'm pulling yours!' and convulsed into laughter.

It was one of those moments Paul would never forget. He was laughing at his joke but suddenly realised no one else was. He stopped laughing and looked around the room. Trudy's Dad looked shocked; her Mum looked puzzled and Trudy looked vexed. None of them were laughing. There was a moment's silence, embarrassed silence. Trudy's Dad's was the first to speak, his voice was raised, his face was red. 'Never in my life have I felt so misled, never have I heard anyone make fun of crime, we are deeply upset and ask you to leave straightaway! Paul noticed Trudy's Mum glance away and cower her face, he glanced at Trudy. Trudy had a tear in her eye. She got up and moved towards the door.

Paul got up and started to follow Trudy. He looked back to Trudy's parents, but both were looking away. Paul mumbled his thanks and followed Trudy into the hall. She was holding the front door open. Paul went to kiss her, but she moved her face away. Paul could see she was upset and crying. Paul felt terrible, just what had he done? The door closed firmly behind him. Paul went straight home.

Paul went in through the back kitchen door. Both his brothers were sitting at the kitchen table. They jumped up and greeted him enthusiastically saying, 'Yo, how did it go?' but then noticed Paul looked crestfallen and his head was bowed. 'Whatever has happened?' they asked and at this point Paul's Mum and Dad came through to the kitchen as well. Paul was still in state of shock; he couldn't believe what had happened. He tried to explain how well it had gone at first, that Trudy looked great, her parents were nice, welcoming people, that the conversation had been lively and that it was a very nice tea, but that during the tea the conversation had dried up. Paul explained he had felt awkward, so he had told the 'Woolworth's story'. Both his brothers said, 'Oh my God! Did you?' Paul's Dad said, 'Oh no!' and his Mum looked really anxious.

Paul's Dad then spoke. He could see Paul was really upset and confused. 'You need to realise that Trudy is their only child,' he began. Paul's brothers were silent. Paul's Dad carried on and his Mum joined in to suggest he should take another bunch of flowers around and offer apologies. Paul did this, but it was late afternoon and he found the house was empty and their car was not on the drive. He left the flowers with the intention of calling again the next day to apologise. Paul then went on to see if he could find Steve, Tony and John for a kick around game of football at the recreation ground.

It was an hour later that the four boys all met. They played football for an hour. It was a very good kick around as they all needed to burn off some energy. Exhausted, they sat down on the grass. It was Tony who spoke first. He explained he still hadn't seen Cecilia. The other three all groaned together and then laughed saying he should just go around to her house, knock on the door and ask if she wanted to see him again? Straight talking was what was needed they said. After all Celia had asked if he wanted to see her again. Tony quietly nodded his head and smiled.

It was John who spoke next, grinning from ear to ear as he spoke quietly about Susan and how well the relationship was going. He had been staying at Susan's house quite regularly after they'd gone out to visit friends or to the cinema. He and Susan slept together every time he stayed. They would wait for an hour after her parents had gone to bed and then John would creep over the landing into Susan's room. He then crept back as the dawn came. So far it had worked really well. Steve grumbled and said how lucky he thought John was as he'd not even found a girlfriend yet.

Paul had remained silent up to this point. He was aware the others were now looking at him expecting an update on Trudy. He told them the whole story. Steve, Tony and John were astonished; they had all thought things were going so well and couldn't believe Trudy's parents had been so upset by the Woolworth's story. 'It was only a bit of fun,' Tony said, and Steve added, 'Well, at least I'm not the only virgin around here.' They all laughed. Paul went on to say he was planning to visit Trudy's house again tomorrow and they all wished him good luck.

The conversation then moved on to exams. 'O' levels were now only six weeks away. They all agreed how tough it was to revise. Steve said his younger brother and sisters were always so noisy in the house, he was distracted. Paul said his two older brothers kept asking him to do jobs around the house. John said he kept thinking of Susan whilst Tony said he just got so bored! It was good to talk about these issues amongst themselves and they laughed when Steve said he had to think of 'Collywobbles' and that strict look to make sure he got on with his revision! They also reflected on how much these exams mattered for their A level selections, yet none of them were sure exactly what eventual careers they might seek. It was confusing and it was stressful.

The next six weeks flew by. There was no time for sport or socialising. Paul didn't go to the copse, partially to focus on his revision and exam preparation but also, he didn't want to meet Trudy with their other friends listening. He had called to her house several times to speak to her, but the door had never been answered. He tried not to think about Trudy too much, but it was hard not to. Maybe she was working hard on her exam preparation too he thought, or maybe he had really upset her and her parents? Paul was confused.

He was also confused by his parents and brothers. There was an assumption he would be joining them at the family engineering business, so his brothers often teased him on why he thought exams were important. Although Paul told them he might not join them and work somewhere else, they tended to ignore him. He just wasn't sure where else he might work or what sort of work he might do. It was unsettling.

Tony had similar conversations with his parents and they were encouraging him to join his Dad at the shop. Tony just wasn't sure. He didn't want to upset them by saying he wasn't interested. He just felt clothing retail was boring and wanted to work in a more exciting environment with regular changes, rather than just following the same routine every day. These thoughts were always in the back of his mind but more so as he sat in his room revising for exams. It was unsettling.

John was unsettled too. He couldn't stop thinking about Susan. Every time he was away from her and trying to focus on his exam revision his mind kept drifting back to things they'd done, things she'd said, things she'd worn. He was annoyed with himself. He just couldn't focus or concentrate. He was besotted! His lack of focus wasn't helped either at home by his noisy elder sister and her friends.

Furthermore, his parents were frequently asking him how he was getting on. Their intentions were good, but their enquiries caused John to feel tense knowing he had to do well. Like Tony and Paul, he wasn't sure yet what that might be, maybe something academic but that was just a passing thought and there was no certainty.

Steve was the most content of the four wanting to do well at his exams but also looking forward to working on his Father's farm after school. His parents had suggested he should go to Agricultural College, but he didn't think this was necessary. He often thought that maybe he liked home life too much and was this the reason he'd not found a girlfriend yet like the others had.

The 'O' level exams started. The pressure the boys felt intensified as they all wanted to do their best. They all had different approaches in their exam preparation; some preferred last minute cramming, others liked to make notes. The most common aspect though was their ravenous hunger and they all laughed about this later. Within three weeks the exams were over and looking back, they all agreed the exam time had just flown by. But what none of them had anticipated was the huge anti-climax they all felt after the exams finished. The contrast from the feelings of full pressure to suddenly having nothing to do, other than to relax, was very strange.

The post exam period, the school summer holidays, was to provide several turning points in the lives of all four boys; none of it was planned or anticipated.

In Steve's case it took the form of a phone call from his father's brother, Uncle Frank. The call came out of the blue, shortly after the exams finished in mid June. Uncle Frank was a keen sailor and had been national champion of the 'Swift' class catamaran. He had a problem. His normal crew had to visit a sick relative at short notice in Australia and with the National Championships coming up in a weeks' time Uncle Frank didn't have a crew. He wondered if Steve would be interested.

Uncle Frank explained to Steve's Father that it was perfectly safe; there were rescue boats and life jackets. They then discussed Steve's lack of experience and Uncle Frank said that if Steve could get over to his house a couple of days beforehand, he would train him as he was impressed with how much Steve had grown and how strong he was now as a young man. In fact, he said Steve had the makings of an ideal crew!

Steve was really flattered to hear this from his Father when he'd finished the phone call, to be called a fit and strong young man by his Uncle! His Father was a little concerned, but as the conversation developed it was clear he was also considering when Steve would return as help would be needed with harvesting. It was eventually decided that Steve could go and arrangements were made for him to travel to Uncle Frank's by train the next day. Steve was excited, he'd been feeling a little 'lost' after all the exam pressure and it was good to go off and do something different. It was also a welcome a break from his younger sisters and brother too!

Uncle Frank met him at the railway station the next day. It had been an uneventful journey, though Steve had felt really excited and looked forward to the sailing as it would be a complete contrast to living at home and working on the farm. Uncle Frank was divorced. It had been a childless marriage and his wife had run off with her boss some years before. Uncle Frank had been really upset by this and had found his interest in sailing helped him to cope with his divorce. They went to Uncle Frank's flat first to drop off Steve's suitcase as the sailing club was only a short distance from the flat. They had a cup of tea and then walked down to the sailing club to rig the boat and go for a late afternoon sail.

On arrival in the boat park, Steve noticed there were several other Swift class catamarans, and some were also being rigged and prepared to sail. Uncle Frank showed Steve where everything was and how to rig the boat and attach the sails. They didn't raise the sails in the boatyard but got changed. Uncle Frank gave Steve a wetsuit to wear and a life jacket. He showed Steve how to wear the life jacket and how to blow the whistle if there was an emergency. They then pushed the boat a short distance down to the beach on a trolley. It was a sunny afternoon and there was a fresh breeze blowing, ideal for Steve's first outing Uncle Frank said. Steve looked around him and thought what a complete difference this was to the farm! He smiled to himself in anticipation.

Uncle Frank showed Steve how to raise the mainsail and foresail with the boat heading into the wind. They then pushed the boat into the shallow water. Steve was asked to hold the front of the boat, still heading into the wind whilst he returned the trolley to the shore. When Uncle Frank got back to the boat, he climbed in and released the rudders to give him steerage, nodding to Steve to jump aboard and they were off! Initially the sails weren't pulled in; they flapped in the sea breeze but just enough to enable the catamaran to nudge through the shallow and into deeper waters. Uncle Frank showed Steve how to drop the centre board whilst he fully released the rudders. They were then ready to pull in the main and fore sails and with a 'whoosh' the boat surged forward leaping over some waves and diving into others, creating great clouds of sea water spray.

Steve had never experienced anything like it! He was elated. It was just great fun he thought. He screamed a great 'whoopee!' and turned to see Uncle Frank smiling from ear to ear too! As the afternoon progressed, Uncle Frank taught him how to adjust the sails and where to position their weight to achieve maximum speed. Steve learned a lot in a short time. Uncle Frank knew his stuff and was so keen, it was an inspirational experience. Whilst sailing up and down the bay, Steve noticed another Swift catamaran. It seemed to be a father and daughter crewing and they were screaming at times too enjoying the weather. Steve waved to them and smiled when the daughter waved back, although Steve didn't think much more about it at the time.

After a couple of hours, they returned to the shore, dropping the sails and pulling the Swift back into the boatyard. Uncle Frank showed Steve how to fold the sails, put the boat cover on and tie the boat down securely in its berthing place. They showered and Uncle Frank showed Steve the way through to the bar to buy him a beer. Steve explained he wasn't allowed one at home as he was just underage. Uncle Frank said 'nonsense' and thrust a pint in his hand. Steve smiled; the beer tasted good after all the gallons of salty sea water he felt he'd drunk!

The bar was quiet, with only about a dozen people there and he glanced around as Uncle Frank started talking with other club members. He noticed a really good looking girl, with long dark hair and dark eyes talking with other people at the other end of the bar. It was at that moment she glanced at him, their eyes met, and she smiled. Steve then realised it was the girl he'd waved to at sea that afternoon. She looked so different out of her sailing clothes. He wanted to talk to her but realised she was with other people and it would not be easy to break into the group she was talking to. Steve focussed back onto the conversation with Uncle Frank but his mind was thinking about the girl and wondering who she might be?

The following morning Uncle Frank made breakfast and they went down to the boatyard. The tide was out, and the wind was light. Over the next few hours, Uncle Frank showed Steve how to carry out some basic maintenance on the boat. During the morning many other boats and crews arrived, all looking forward to the National Championships. Uncle Frank knew a lot of them, and the morning flew by quickly as old friendships were renewed. Lunchtime arrived and Uncle Frank took Steve back to the bar. They didn't have a beer though as they planned to sail that afternoon. The wind was freshening, and they needed to practise more. Steve glanced around the bar several times during lunch. There were many more people than last night but no sign of that good looking girl he'd noticed yesterday. Where was she, he thought.

The afternoon practice was again great fun, and the wind was not as fresh as the previous afternoon. There were many more boats on the water now and Uncle Frank spent some time talking through the tactics for the first race the following day emphasizing the importance of a good start. Steve began to feel more confident as he increasingly understood the race arrangements and felt he was developing good teamwork with Uncle Frank. They returned to the boat park, de rigged, put the cover on, tied the boat down securely as before and then showered. It was as Steve entered the bar that he quite literally bumped into that good looking girl. She was at the tea machine by the entrance and trying to carry two mugs of hot tea. Steve offered to help, she smiled and handed him one to carry.

She led him over to the other side of the bar to a table and having put the tea mugs down, they introduced themselves. Her name was Jan. She chatted easily, explaining she lived in the town and had been working in her Mum's shop all day. Steve thought Jan had a very nice smile explaining he was just an apprentice at sailing but that he was really looking forward to the Championships. Jan had been sailing all her life and said that Frank had a really good reputation in the Swift class, so she expected them to do well. Steve smiled. He wasn't so sure and was just looking forward to a weekend of competitive fun.

They carried on chatting and discussed the events over the weekend. There were four races altogether, two on each day. Steve hadn't realised there was an informal drinks reception that evening, followed by a disco after the racing on Saturday evening and then an early evening Awards meal on the Sunday. Jan had clearly been to these Championships before and knew a lot about them.

Jan's Dad came over to say hello and at this moment Uncle Frank came over as well. It was clear they knew each other and they both offered Steve and Jan drinks. Steve asked if could have another beer while Jan asked for a glass of wine. Uncle Frank and Jan's Dad carried on chatting as they went to the bar, leaving Steve and Jan to carry on getting to know each other.

It turned out that Jan was the same age as Steve and had just completed her 'O' levels as well. They chatted together, sharing stories of their friends and the stresses and strains of exams. Steve explained how ravenously hungry they'd all been while Jan described how close to tears her friends had been as they all wanted to do so well. Steve went on to say how weird it was that none of his friends really knew what they wanted to do, but that he was looking forward to working on his Father's farm. Jan explained her Mum had been a buyer with one of the large Oxford Street stores and that she also hoped to go there after her 'A' level exams but she needed good grades!

Time slipped by quickly as they chatted happily. Uncle Frank and Jan's Dad came over several times to top up their drinks. Steve had never drunk more than one pint before and was feeling somewhat 'woozy', Jan said she felt 'tipsy'. They laughed as they debated the difference between 'woozy' and tipsy' with no real conclusion. It was a bit of a relief when Uncle Frank came over to say they should head back for a good night's sleep as it was a big day tomorrow! Everyone agreed, said 'goodnight' and left. On the walk back Uncle Frank asked if Steve had enjoyed everything so far with a glint in his eye. Steve just smiled and said, 'Yes thanks.' They slept well that night.

The following morning the sun was shining and there was a light breeze. Steve watched the forecast with Uncle Frank over breakfast. It suggested the light breeze would freshen during the day but that from tomorrow, Sunday, it would get quite strong as a new weather front moved in. After breakfast, Steve and Frank walked down to the boat park; it was busy, thirty five boats had entered, and they all realised they needed to be rigged and on the water before the Starter's guns went off. Steve worked hard to help Uncle Frank. He now knew what to do but hadn't anticipated the happy chaos in the boat park and how much all the competitors would get in each other's way.

They got changed in good time and headed off with the boat on the trolley to the beach, Steve realised with all the commotion that he'd not seen Jan and wondered if she still felt a little 'tipsy' after the drinks last night. It was only once they were on the water that he spotted her crewing with her Dad. The Starters gun was about to go off so there was no time to wave, everyone needed to concentrate.

The tension mounted. There were a lot of boats in close proximity to the Starters Line. Uncle Frank kept tacking and tried to manoeuvre to the best position. All the other boats were trying to do the same as well though! Two guns were fired and flags unfurled at six and then three minutes before the start. Then a further three minutes after the second flag, another gun was fired. All the flags were dropped, and the race started! If you were over the start line you had to tack around and cross it again. Steve had thought his 'O' levels were stressful, but it was nothing like this!

Before the Starters gun had gone off there was a complete melee of boats heading in all sorts of directions and different speeds. Now, in contrast, all the boats were heading in the same direction, towards the first buoy with complete focus on wind fluctuations and surrounding boats. The concentration was intense! Steve peered around him. Uncle Frank seemed to have made a good start, they were certainly in the leading ten boats. Ten minutes later and they were around the first buoy. Steve realised they were in fifth position!

The race carried on around a triangular course over three laps. Steadily Uncle Frank got closer to the leaders and in the final lap they did really well and went over the finishing line in second position! Uncle Frank seemed pleased, but Steve was elated. He really liked sailing, this was his first ever sailing race and they had come second in the National Championships. That wasn't bad was it?!

Steve looked back and noticed Jan and her Dad were crossing the line in about tenth position. He waved to her, she waved and smiled and gave a 'thumbs up'. Steve smiled and gave her a 'thumbs up' too. Back on the beach it was then time for a quick lunch in the clubhouse. Steve sat with Jan and her Dad and joked that none of them wanted alcohol after the previous evening. Jan teased Steve, saying how well he'd done and doubted that he was an apprentice. Jan's Dad concurred and said that Steve had done very well. Feeling flushed with success Steve said, 'Just followed the Captain's orders,' and they all laughed.

The second race in the afternoon was even better for Uncle Frank and Steve. They rounded the first buoy in first position and managed to hold that position all the way to the finishing line. Steve couldn't believe it. He turned to Uncle Frank as they crossed the finishing line. Frank just smiled. In the boat park, Steve was tying the boat down to secure it when Jan came over. 'You two just flew today,' she said and offered congratulations. Steve tried to suppress his pride and appear modest; it was hard work! Jan explained they'd had a bad race, collided with another boat and came in around twentieth.

She seemed disappointed but was able to tease Steve, casting further doubt on his claims to be an apprentice. They laughed together and agreed to meet at the disco that evening.

Steve showered and got changed back at Uncle Frank's flat. He thought a lot about Jan, he really liked her. He put on his best shirt and then walked back to the club with Uncle Frank. Jan wasn't there when they arrived, so Steve enjoyed a pint as many other sailors came up to congratulate them on the win and discuss the following day and the final two races. The forecast indicated stronger winds and it was generally agreed it would be a good day's racing.

After half an hour Jan walked in and she looked stunning. Steve broke away from the conversation and went over to talk to her. As he approached, she turned towards him, smiled and said, 'Hello apprentice!' Steve laughed with her and she then asked if he was an apprentice at dancing also and would he dance with her later.

They carried on talking easily about the day and the prospects for the following day while Uncle Frank and Jan's Dad bought drinks again. The disco started and the room was soon buzzing with singing and dancing activity. Steve and Jan didn't dance together initially but joined in with various people they'd met that day. It was really good fun with many of the sailors play acting and singing along with the songs.

It was later in the evening when the music slowed that they danced together. The room was hot, and Steve suggested they should walk onto the Clubhouse rear patio for some fresh air. Jan readily agreed and once outside they strolled into the boat park. It was a great evening, quite dark with amassing clouds overhead but warm with a fresh breeze.

Behind them they could hear the disco music and Steve reached out to hold Jan's hand asking if she'd like to carry on dancing on the boat park. Slow music played as Steve drew Jan closer to him and they kissed. It was a long lingering kiss broken by the sound of Uncle Frank calling out from the patio. He asked if Steve was in the boat park as he couldn't see in the dark and if he wanted another drink. Steve and Jan broke off the kiss and laughed. He called back to say he was just checking the boat and yes, he'd be back shortly.

Steve and Jan returned to the Clubhouse just as the DJ was announcing the final dance, it was a slow number and they danced together. Uncle Frank and Jan's Dad noticed and commented that there seemed to be a new friendship in the air! They both smiled, Steve and Jan joined them for a final drink when the music had finished. They all toasted each other on a good evening and looked forward to a good day's racing the following day.

The following morning was breezy. There was a real buzz in the boat park, plenty of laughter and banter as the crews anticipated a good day's sailing. Uncle Frank was thorough in his preparation, double checking all the shackles and cleats, making sure all the equipment was stowed securely and then double checking his and Steve's lifejackets. Steve was unprepared for the speed of the boat as they cast off and crashed into the waves, it was really exhilarating. Uncle Frank was very amused to hear Steve as he screamed a great 'whoopee' but then they had to focus and prepare for the start.

The start was difficult; all the boats were trying to avoid collisions, with many having difficulty controlling their speed. As the starting gun went off, Uncle Frank and Steve found they were in a poor position with other boats ahead of them affecting their wind flow. Uncle Frank then tacked away to clearer waters, but they were only in around tenth position as they rounded the first buoy. It was then that conditions worsened. The wind strength increased noticeably and hit them as they went on a downwind leg. The speed of the boat was phenomenal; the bows were crashing into the waves causing large sprays of water. Steve couldn't look forward. Uncle Frank peered around Steve and said later that he was a good water shield! They both moved further back towards the stern of the boat to reduce the impact as they crashed into the waves. As they sped along Steve was aware that other boats had capsized and they reached the second buoy in fifth position.

The next two legs were easier as they were on a reach with the wind coming from the side of the boat and then tacking with the wind ahead of them. Whilst sailing, Steve looked around and was surprised to see there were only around seven boats still racing, many were capsized, and others had returned to shore.

As they rounded the next buoy, they were in third position, but the next leg was downwind. The boat leapt forward and increased speed markedly. Steve certainly couldn't see where they were going, and he couldn't see Uncle Frank or hear him either but was aware he was beside him. It was then that they lost control of the boat; it seemed to bounce off the top of one wave and then just fly. The boat plunged into the sea and turned over.

Steve looked around him and was alarmed that he could not see Uncle Frank. He called out and heard a faint cry. He then saw him on the other side of one of the hulls. Uncle Frank's face was red, and he looked exhausted, with his eyes wide open. Steve felt he had bruised his ribs. He had swallowed some sea water and felt his legs were tangled in some of the ropes but realised he needed to get over to Uncle Frank and help him.

Steve freed his legs, then clambered over the hull and swam towards Uncle Frank. He could see he was having trouble breathing. He grabbed him by the back of his safety belt collar and pulled him back towards the upturned hull. They were both freezing in the water, despite wearing wet suits. Uncle Frank seemed a little dazed and didn't say much. Steve wondered what he should do next. He was not sure. It was then he had one of those moments he'd not forget for the rest of his life. He heard the noise of a powerful outboard engine approaching fast and looking up, saw it was an RNLI lifeboat. What a relief!

The lifeboat crew knew what they were doing. They helped Uncle Frank out of the water first, hauling him into the lifeboat. He seemed to be exhausted. They wrapped him in foil and then helped Steve on board. They managed to drop the sails on the boat and right it too. They then towed it back to shore. The wind was still strong, and the waves were rough but seemed to be getting calmer.

On shore they were helped by club members. Uncle Frank was taken to hospital by ambulance while Steve stayed at the club to help clear up. They returned Uncle Frank's boat to its berth and tied it down. Sailing was cancelled for the rest of the day. It was whilst Steve was at the club that his thoughts turned to Jan. He asked other crews if they had any news and was told Jan and her father had beached their boat down the coast and that a vehicle with a trailer had gone to collect them.

Steve changed and returned to Uncle Frank's flat with all his clothing and equipment. He then caught a taxi to the hospital to find Uncle Frank in a recovery room. He'd suffered mild hypothermia and was told to stay in overnight for observations. They agreed Steve should return home as Uncle Frank had friends and neighbours who could help, and Steve was needed back on the farm. It was on the train home later that afternoon that Steve's thoughts turned to Jan.

It was then the whole impact of the events hit him. He was exhausted from the physical exertion. He wondered if Jan was ok and also reflected on how close he and Uncle Frank had been to a serious outcome. It was all a bit scary. Steve found he was shaking and felt cold. He had no contact information for Jan but decided he would call Uncle Frank the following day to check he was well and ask if he had a phone number for Jan.

It would be years later the four friends would reflect on this period of their lives, the emerging interest in girls yet the sometimes awkward approaches they had made. Paul would anguish forever about his visit to Judy's parents and the disastrous outcome yet in contrast had Steve found his perfect match in Jan and likewise John with Susan? Tony had not seemed to have found a match for him at all and yet ...

CHAPTER 7

DESIRE PHASE
(18+ YEARS OLD)
Boys are Men

♂ **MEANWHILE, THAT WEEKEND,** the unexpected was happening to Tony as well. He went down to the local shops and as he was walking out, he literally bumped into Celia! They both apologised and then laughed saying, 'Hello, how are you?' at the same time causing then both to laugh again. It transpired that Celia had been away visiting her sister in America who had been quite ill but had now recovered. Celia asked how Tony was and if he like to call around sometime. Cecilia smiled as Tony readily agreed and explained he was free now if it suited her. Broad, happy smiles were exchanged. Celia finished her shopping and they then drove back in her red sports car to her house.

Tony helped carry Celia's shopping back into the house. With the door closed they smiled at each other; Tony dropped the shopping in the hall. Nothing further needed to be said, they smiled and kissed eagerly removing clothing and shoes as they went up the stairs and into Celia's bedroom. Afterwards Tony glanced over to Celia and pointing to the small dormer window asked if she wanted him to close it again?

They both laughed, the situation just felt so good. They spent the rest of the day in bed talking and making love. Celia explained she'd missed Tony and had not known how to contact him. Tony explained he'd been stretched with exams and it was probably just as well she'd been away. Celia kept stroking his moustache as they talked. Tony told her the story of the Manchester Police Sargent and this brought tears to her eyes.

Tony then explained how his parents wanted him to work with his Dad in the clothing shop and how unsure he was; he really wasn't interested but didn't want to hurt their feelings. Celia told the story of her divorce and the sadness and anguish she felt once she'd discovered her husband was having an affair with his secretary. 'He's paid for that though in the divorce settlement,' she said with a despairing look. She was clearly still upset by her husband's affair. The afternoon flew by and Tony realised he needed to go back but they arranged to meet up the following day to go out for a ride in her car. Tony smiled to himself walking home. Only a few hours ago he'd been anticipating a long summer holiday with nothing to do; now he could see a lot of fun ahead. It was just unbelievable how quickly circumstances could change!

Paul was also in a period of unexpected change. He'd been distracted and upset by the way the relationship with Trudy had finished so suddenly. He'd been teased by his brothers relentlessly and his parents had been concerned that it might affect his exam performance. They had encouraged him to follow an exam timetable and focus on his revision. Their encouragement helped. But now with the exams all over and still no sign of Trudy what might he do?

It was his Dad who surprised him one evening when he explained that one of his customers at his engineering business was in some difficulty. His son had been due to work in America all summer in one of the camps but had fallen ill and could no longer go. Would Paul be interested to go instead? They discussed it further. Paul just qualified on age, he enjoyed sport and could evidence his sporting certificates to help his application. Everything would need to be completed, submitted and agreed within five days. Paul said yes readily, he felt a break from routine would be perfect and what an exciting trip too!

The next few days were frenetic; forms were filled, phone calls were made and on the fifth day Paul travelled to London with his Mum for an interview, his first ever interview! The interview went well, it was agreed Paul could go, he needed to call back to the office the following Tuesday to collect his tickets and then onwards to Heathrow Airport the same day. As he and his Mum walked away to get their return train, Paul smiled to himself. Although unknown to him, he was having the same thoughts Tony had had but very different circumstances! Only a few hours ago he'd been anticipating a long summer holiday with nothing to do. Now he could see a lot of fun ahead; it was just unbelievable how quickly circumstances could change!

The unexpected circumstances that Steve, Tony and Paul were experiencing were much less worrying than the unexpected circumstance that John found himself in. John and Susan had discussed and looked forward to a long happy summer together post exams. The exams had been a stressful experience and they had plans to work together harvesting on local farms, fruit picking, weekend trips to music festivals and friends to visit too. There was a lot to look forward to! However, one week after the exams John arrived at Susan's house and found she was really distressed. John was puzzled and couldn't at first understand what the matter was. It was then she uttered, between sobs that her normal regular monthly period had not happened. She was worried that she might be pregnant!

What would her parents say, would they have to let them know they'd abused her parents trust and slept together in their house? What would it mean to their hopes for further education and careers, how would they cope financially to bring a child up when neither of them had a reasonable job? Susan sobbed as she shared her thoughts with John, she was really upset. John was dumbstruck, this was a real surprise! He listened to Susan and just didn't know what to do.

He then had an idea. There was one person who might know what to do, his sister! John had often heard his sister talking with her friends. She was a lot older than John and he had sometimes overheard them referring to friends who had become pregnant and how they had coped with this situation. John aired his thinking with Susan; he thought they could take his sister into their confidence and work out what to do. Susan calmed down a little as she listened to John. She felt a little better that they could talk to someone, in confidence, who might know what to do. It was agreed John would go home and find out where his sister was and arrange to meet her as soon as possible.

When John arrived home, it was mid-afternoon. His luck was in, his parents were out but he could hear music from his sister's room. He went up the stairs and knocked on her bedroom door. There was a pause and then he heard his sister say, 'Who's that?' She wasn't used to visitors mid-afternoon and was surprised when John answered and furthermore, even more surprised when she heard him say, 'I need your help.'

She opened the door and thought he looked a little anxious, 'Come in tell me what's up?' she said encouragingly. John sat down on her bed and told her the whole story and finished by asking what she thought they should do? His sister could see he was worried and could see he needed help. She pondered further how Susan must be feeling and realised they were very anxious. 'The first thing we have to do,' she said assertively, 'Is to get Susan to see her doctor as soon as possible and get a pregnancy test. It may just be she is late and there is nothing to worry about!'

John asked if she could meet him and Susan explaining that Susan would welcome a conversation. John knew Susan was worried her Mum may find out if she'd been to her family doctor and there were other concerns as well. They arranged to meet for a coffee in town the following morning. John went back to Susan's house and told her what his sister had said. Susan seemed better; she was pleased there was someone she could talk to. The following morning couldn't happen soon enough. Susan and John arrived at the café before his sister and found a table in a quiet corner.

When his sister arrived, John fetched the drinks and was pleased when he got back to find his sister and Susan were in deep conversation. He passed the drinks around and listened. In hindsight, the situation was quite straightforward, Susan was concerned that her approach to their family doctor would be confidential; John's sister was able to reassure her of this. John took Susan back to his parent's house and they phoned the Doctor. An appointment was made for the following morning.

The rest of the day was difficult. John and Susan went for a walk as a distraction, but the subject of Susan's pregnancy was on their minds. Susan was rehearsing what she should tell her doctor and how she might say it. The following morning John escorted Susan to the doctors but waited outside rather than going in. Time seemed to stand still for John; he couldn't believe it would take so long.

Suddenly though Susan appeared at the door and, much to John's delight, he could see she was smiling and seemed relieved. He rushed over and took her hand and they talked as they walked up the street. Susan explained how nervous she'd been but that the doctor was female, had been very helpful and had reassured her everything was confidential. The test had revealed no pregnancy, but the doctor had recommended and prescribed the pill as an alternative to the condom. John was relieved to see the complete change in Susan. They could now laugh together again!

So, although all the friends had initially felt a post exam anti-climax there were now significant changes happening in their lives. Boys were now becoming men. Steve had survived a storm and found a potential girlfriend in Jan, Tony was over the moon with Celia, Paul was off to America and John was so relieved that his and Susan's concerns were unfounded. They could now look forward to a great summer!

The summer weeks flew by. Steve was working long hours on the farm. He called Uncle Frank one evening during the first week he was back and was pleased to hear he had been released from hospital. Complete rest had been recommended along with some medication. Uncle Frank's neighbours were being very supportive and were calling regularly at the door to see if he needed anything. Uncle Frank said he didn't like to trouble anyone but welcomed the help. His main focus now being to watch the cricket test series, rest and recover his strength. They discussed the race and Uncle Frank explained he had had not experienced that strength of wind before, it had been quite unusual.

In passing conversation, Uncle Frank referred to Jan and her Dad saying their boat had been badly damaged, but they were unhurt. At this point Steve asked if Uncle Frank if he had their phone number as he'd like to call and check they were ok as well. Uncle Frank chuckled down the phone asking if there was any other reason to call them. Steve smiled with him and made a note of the number.

It was Jan's Dad who answered the phone. Steve explained he was calling to ask if they were ok and a long conversation ensued in which Jan's Dad described the damage in great detail and that he thought the boat would be written off by the Insurance Company. Apparently, as they had been driven ashore, the boat had capsized suddenly in the shallow waters, snapping the mast and cracking the catamaran's cross beam. Both Jan and her Dad had been thrown from the boat as it capsized. Jan had been bruised, her Dad too and had also fractured his forearm and it was in a sling. It was at this point that Jan's Dad casually said, 'Would you like to speak to her?'

At last, Steve was able to talk to Jan. He asked her how she was, and it was clear in the way she spoke that her Dad was still within hearing distance. They discussed the race with Steve explaining what had happened to him and Uncle Jack. He really praised the RNLI saying that he thought it was a lifesaving operation and how well trained they were. Steve went on to explain that Uncle Frank was now recuperating at home, that he was planning to visit the following Saturday, and would Jan be interested in meeting? She readily said, 'Yes' and they made arrangements. Steve would call on Uncle Frank in the afternoon and then meet Jan early evening for a couple of hours but would have to return to harvesting the following day.

Steve wasn't prepared for what he saw when he walked into Uncle Frank's flat the following Saturday. A neighbour opened the front door and when Steve walked into the living room, he found Uncle Frank hunched up in his chair with some blankets over his lap. When Steve said, 'Hello,' cheerily, Uncle Frank looked up, smiled and said, 'Oh, hello Steve,' but Steve could tell this was an effort. It wasn't the engaging, smiling Uncle Frank he was used to. The neighbour left, Steve thanked her for her help and then made him and Uncle Frank a cup of tea. Steve sat with Uncle Frank in his living room for the next two hours and they talked nonstop.

Initially the conversation reflected on the race, the strength of the wind, the response and help from the RNLI. Uncle Frank reflected on the fact that he had been completely exhausted and if it hadn't have been for the RNLI, he would not have survived. They then discussed the hospital care and medication and it was clear Uncle Frank needed to build his strength and energy and that it would take time.

This then led to a lengthy conversation in which Uncle Frank revealed he felt he was just not the man he used to be. Although only in his late fifties, should he really be sailing? He seemed quite gloomy in his mood saying it had been perfectly alright when he had been Steve's age, but should he be sailing now? The conversation moved on and Uncle Frank explained that several friends of the Sailing Club had kindly called in to check he was ok and that one in particular had struck a chord. This friend was apparently a similar age to Uncle Frank and referred to the 'Male Menopause'.

Uncle Frank went on to say he had never heard of the 'Male Menopause'. He had of course heard of the 'Female Menopause' and understood it referred to the change in the physical conditions of females. Uncle Frank's friend had explained that the 'Male Menopause' referred more to the psychological changes in males, that ageing males thought they could still do as much as they could when they were younger and failed to reduce their activities. 'He told me my case of the 'Male Menopause' was a classic one,' laughed Uncle Frank. Steve laughed too though this was all new to him.

After two hours Steve explained he'd arranged to see Jan whilst he was in the area and that he needed to go. Uncle

Frank smiled broadly; the best Steve had seen all afternoon. 'That's great news,' he said and gave Steve a friendly punch on the arm. Steve explained he was planning to come back the following Saturday and if convenient could he bring Jan as well? Uncle Frank readily agreed and said he would look forward to it. He gave Steve another friendly punch on the arm and smiled again as they parted.

Steve was standing under the clock in the town's bus station at five in the afternoon as arranged, but there was no sign of Jan. Was he in the right place he wondered? He then had a tap on his shoulder and there she was with a great beaming smile. She looked great. He bent down and kissed her, she responded but then glanced around to see if anyone had noticed. No one had. They knew Steve only had a couple of hours before he needed to catch the train back. They had agreed to fish and chips and a walk in the park. Jan said she knew 'the best fish and chip shop in town' so they set off there and then she took them into the local park where they just chatted.

The conversation was easy; it was as if they'd known each other for years. Jan told Steve how terrified she and her Dad had been once the wind blew up in the race explaining they had really lost control. Her Dad was still in discomfort with his arm (they smiled about the long telephone conversation Steve had had with Jan's Dad) and Jan explained that although they were likely to get the full insurance money for the boat she wasn't sure if they'd buy another one. Steve told Jan the full story about Uncle Frank. He described his surprise to find Uncle Frank was so weak and hunched up when he'd visited earlier that day, and would Jan like to visit with him next Saturday? Jan eagerly agreed.

Jan then described in more detail the work she did with her Dad in his shop. She wasn't sure though if she wanted to work there all her life and like Steve, was awaiting her 'O' level exam results and then would decide on choices of 'A' levels and future directions. Steve described his life on the farm with his Father and younger brother and sisters. As he spoke his enthusiasm and interest were evident. He glanced back at Jan as he described some of the tractors and then realised that she might not be as interested as he was!

The conversation then slipped back to Uncle Frank. Steve told Jan about the friend of Uncle Frank who thought he had a condition known as the 'Male Menopause'. Jan frowned inquisitively as Steve spoke and repeated the conversation he'd had earlier with Uncle Frank.

'There's no such thing as a Male Menopause,' said Jan and they laughed and debated a little longer the physiological evidence of the female menopause alongside the varying psychological situations behind the so called 'Male Menopause'. Two hours had flown by quickly. Steve glanced at his watch and realised he would need to run back to the station. Jan ran with him, there was just time for a brief kiss at the station barrier. He then ran for the train glancing back with a quick smile. Jan turned and walked home but with a spring on her step. She liked Steve and was looking forward to the following Saturday.

That same weekend Tony was with Celia. He stayed at her house on Saturday and Sunday evenings. He'd told his parents he was seeing 'a girl' but hadn't explained she was nearly twice as old as him! Tony liked Celia, she was fun to be with and the love making was endless. Celia liked Tony's enthusiasm and energy for everything. They often discussed their relationship and that it 'couldn't possibly last long' because of the age difference but in the same sentence agreed, 'Let's enjoy it whilst we can!'

Celia was fascinated by Tony's moustache and often said it tickled her, this would make them both laugh. They often discussed Tony's future, how young he was, only just completing his 'O' levels, his anxieties about working with his Dad in retail and his uncertainty on just what he did want to do in his working life. Tony found Celia was a good listener and that her questions made him think but there were no real conclusions, yet!

At one point, they both came to realise something. Celia was recently divorced with plenty of time and money too and Tony had a whole summer ahead of him, plenty of time but little money. 'Let's go on holiday!' said Celia to Tony. She reassured him that she would pay, it would be no problem. She then went on to suggest they should go in her car on a two week touring holiday of France! Tony's broad smile at her suggestion said it all. He'd love to go, two weeks in France in a great car with Celia, who wouldn't say yes to that! He then thought of his parents, they would need to know, but that seemed a minor consideration. They agreed to go into the local Travel Agents the following day to make arrangements.

When Tony got home that evening his Mum asked if he'd had a good time. She noticed he coloured slightly as with he said, 'Yes'. Her 'mothers' intuition' kicked in to realise her son was growing up fast. She was a little taken aback though as Tony added that he and Celia (it was the first time she'd heard him refer to that name) were thinking of going on a two week touring holiday of France. His Mum just said, 'Oh that sounds nice,' and added, 'Let's discuss it further when your Dad gets home.' Her immediate concern was not only money but she also realised the relationship was quite serious and yet her son was still so young, she thought.

Tony's Dad arrived home shortly afterwards and cheerily asked Tony if he'd had a nice time at his friend's house, Tony responded in the same cheery voice saying, 'Oh yes!'. They were sitting down, and Mum was dishing up the evening meal. She said, 'Tony is thinking of going on holiday with his friend over the next two weeks.' Tony could tell his Mum and Dad were more than just curious and decided he should tell them everything. Tony's Dad remembered Celia from the garden barbeque party they'd all been to recently. He'd privately noticed what an attractive woman Celia was and felt really impressed with Tony. By contrast, Tony's Mum was anxious, her motherly instinct was to be cautious, there was such an age difference and Tony was so young. He'd only just passed the age of consent!

Tony explained he was going to the Travel Agents with Celia tomorrow to book the Channel crossing to France and some hotels as well. It was at this point the subject of money came up and Tony's parents were both surprised to hear that Celia would be paying for everything. Tony's Dad laughed and said he guessed Tony wished he had paid more attention in his French classes at school? Tony explained that Celia was fluent in French and had visited there many times but yes, he hoped to learn more! With a grimace Tony's parents realised there was not a lot they could do; they quietly accepted their boy was growing into a man.

Meanwhile Paul had arrived at a US summer camp in Richmond, Virginia. Talk about being thrown in at the deep end. The group of ten boys he was responsible for were due to arrive the day after him so Paul had only one day to acclimatise. Not only was the weather such a contrast to the UK, it was hot and very humid, but he also had to get familiar quickly with the facilities in the camp, meet his colleagues and get to understand the day to day programmes of activity. Paul was to be known as a team leader and would be working for a group leader who had another ten boys. There had been a lot to take in!

The facilities in the camp were impressive with a large acreage of sprawling woodland and lakes, full of wildlife. There were marked walks through the woodland and organised trekking took place every day. The lakes were numerous with areas designated for swimming, canoeing, and sailing activities. Little did Paul and Steve know they were both learning about sailing at the same time but in very different circumstances. The lakes in the woodland were much calmer than the sea, though you needed to be aware of sudden gusts!

The accommodation was basic but charming. There were log cabins scattered throughout the woods with shower and toilet facilities. They were all sited within walking distance of a large, grassed area in the centre of the camp where the main dining and meeting hall was located along with a small administration office. Paul met all the other leaders in the main hall at the end of his first day; it was a briefing session from the Camp Director as a new intake of campers was expected the following day. The camp was for boys and girls in the 11 to 15 age category. Paul realised he was one of the youngest leaders but whilst walking into the main hall that evening for the briefing session, he noticed there were a lot of good looking female leaders! It was then that his mind cast back to Trudy, wondering what she might be doing and where she was. He realised it was the first time he'd thought of her for several days.

The Camp Director was assertive; he was clearly a good leader and gave an impressive presentation to all the camp staff. There was an understandable emphasis on safety but also a lot of administration issues that needed to be understood. It was all new to Paul as he sat by his group leader who later explained everything in more detail. As the meeting closed, a small buffet had been arranged which was the first opportunity Paul had to meet many of the other staff.

Without exception every American he spoke to commented on his accent. All were complimentary and some asked if he had met the Queen. A couple of the girls Paul chatted with were particularly kind. They were both blonde haired and very good looking Paul thought. They lived locally in Richmond and were intrigued to know what life was like in the UK. Paul was taken aback; he'd not appreciated the differences between the UK and America. He realised there was a lot to learn. He explained how anxious he was to look after the first group of ten boys tomorrow. He was pleased with the reassurances the girls gave, that apparently it was all straightforward and that he should just ask about anything he was unsure about. It all sounded so easy! Their conversation was then interrupted by the sound of a loud gong. The Course Director explained it was time to break the meeting up and to return to the log cabins for final preparation and then sleep.

Paul said goodnight to the two blonde girls. They wished each other good luck and that they looked forward to meeting again soon. Paul then found his Group Leader and they walked back through the woods to their log cabins. It was dusk and they had difficulty finding the right trail. They spent a couple of hours finally preparing the cabins and then, feeling exhausted went to bed. As Paul lay in bed, he listened to all the strange sounds in the woods; it was both eerie and exciting. The next thing he knew he was being shaken by his group leader. It was morning and time to shower and breakfast as the campers would be arriving just after breakfast!

The next few days flew by for Paul. The campers all came from different towns and different schools in Virginia. They were only staying in the camp for a week but in that time the schedule was frantic as all the activities needed to be included. Paul was surprised that he really enjoyed it! The ten boys looked up to him and by and large did as they were asked. The group dynamics were interesting too. There were some fall outs and disagreements in which the campers looked to Paul to adjudicate.

They were growing boys, appetites were huge so when returning to the dining hall from a morning's trek in the woods or a sailing session on one of the lakes, food was devoured ravenously. By evening they were all exhausted. After the evening meal there was normally some singing by the campfire. By the time they returned to the log cabins there was initially a lot of excited banter and teasing as they shared stories of the day, but this quickly fell away to sounds of heavy sleeping.

Paul always liked that time of day, when everything was quiet; it was the only time he got to himself. He'd noticed the blonde haired girls during the week at the dining hall. Like Paul they were busy supervising their groups but there had been time for fleeting glances and thumbs up signs across the hall. Paul wondered if there would be time to talk to them again. He was thinking of Trudy less and less. He was also thinking about his Dad and the family engineering business. He was enjoying supervising the groups at the camp and wondered if he should seek a supervising role in a business back in the UK. But this was only a passing thought at that time as he also fell into a deep sleep.

Paul needn't have worried about seeing the blonde haired girls again. The first real opportunity was at the weekly handover; when the parents arrived at the end of the week to retrieve their children. There was a lot of excitement and big hugs to say 'farewell' but then the camp became noticeably silent as the campers drove away. Paul walked over to the two blonde haired girls as they waved their campers off. They smiled at him as he approached and then talked animatedly about the experiences they'd had with their campers. They couldn't talk for long as they needed to return to their log cabins and prepare for the next group of campers who were due to arrive that afternoon.

It was the following week that Paul got to know one of the girls well during a trek which had been arranged deep into the woods and halfway up a small mountain. It was arranged for a mixed group of girls and boys. Paul was to lead the boys. He didn't know until they assembled at the main hall that morning that one of the blonde girls was to lead the girls group. She was the overall leader as she had taken campers on this trek before. There was a log cabin at the end of the trek where they were due to camp that night and then trek back early the following morning.

The trek was longer than Paul had expected and hard work. In part they followed an old Indian trail called 'The Appalachian Way' which was beautiful. It wound its way through deciduous woodland and colourful pastures in the foothills of a small mountain range. The campers were tasked to identify wildlife during the trek but as they were initially excited and noisy, they scared any wildlife away. As they ascended though they became noticeably quieter; the views were stunning and the whole group seemed to settle down and enjoy the trek.

They arrived at the log cabin late afternoon and set up camp. The facilities were basic. The campers rolled out their bedding in the cabin on hard beds. A log fire was lit to warm the pre prepared food. The camper's excitement grew again as they speculated that this was what it might have been in the old 'wild west' days. After the evening meal, there was singing into the night around the campfire and various games were played too. The campers went to bed exhausted and were soon asleep. All went quiet. Paul stepped outside the cabin to check the fire had doused down. He was sitting on a log staring at the embers and reflecting on the day. It had been a good day, what an experience! He was startled when the blonde haired girl came up and sat down beside him.

They spoke in whispers, anxious not to wake the campers. The conversation was easy as they shared the experiences of the day. As the embers died down and the night air became cooler, they moved closer on the log. One thing led to another, she was eighteen and nearly two years older than Paul. When Paul moved his arm around her to keep her warm, they looked at each other, smiled and kissed. The kissing went on for some time but they both realised they also needed some sleep and tip toed back into the cabin.

The following morning, they awoke to a brilliant sunrise. Breakfast around the rekindled fire was followed by chores to tidy the cabin, sweeping all the floors and cleaning all the plates and cooking equipment. It wasn't until mid morning that they descended back to return to the main camp. It was a happy group; new friendships had been made and that included the leaders as well as the campers! On the way back down, Paul often caught the blonde haired girl's eye and they smiled, she looked great Paul thought.

As they approached the camp, Paul caught up with her and walked alongside. He casually mentioned he'd enjoyed the previous evening and tentatively asked if she would like to meet again? She smiled. They discussed the camp routine and realised the best time to meet would be after lights out. Paul would walk through the woods to her cabin. There was a lot to be done that day returning to camp, so they arranged to meet the following evening. Paul was excited and contemplated what might happen. She seemed to like him and kept saying how much she enjoyed his accent and had he met the Queen? He enjoyed their banter; she was really nice looking and a great kisser too.

The following evening couldn't come soon enough for Paul. He was lucky as the group of campers had enjoyed an energetic day and were soon sound asleep. He was a little concerned about leaving them as technically his job was to be there in case anything happened. As he crept away from his cabin and all seemed to be quiet, the concerns for his campers were quickly overwhelmed by the excitement he felt as he approached her cabin. He peered ahead along the path towards her cabin and there she was sitting outside, waiting and looking amazing!

He cupped his mouth and softly made the sound of an owl. She spun around smiling and holding her finger to her lips, told him to keep quiet. As he approached, she grabbed his hand, still indicating to him to keep quiet and led him away from her cabin. There was another, older cabin a short distance away which was unoccupied. Paul had been looking forward to more kissing. He was wrong. As soon as they got into the cabin, they kissed initially but then she stood back, pulled off her T shirt, pulled down her shorts and lay on the bed. Paul hadn't anticipated this forwardness but with a smile, stripped as well and lay alongside her. The next two hours were passionate; her appetite for sex seemed relentless. It was the first time Paul had made love. It was a night he would never forget and he learned a lot from her.

After two hours, they realised they should return to their cabins. They kissed and parted with whispered salutations, 'See you tomorrow!' Paul smiled all the way back to his cabin. Everything seemed quiet on arrival, just the sound of contented camper snoring. Paul grinned as his head hit his pillow, he just couldn't believe what had happened, she had been amazing. The next thing he knew it was morning. He had to get up and whilst waking his campers, found that although feeling drowsy his recollections of last night made him smile. All seemed well with the world he thought, and he looked forward to seeing her again. The day followed the normal routines of camp exercises and activities, plenty of laughter and good fun.

That evening Paul had to take his group over to the main hall for their evening meal. They arrived early and had to wait outside whilst the catering team finished their preparations. As he waited, he looked up and saw the blonde girl approaching with her group as well. He smiled, and she smiled back but then beckoned him over.

They both stepped aside from the campers and out of earshot. Paul said how much he had enjoyed the previous evening, that it was amazing, and he just couldn't believe it. He was taken aback though as when he looked at her, she seemed sad, there was a tear in her eye. She then spoke and explained she had really enjoyed the last night also but that she had been thinking during the day and realised Paul would be returning to the UK soon, so there was no future in their relationship and no point in seeing each other again.

Paul couldn't believe his ears. It was difficult as although they were out of earshot from the campers they were in full view, and only a few steps away. It was then the main hall doors were opened. She turned and glanced at him, there was still a tear in her eye as she mouthed the word 'sorry', then turned and followed her group into the main hall. Paul was stunned, from feeling so happy one moment to then feeling so dejected the next. He just couldn't believe it. He then also followed his campers into the main hall, trying to conceal his feelings of rejection and total dejection.

John's summer holiday break didn't involve the overseas adventures of Paul and Tony. Like Steve, he remained in the UK spending all the time he could with Susan. They were not just happy but also mightily relieved that Susan was not pregnant. John often thought how embarrassing it would have been as her parents would have realised their hospitality had been abused, that John had been creeping into Susan's room at night. Their relationship seemed much better for it though, Susan felt more confident being on the pill and they often made love during the day at either of their houses whilst their parents were out. Susan had met John's parents and developed a close relationship with John's sister who felt pleased they had confided in her and that she had been able to help them.

John and Susan spent the summer in part time work, picking fruit on local farmer's fields. The initial soft crops of blackcurrants, raspberries and strawberries were followed later by plums, apples and pears. They worked some days in the orchards on Steve's family farm and often saw Steve driving past on one of the tractors. There was no time to talk but just a fleeting wave and smile as he sped past. It was during this time though that Steve took the train back to see Uncle Frank for the second time and had arranged to collect Jan on the way.

Steve smiled broadly as he walked towards the exit barrier at the station; Jan was waiting for him the other side of the barrier. Steve had thought about Jan a lot, he had missed her. They kissed and then, holding hands, slipped into the station café for a drink and a catch up chat.

Jan wanted to talk again about their boat being written off by the insurance company. She told him that her Dad was waiting payment but actually he had not expressed any enthusiasm for buying a new boat. Jan felt he had been affected by the stormy conditions. Steve explained he had not heard from Uncle Frank since last week but that he understood from his parents he was still resting in his flat.

Uncle Frank's flat was only a short distance from the station. They set off holding hands. On arrival it was Uncle Frank who answered the door. Steve was pleased to see he was up and about but as he stepped away from the door to lead them into the living room, he walked with obvious difficulty, he was stooping, and his back was badly hunched. Jan noticed this immediately, you couldn't fail to and she was quite taken aback and felt she wasn't ready for this. It was such a contrast to the Uncle Frank she'd known strutting around the boat park with confidence and engaging everyone in hearty conversation.

As they sat down Steve offered to make some tea leaving Jan with Uncle Frank in the living room. The conversation was awkward at first, Jan didn't want to say the wrong thing. Uncle Frank was mentally alert but physically weak. They discussed the race and Uncle Frank was interested to hear Jan's father had made a successful claim on his insurance but that he was unlikely to buy another boat. When Steve brought in the tea, Uncle Frank updated them with his condition. He was taking a lot of medication, but the focus was on complete rest and eating well. He was fortunate to have good neighbours who were helping him with shopping and even cooked some meals for him.

Uncle Frank relaxed with his cup of tea and then chuckled saying, 'Of course, I'm not sure if Steve has told you but one of my friends has told me I'm going through the 'Male Menopause'. Jan looked quizzically at Uncle Frank and said nothing, she didn't want him to know that she and Steve had been talking about him and had discussed this. Uncle Frank explained further that the Male Menopause was, to the best of his knowledge, not recognised as a medical condition.

He explained the Male Menopause was more psychological rather than the more obvious physical changes that happen to women. Men classically try to do things in their later years that they did well when they were younger but now lacked the stamina and strength to perform well. 'I'm a classic case,' he continued, 'Sailing competitively at my age, I should have known better and certainly that gale we encountered sorted us all out didn't it?' Steve nodded and tried to gently steer Uncle Frank away from the idea of a Male Menopause but was surprised when he referred to a further visit from his friend during the week and that they'd discussed it in more detail.

The next hour passed quickly as Uncle Frank discussed what his friend had said, 'It all starts with the origins of the male species as cave men,' he started, Steve's eyebrows raised at this as Frank explained that the cave men were driven by three motivations, all centred on the family groups they led, 'Simply they had to protect, provide and procreate,' he said. Steve and Jan glanced at each other and smiled at the mention of the word 'procreate' but turned back to Uncle Frank as he was in full flow now explaining his thoughts further.

'I'd not really thought about it before,' he went on, 'but sitting here all day at the moment as I am, the idea of protection, provision and procreation all makes sense to me.' Steve and Jan could see Uncle Frank was enjoying sharing his thoughts with them. He went on to explain that in the case of the cave man he had to protect his family from wild animals and other tribes and that to do this he needed to be strong and skilful. In the case of modern man today, sport is now important Uncle Frank said. 'Modern man is trying to remain fit and skilful to protect his family.' He went on to talk about provision, Cave man had to hunt and grow crops to feed his family, whereas modern day man studies hard to get a good job and earn a good salary. 'Procreation' Uncle Frank went on, 'has not really changed since the cave man, boy meets girl as you two know', he said and winked noticing that both Steve and Jan were blushing, but he also saw they exchanged a smile as well.

'So, modern day man finds his origins in caveman: provision, protection and procreation,' he summarised. 'It all seems so simple and obvious now,' he said with a resigned grimace. A conversation then took place between the three of them, largely dominated by Uncle Frank thinking through all the sports he had tried and how competitive he'd been, all the exams he'd worked hard for and how important good results were. He reflected on his life, realising all his hard work and competitive sporting life had been driven by cave man instincts and that he'd never thought about it before, but by understanding these he realised, the behaviour of modern day man can be better understood. There was no further discussion around procreation as Uncle Frank didn't wish to embarrass his two young visitors.

The conversation on the Male Menopause had certainly raised Uncle Frank's spirits as he'd shared his thoughts with Steve and Jan. There was more of a spring in his step so to speak, but after an hour Steve and Jan could tell he was weakening and got up to leave. They asked Uncle Frank if there was anything they could do for him. He explained again that he was lucky to have such good neighbours and there was nothing further to be done. Steve and Jan bid him goodbye. Steve indicated he was planning to return the following Saturday and that he enjoyed the trip over on the train; it was a welcome relief from harvesting!

Once outside Uncle Frank's flat and walking down the road, Steve and Jan looked at each other, smiled and then kissed. They had both been concerned seeing Uncle Frank in such a weakened state but also, they were intrigued by his thoughts on the Male Menopause and even more by his references to procreation. Steve explained to Jan that he had only heard the word 'procreation' when his friend Tony used it, saying it was the posh word for sex. They both laughed. Steve suggested they should walk back into the centre of the town for a coffee, but Jan then explained her parents were both working in the shop and would he prefer to go back to her house instead? Steve readily agreed.

Jan's home was an old Victorian semi-detached on three floors with high ceilings and large bay windows. Once the front door closed Jan turned to Steve and kissed him eagerly. They never got around to making coffee but spent the rest of the afternoon in her bedroom on the third floor. It was the first time either of them had had sex, their appetite seemed insatiable and between making love they could only lie looking at each other in the eyes and smiling, it was wonderful. Jan whispered to Steve that she had heard making love was good but had never imagined it would be this good!

It was late afternoon when Jan looked at her watch and panicked as she suddenly realised her parents would be back from the shop in half an hour! They leapt out of her bed, dressed, and ran down the stairs and into the main entrance hall. There was time for one last lingering kiss and a nodded understanding they would see each other again the following Saturday. Steve slipped out of the front door and headed for the station. Jan ran upstairs to tidy her room.

It was only a few minutes later that she heard her parents coming through the front door. She called down and cheerily asked if they'd had a nice day, they both responded to ask if she had also. Jan blushed a little as she replied back that she had, it was good they couldn't see her face she thought and then smiled as she thought of Steve and their afternoon.

And so, the summer days rolled by quickly and happily for all four friends. Their activities had varied considerably. There were really only two common themes for all of them being the anticipation of their exam results at the end of August and the discovery of women and making love. Quite a contrast!

The 'O' level results day then arrived. Tony, John and Steve had to go to the Grammar School to collect their results; Paul went to his Technical School. They returned to their homes initially to discuss the results with their parents and families. They had arranged to meet later that afternoon to play football and catch up. A whole summer had passed by and they'd not seen each other, there was a lot to catch up on!

Tony was the last to arrive at the recreation ground. The others laughed as he strode towards them calling out, 'Bonjour, ca va?!' with a wave, a cheery smile and a perfect French accent. They all knew he'd spent the holiday in

France with Celia, the football was put to one side, they sat down and started talking.

It had been almost eight weeks since they last met. There was a brief conversation about the exam results, they had all done well, but then the conversation quickly moved on the girls, Tony spoke first describing his time with Celia. Although there was a huge age gap, they had got on really well, Tony said, 'She's quite trendy really!' and the others laughed. Tony described her fast car, the Péage routes, the towns, the coastal areas, the food, the wine, the language and the sex saying he was completely wasted, and that Celia had an enormous appetite; they all laughed.

With a more sombre expression, Tony explained his parents had been unsure about Celia knowing that she was a lot older but that they had now met her and there was a better understanding. Still with a sombre expression, Tony went through his 'O' level results explaining he'd failed English Literature saying he 'couldn't understand that Bill Shakespeare bloke', but adding he passed the other eight exams with six 'A' grades and two 'B' grades. He was particularly pleased he'd passed English and Maths with 'A' grades. He was concerned though that he still wasn't sure what he wanted to do at 'A' level, and he was also concerned that he needed to let his parents know he definitely didn't want to go into retail as they had done.

It was Paul who spoke next saying he could beat Tony's trip to France as he had been all the way to America! Although Steve, John and Tony knew this they all said 'oooh' in anticipation of Paul's stories. They knew Paul had gone at short notice and that the trip had been in the back wash of the sudden fall out with Trudy. They listened as Paul described the trip, the flight into New York, the travel by bus to Richmond, the camp activities, the climate and the meals and so on but their attention was really grabbed by Paul's reference to the two blonde haired girls.

Paul's face blushed as he described the overnight hike into the mountains with one of the blonde girls and the subsequent love making on return to camp. He got the 'thumbs up' from his friends as they heard the story, but then a frown as Paul explained it had turned out to be only a one night stand.

They asked if Paul had seen Trudy since he'd got back; Paul said he had knocked her door and her Mum had answered to say Trudy had spent the summer away at a cousin's house and also, that her Mum had indicated that Trudy was seeing someone else. Paul seemed saddened and puzzled by this, it was only a story he'd told that had gone wrong, wasn't it? Paul went on to explain he passed all his 'O' levels, but the grades were generally 'B's and 'C's with one 'A' in Physics which his Dad had been pleased with. His Dad was still encouraging Paul to join the engineering firm with his brothers after school, but Paul still wasn't sure, particularly after all he had experienced and seen in America. Paul commented that he needed to have a serious careers chat with his Dad!

Whereas Paul and Tony were unsure what careers and jobs they wanted to pursue, Steve was now happily committed to working on his family farm with his Father. Steve's exam results reflected this. He had not tried as hard as the others as he felt his exam results were not as important. Although he had passed all of them it was only 'C' and 'D' grades. The other boys had anticipated this but what they hadn't anticipated was Steve's story about Uncle Frank and also Jan!

Steve told the story of the races in the catamarans, meeting Jan, the gale, then the capsize, the rescue by the RNLI and the subsequent trips to see Uncle Frank and how the relationship with Jan had developed. He had a broad grin as he described his relationship with Jan; the others 'whooped' and Tony even slapped him on the back.

However, the smiles all turned to frowns as Steve described the declining health of Uncle Frank and his thoughts about the Male Menopause. They dwelled on the Male Menopause. Steve explained Uncle Frank thought modern day men still exhibited their 'cave man' origins and that their behaviours were based on the three Ps – Protection, Provision and Procreation. 'Maybe Uncle Frank has a point' said Steve, 'Just look at our conversation this morning where the 'Provision' part has been under discussion. We're all keen to get good exam grades and good jobs to provide, aren't we? And as to the 'Procreation' part, well we're all into that, now aren't we?' They all laughed as John said, 'There's no such thing as the Male Menopause!'

It was John who then updated them last. In his quiet voice he seemed almost embarrassed as he mentioned he had passed all his 'O' levels with 'A' grades. The others all 'whooped' again and patted him on the back. They asked John what he wanted to do with his career. John replied to say he didn't really know but maybe 'something academic' with a shrug of his shoulders.

John then went on to tell the story of Susan and the concern at the beginning of the summer holiday that she might be pregnant, the subsequent advice from his sister and the visit to the doctors. The others all felt relief for John when he explained that the pregnancy tests had been negative, that Susan was now on the contraceptive pill and that they'd had an enjoyable relaxing summer picking fruit and added, 'not like the adventures of you lot!' with a broad smile.

The boys had been talking for over two hours and hadn't kicked the football; it had just been great catching up with each other, a lot had happened in a short space of time. One thing was apparent, that with the 'O' level exams behind them and now that all of them had experienced sex, they really were no longer boys, in fact the boys had become men!

One story was to stick in their minds for many years though wouldn't be discussed a great deal until they were older. Uncle Frank's thoughts about the Male Menopause had interested them. It had particularly affected Steve as he had heard them at first hand. He often reflected with Jan on what became known as the 'MM' conversation, commenting on his friends often as he observed how his friends were coping with the pressures of growing older, coping with families, home ownership and careers.

In many cases the stories were amusing but it helped Steve understand what was important. He was to find his friends were more open to discussing it once they reached retirement age and could reflect with him.

CHAPTER 8

DEMAND PHASE
(18-25 YEARS OLD)
Men meeting Women

IMPORTANT DECISIONS WERE made by all four boys (now men!) in those few vital days after the 'O' level results had been announced. John and Tony decided to stay on at Grammar school to study for their 'A' levels; in John's case he thought he would like to be a teacher, but in Tony's case he still wasn't sure about the career he wanted to pursue. He believed further education would open up new doors and extend his opportunities. In fact, anything to avoid working with his Dad in retail!

Steve had wanted to leave school and work on the farm; his parents had welcomed this but encouraged him to go to a local Agricultural College on a day release scheme to broaden his knowledge. Steve was reluctant to do this at first but would later appreciate it more than he could have imagined. Paul had the most difficult discussions with his Dad and brothers making it clear that the trip to America had opened his eyes to all sorts of career opportunities. He was interested in Engineering and would stay at the Technical College to study his 'A' levels but wanted to travel afterwards to, 'see the World!'. His brothers felt he was being spoilt as they had left school at the earliest opportunity to work with their Dad. Paul's Dad raised his eyebrows; he could detect the tension amongst his sons but recognised a maturity in Paul that he'd not seen before.

Tony, Paul, John and Steve talked regularly in the last remaining days of the summer holidays to develop their ideas. But all too quickly the summer holidays were over, the autumn term had begun, and new routines were underway! The days flew by for Paul, Tony and John. They still went to the same school to progress their studies but found it a lot more intense than 'O' levels. Steve's routine changed the most as he was now working almost full time with his Father; it was going so well but he started to look forward to his days at Agricultural College as a release from his daily routines on the family farm.

However, Steve had not anticipated a further change in his life; Uncle Frank died.

It was a Wednesday evening and Steve returned late from college and walked into the kitchen to find his Mother and Father sat at the kitchen table with sombre expressions. Steve knew something was wrong. In some ways the news of Uncle Frank's death was not a surprise as he had just seemed to be getting weaker and weaker, yet Steve had not contemplated he would die. He had not imagined that possibility. He was really shocked.

His parents were also upset; Uncle Frank was Steve's Mother's brother. She was crying uncontrollably, repeatedly saying that he seemed just too young to have died. Steve's Mother suggested he should call Jan as she had got to know Uncle Frank quite well in recent weeks. Steve wasn't prepared for Jan's reaction either when he called her. Jan was also shocked, she sobbed and cried like Steve's mother, saying what a nice man she thought Uncle Frank was and that she would miss him. Steve explained no funeral arrangements had been made yet and that he would call her back as soon as he knew.

That evening was quiet. Steve's siblings hadn't known Uncle Frank as well as Steve and their parents, but it was clear the news had been upsetting. They finished their homework and then went to bed quietly. Steve sat in his bedroom recalling memories, particularly those of the last few months. The racing in the catamaran had been more than just fun, it was thrilling, and the recollections gave Steve a sad smile. There were so many memories of the day of the gale, the rescue by the RNLI and the look of exhaustion on Uncle Frank's face after they had capsized. Then there were the happy memories of meeting Jan and everything that had happened since. It was such a mix of emotions, Steve felt really upset; he was close to tears but didn't cry. He reflected though on how much his Mother and Jan had cried yet he had not? It must be something to do with the genes he thought and that men are different to women? He had not noticed his Father crying.

Several days passed before the funeral arrangements had been made. Steve had called Jan on numerous occasions, mostly in the evenings and they discussed many memories, often laughing and then sharing silences as they reflected. They both said how much they missed each other and looked forward to meeting soon but in very sad circumstances. Jan was concerned that she had not met Steve's parents or his siblings either and was reassured as they realised the main focus would be on the collective memories of Uncle Frank.

The day of the funeral arrived. Some days before, Steve had told John, Tony and Paul the news about Uncle Frank. None of them knew him but they could see how upset Steve was. In particular Steve told them how very upset his Mother and Jan had been, that they had both cried, Steve said he felt very upset but hadn't cried, nor had his Father. Steve pondered on why women seemed more able to display their emotions openly whereas men generally couldn't. They could tell Steve wanted to talk more and in particular share memories about Uncle Frank's thoughts on the Male Menopause saying 'There's no such thing as the Male Menopause' which had made them all smile.

Steve was travelling with his family in their car to the funeral and found he was thinking through the discussions he'd had with his friends and how they had helped him. He thought ahead to meeting Jan again and felt excited; it was going to be a day of mixed emotions for sure he thought.

Jan looked beautiful. She wore a plain black dress and shoes with a simple shawl draped over her shoulders. Steve felt an intake of breath as he saw her standing at the church gate. It was at that moment that she saw him too and gave a great welcoming smile though she quickly became more serious as she realised Steve was with his family and she wanted to show her respects as they walked towards her.

Steve stepped forward and kissed Jan on the cheek, he then introduced her to all his family. Steve's parents then led them up the church path followed by Steve's siblings. Steve and Jan held hands and followed behind them, he gripped Jan's hands firmly and glanced at her with a reassuring smile and whispered, 'You look lovely!' Jan smiled back.

The church was packed. Steve recognised a lot of people from the sailing club. Two of the four eulogies were from sailors that Steve had met and they both paid testament to Uncle Frank's achievements; not only had he been a key member of the sailing club committee, but they also recognised his achievements over the years in racing and that he had won the Swift Catamaran National Championships twice. There was reference to the exceptional weather conditions during his last race. Clearly his passing had affected a lot of people; they had either participated themselves or knew people who had. Although Uncle Frank's death wasn't directly attributed to the race it was clearly a major cause and on people's minds.

The other two eulogies were from work colleagues who paid tribute to his achievements at work and how much he would be missed. Significantly, Steve thought, there was no mention of his childless marriage or any family matters and it was noticeable that his ex-wife did not attend.

The wake afterwards was held at the sailing club. Steve sat in a corner of the clubhouse with Jan. They had hoped to talk but there was a constant stream of well-wishers who came over to offer their condolences. One person, who introduced himself as 'Tim' explained that he had been a lifelong friend and had visited Uncle Frank several times whilst he had been unwell. Tim went on to mention that they had discussed the Male Menopause in particular. Steve smiled and then explained that Uncle Frank had mentioned Tim's visits and the conversations several times; he had been very interested in the subject and noted his concern that the condition wasn't medically recognised.

Steve's response surprised Tim, he hadn't realised Uncle Frank had been discussing the Male Menopause with anyone else. Tim was encouraged to know this and went on to say that Uncle Frank had been particularly interested in the idea that modern day man's behaviour is based on the three primary instincts being provision, protection and procreation, that he felt he had succeeded in two but failed in one. Steve certainly hadn't heard Uncle Frank talk in these terms and listened further as Tim indicated that he thought it was a good idea that Uncle Frank's ex-wife had not attended today as this part of his life had not worked out. He went on to add though that by contrast it was right that his excellent achievements at work and in sport had revealed his provision and protection instincts,

Tim added he was really pleased that these had been fully acknowledged in the eulogies today.

Steve had not really thought about Uncle Frank in these terms and realised there was a lot more to this than he had first thought. The conversation with Tim could have carried on for some time were it not for the intervention of Steve's Mother who indicated they needed to leave and get back to the farm. Steve and Jan stood up; Steve shook Tim's hand and said he hoped they would meet again. There was a knowing smile as they realised, they should definitely talk further about Uncle Frank and the Male Menopause. Steve then took Jan's hand and they followed Steve's Mother out of the clubhouse. They waved goodbye to people they had met and made their way to the car park.

It was only as they approached the car that Steve suddenly thought about Jan and when he would he see her again. He need not have worried though, as at this moment his Mother spoke to Jan to say how pleased she'd been to meet her and asked if Jan would like to come over to the farm and stay for a few days. The smiles from both Jan and Steve were evident, Jan readily agreed, and arrangements were made for the following weekend. Steve and Jan kissed briefly, they were both aware Steve's siblings were watching and felt a little embarrassed.

That evening Steve met Paul, John and Tony on the recreation ground for a kick around. Afterwards Steve told them about Uncle Frank's funeral and reminded them of their conversation before the funeral in which they had said, 'There's no such thing as a Male Menopause.' They all smiled at this but then Steve told them that he had met Tim, Uncle Frank's friend at the funeral and that Tim was certain that the Male Menopause condition existed but that it is just not understood.

Steve went on to say he'd been surprised by Tim's assertions that Uncle Frank felt he had failed to achieve his founding instinct of procreation but that this had driven him to excel in the other two as he had been a very successful sportsman and built a successful career and business. 'You know,' said Steve, 'there's more to this Male Menopause than I first thought!'

They discussed it further and reflected on themselves all working hard to achieve good exam results at School and College and find ways to earn good standards of living. Tony commented that the 'provision' instinct was strong in all of them and added further that it was nearly as strong as the 'procreation' one. The others could all see he was thinking of Celia, there was a knowing glint in his eye! Steve smiled and explained that Jan was coming over to stay the following weekend and they decided to meet. They laughed together more acknowledging that the 'procreation' instinct was strong in all of them!

The weeks flew by; all four friends were focussed on their further education. Tony and John were finding that there was more to the 'A' level syllabus than they had imagined, particularly the course work assignments. Paul's 'A' level studies at Technical College involved a lot of technical work which he enjoyed. Steve still found his day release at Agricultural College was a welcome change to the day to day routines on the farm.

Sport was also of increasing interest to the four friends; they had all played competitive football at school and joined junior football clubs outside school. Their parents had encouraged this and taken them to both practice sessions and matches. There was a good feeling of 'team spirit' whether they won or lost. Their coaches had always said it was the taking part that was the most important thing.

Paul's brothers played for the local rugby team and took him along to play in the colt's section. Paul really enjoyed this and found the 'team spirit' even stronger in rugby. It was much more physical than football, the tackling was hard, and he found it was more physically exhausting than football. Winter rolled into spring and then summer and with the changing seasons the football and rugby seasons came to an end. The four friends played cricket and tennis through the summer months both for school and club teams. Again, it was highly competitive, and tested out their physical abilities and stamina as they continued to develop into young men.

Alongside their development into young men, the four friends continued to develop their interests in 'Procreation' and their relationships with their girlfriends. Everything seemed to be developing well for Tony, Steve and John but it was Paul who anguished over his failed relationship with Trudy, he had learned she was now in a serious relationship with someone else. Paul couldn't believe he'd messed things up so badly in telling that story about Woolworths. He felt he couldn't share his anguish with his brothers who would just tease him or his parents who wouldn't understand. Paul surprised himself however as he found he opened up his feelings one evening to his Rugby Coach as they sat in the Clubhouse after a strenuous training session.

He respected his Coach; he was a lot older than Paul and had been a really good rugby player in his day. They were in the middle of a general chat when the coach asked if he had a girlfriend. Perhaps, Paul thought later, it was the opportunity he'd been waiting for, to tell the story to someone he respected but who was entirely neutral. Paul told the story of his relationship in full and included the Woolworths story. When he finished the coach laughed uncontrollably, there were tears in his eyes and he slapped Paul on the back.

Paul was puzzled. Why hadn't Trudy's parents found it funny also he asked. The Coach drew in a deep breath, raised his eyebrows and smiled as he turned to Paul and explained he needed to see the story from Trudy's parents' perspective. Here was a boyfriend (maybe a future son in law!?) of their only daughter telling them he had a criminal record and then, even worse it turns out this boyfriend is misleading them all!

Definitely not the audience for this story the coach said and as he looked into Paul's eyes, Paul realised the bad error he'd made and why it had upset Trudy so much. The Coach could see Paul's troubled state and gave him a friendly punch on the shoulder and reassuring him that he would find a girlfriend before too long; 'You're a fit, intelligent, good looking bloke,' the Coach said, 'You'll meet someone soon and you'll soon forget that Trudy,' he continued, 'And in case you ever find the need to tell another story can I tell you mine?' Paul felt really much more confident and reassured by his Coach's responses and nodded in anticipation.

The Coach started by saying that this story was about President Charles De Gaulle and had until recently been restricted under 'The Official Secrets Act.' Paul was hooked and leaned forward as the Coach told the story.

It was the summer of 1969; the constitutional referendum that was held in France on 27 April 1969 had forced President Charles de Gaulle to resign. The British Embassy in Paris decided to invite the great President to a formal lunch reception to celebrate his excellent career. The day arrived and the sun shone brightly as the President drove up the Champs-Élysées with his cavalcade. He was in his grand chauffeur driven, open topped limousine accompanied by his wife and Police outriders. He waved grandly, smiling to the cheering and adoring crowds as they approached the wide red carpet laid out at the doors of the main entrance to the Embassy.

The cheering increased significantly as the limousine glided to a halt at the end of the carpet and then the President and Madame Charles De Gaulle were assisted from the limousine and onto the carpet. The President paused with his wife and with great 'Presidential aplomb,' looked around him, smiled broadly, then waved and nodded his appreciation to the entire crowd. The crowd went wild with excitement. (Paul was at this stage completely engrossed in the story; the Coach could certainly tell them well!).

Inside the Embassy the staff could hear the roar of the crowds and smiled at each other in anticipation of a grand event. As the President entered the reception lobby he was greeted by the British Ambassador. He and his wife were then offered a correctly chilled glass of Moet Chandon champagne, the very best that France could offer of course! With the formal welcome completed, the Embassy ladies, (all dressed in their very best with glittering jewellery) swarmed excitedly around the President's wife, with one of them asking her what she was looking forward to most in her retirement. The President's wife smiled, she paused for a moment as if to suggest she was thinking deeply about the question and then, raising her glass and speaking in broken English, she said; 'My dears, ze sing I look forward to most in retirement is ...' She paused again and then said, 'a penis!' and smiled to all the assembled ladies.

A great hush hit the room; no one could believe what the President's wife had said, no one knew what to say! Fortunately, the President was close by and having heard his wife's announcement, he calmly stepped forward and said, 'Cherie, I think when you pronounce this word in English it is 'happiness'!

It was at his point that the Coach and Paul fell about laughing, there were tears in their eyes. Even though the Coach had told this many times he still found it hilarious. The Coach then noticed that Paul had stopped laughing and had a serious, reflective look on his face. 'What's up?'

said the Coach and Paul looked at him and said, 'There's no way of course I could use this story with prospective in laws and mention the 'penis' word!? The Coach laughed and said, 'No you're completely right, many apologies, I just wanted to tell you a story to cheer you up!' and added he would think again and come up with a better story. They both laughed together, and Paul felt a lot better and as if a great weight had been lifted off his shoulders.

Meanwhile, a problem was emerging for Tony. The relationship with Celia was going very well, too well. The physical side of their relationship was great. Tony was spending several nights a week at her house overnight. In the daytime Tony found he couldn't stop thinking about her; he thought Celia was just amazing, that she was beautiful, a great lover and wealthy too. But, overall, just good fun to be with. He was very happy; she was everything he could hope for in a woman. The fact she was nearly twenty years older than him rarely crossed his mind. He just couldn't stop thinking about her and now knew what the word 'besotted' meant!

The problems were with Tony's parents. They were deeply concerned that Tony was completely distracted when he should be more focussed and spending more time on his 'A' level studies. The tensions were increasing at Tony's house and it was his Mum who was particularly anxious. The initial discussions had progressed to more regular arguments. It was Tony's Dad who tried to calm the situation. Whilst showing that he agreed fully with his wife, he realised the increasing arguments could have a negative effect and that Tony would spend more time with Celia rather than enduring the bad atmosphere at home. Tony's Dad decided to arrange a quiet pint with his son.

It was rare for Tony and his Dad to go out together; Tony suspected what the reason might be, and he wasn't wrong. Actually, Tony was too young to be drinking. He was just seventeen but looked well over eighteen, the legal age. With pints on the table and the first sups taken, they relaxed. Tony's Dad coughed to clear his throat and then with a little awkwardness that Tony noticed, explained that he thought it was time they should have a conversation about making babies and sex? It was then that Tony, with a big smile leaned forward towards his Dad and said, 'Sure, what do you want to know?' His Dad was stumped, he hesitated and looking back at Tony's smiling face roared into laughter, they both laughed together catching the attention of others in the bar, and just enjoying the humour of the moment. The tension had gone, they could now talk openly.

Tony's Dad was still chuckling and wiped a tear from his eye. He then started the conversation by saying how concerned he and Tony's Mum were about Tony's progress with his exams. He went on to say what a lovely women Celia was (in fact, Tony's Dad quite fancied her himself but didn't say so), that Tony was now a man and needed to focus more on his studies over the next few months. Tony smiled as he responded saying he would have been disappointed if his parents didn't care but that he had found his Mum in particular was nagging him just too much. They reflected together on some of the recent incidents and Tony's Dad agreed he would try to calm his wife's anxieties. They both slapped hands and it was then time for another beer.

With the second beer in hand, Tony realised it would be a good opportunity to chat with his Dad to explain he wasn't really interested in following him into the shop. Tony was surprised by his Dad's reaction, as although he had encouraged Tony to join him in the shop ever since he was a young boy, his Dad was now more reflective. They talked generally about all of the career opportunities that Tony might pursue, in fact Tony's Dad added some new ideas and they were all mainly based on sales roles.

Tony was happily surprised how open his Dad was and asked why his Dad wasn't encouraging him to join him in the shop. His Dad smiled and said, 'The world's your oyster, you need to be your own man,' and then referred to the salt and pepper incident and the expulsion from School following the cake incident with Mrs Collier. They both laughed together as they recalled those incidents from years ago with Tony's Dad saying, 'Just be your own man,' and the beer glasses were clinked again. A good understanding had been achieved; it had been a good pint.

Meanwhile, John's relationship with Susan had gone from strength to strength; content in each other's company they saw each other every day. They were both studying for 'A' levels in Arts subjects and shared similar interests. With hindsight, the pregnancy scare had brought them closer together. They made love frequently and mainly at each other's houses when their parents were out. John's sister could see how close the relationship was becoming and often shared a knowing smile with them.

It was during the start of their second year of 'A' levels that John commented to Susan that he'd been interested in playing Rugby. He had been talking to Paul and it seemed a really good sport to try? Susan encouraged him; she could see how keen John was to try a new sport. John had been playing in the same football team as Tony and Steve and neither of them were pleased to hear that John might be leaving their team to play Rugby with Paul. A strong discussion took place about team loyalties. In some ways it flattered John that Tony and Steve felt that way, but he wanted to try something new and was interested in the different level of physicality that rugby offered. The beer and post-match singing were also of interest!

John initially attended some rugby training sessions. The coaching was good, and John found there were plenty of new techniques to learn. The ball handling and tackling were all so different to football and the players were all really welcoming, and friendly. The Coach was good, very thorough and he said he thought John's best position would be in the front row, probably as a Prop. John told the Coach that he was a good friend of Paul's and that Paul had told him the President Charles de Gaulle story. They both laughed and John felt pleased he'd made the move and looked forward to his first game.

For Tony, Paul and John, it was their second and final year at 'A' level. Steve had exams in college, but they were primarily practical tests and assessments. The stress, the apprehension and tension, was increasing amongst all of them but it was good they could still laugh amongst themselves whenever they met. The weeks rolled by quickly that Autumn Term and then there were parties and celebrations over the Christmas period.

It was at one of these parties that Paul first met Jenny. Their eyes met across a crowded room and they just smiled.

In years to come, Paul and Jenny would often refer to that moment and laugh; eyes across a crowded room, surely the stuff of fiction but it actually happened to them. They had never met before and yet as Paul walked over and started talking with her, it was as if they'd known each other all their lives.

They talked all evening; it was nonstop yet so relaxed. Jenny had two elder sisters, she was in her final year of 'A' levels and didn't know which career route to follow. The family ran a hotel, and she was being encouraged to work there, but she wasn't sure. It was almost a complete mirror image of Paul's situation with his Dad's engineering business. They laughed together so much, and the evening passed by very quickly.

The first kiss seemed so natural; it was an initial peck and then a strong embrace. It didn't happen until later in the evening as they'd been talking so much, everyone else in the room were engrossed in their own conversations and didn't notice particularly. Paul looked down to Jenny and she looked up to him. They both knew this was special. It was getting late, people were leaving, and Paul explained he was walking home, Jenny explained she had come in her own car and could give Paul a lift.

Jenny parked outside Paul's house. They had talked incessantly all the way back. As Jenny turned off the engine, Paul lent over and they kissed again, it just felt so good and if they had not been outside Paul's house, it could have easily progressed. They agreed to meet the following evening, Paul would collect Jenny from the family hotel. The following day dragged for Paul, he just couldn't stop thinking about Jenny, her smile, her laugh and all the different things they'd discussed. His brothers noticed his buoyant mood and asked if he'd had a good time last evening. Paul's broad smile told them everything straight away and learning her name was 'Jenny,' they proceeded to tease him at every opportunity.

Eventually it was time to get ready, well actually Paul had started to get ready sooner than he needed to as he was so excited about meeting Jenny again. When he walked casually into the kitchen he was greeted with 'wolf whistles' from his brothers. One brother offered some of his 'special' aftershave. Paul's Mum looked on with parental pride realising her children were children no more and then handed Paul the keys to her car asking him to make sure he looked after it.

Paul was impressed by the hotel; he had known of it before but hadn't really appreciated how large it was. The reception was busy, and Paul had to wait in a queue but when he got to the desk and asked for Jenny, the receptionist smiled warmly and said, 'Oh yes, we've been expecting you!' At this point an older man stepped out of the office, having heard the receptionist's greeting and offered his hand to Paul and with a firm handshake asked him to follow him. Once away from the throng of the reception area, the man turned to Paul and said that actually he was Jenny's Dad and how pleased he was to meet Paul. He seemed very friendly, and Paul was shortly to find out why he was so welcoming.

He led Paul through a door marked 'Private' and into a large lounge. Jenny was there, Paul couldn't help grinning as she looked so stunning. She stepped forward giving him a welcoming hug and a kiss. But Jenny wasn't on her own, her Mum and two older sisters were there too. They all welcomed Paul and gave him a peck on the cheek. Paul felt quite overwhelmed and flattered by the attention. One of Paul's sisters noticed his slight awkwardness and explained they had really looked forward to meeting him as Jenny hadn't stopped talking about him! Jenny blushed and Paul smiled as he realised Jenny's sisters were teasing her just as his brothers had teased him!

The conversation flowed easily. Jenny's sisters were eager to find out about Paul's family but showed disappointment when Paul explained his brothers already had girlfriends. They were really interested to find out he had worked in America and that he was studying Engineering at the Technical College. The time flew by quickly until Jenny's Dad did a muffled cough and looked at Jenny whilst glancing at his watch. Paul wondered why and then noticed Jenny seemed a little awkward. Jenny turned to Paul and said, 'We have a little problem this evening; I was booked to run the bar, but my relief can't make it, is there any chance you could work with me behind the bar?".

The two sisters looked on and were impressed as Paul said of course he could, but that he hadn't worked behind a bar before! The two sisters clapped and teased Jenny that this was going to be an unusual first date. Jenny flushed as she thanked Paul profusely and explained she would show him everything there was to know. With that they decided to go and check the bar. Paul said goodbye to Jenny's Mum and her sisters who giggled saying they hoped they'd meet again. Jenny's Dad explained he was also on duty and would be seeing them several times during the evening.

The bar was busy; it was not only for residents but also, being near to the town centre, there were a lot of shoppers and local businessmen. Paul and Jenny were rushed off their feet. Paul found the beer pulling was quite easy, but he took longer to get used to the till. It was the spirits and mixed drinks he found really difficult and had to keep asking Jenny for help. Collecting and washing the glasses was a real chore and had to be fitted in when there were no customers seeking drinks. As the evening progressed, Paul kept glancing at Jenny; she just looked superb he thought and her interaction with the customers was great, she was just so friendly. Occasionally their eyes would meet which made Paul tingle with excitement. He looked forward to closing time!

Collecting glasses, cleaning and cashing up all took a lot longer than Paul had anticipated but with the bar to themselves they discussed the customers and various incidents that had taken place. At one point Jenny's Dad came in to collect the cash for banking the following day. He paid Paul and thanked him for his help; Paul said he really enjoyed it and as he said it realised that he actually had! Jenny's Dad offered him the taxi fare home, but Paul explained he had his Mum's car. Jenny's Dad appreciated Paul's honesty.

Finally, everything had been cleared up; Jenny turned off the main lights and poured them both a well-earned drink. They then just sat in the bar and talked. Again, the conversation just flowed so easily, it was as if they'd known each other for years, not just a few days. They both knew this was something special, though neither said so specifically. Paul leaned forward and kissed Jenny. Her response was warm, and they kissed for a long time. At the end they just looked into each other's eyes without saying anything. It was early morning when they parted as Paul realised, he had to get his Mum's car home. There was a parting kiss, a long one and again, a further knowing smile.

On the way home Paul realised he was shattered but kept smiling as he recalled the day's events. His main focus was Jenny, but another thought crossed his mind too; he had really enjoyed working in the bar. Could the hospitality industry be a career option for him, rather than his Dad's engineering business? As his head hit the pillow and drifted into a deep sleep, he could see life was full of opportunities.

With only a few weeks to go to the 'A' level exams or in Steve's case his course final exams, all four men were now in active relationships. The weeks were flying by with little time to meet up and play football at the recreation ground as they had used to. The exam pressure was mounting; they'd been used to similar pressures at 'O' level stage, but this was different and relied more on self-discipline. They each found they needed to plan ahead.

In John's case this was no problem as Susan was on a similar course and they often revised together. Steve spoke to Susan in the week several times by phone and discussed the course work they were doing. Similarly, Paul and Jenny realised they had to set time aside to revise.

It was Tony who was in the greatest difficulty; Celia wanted to see him, yet his parents were concerned he should remain at home and revise. When Tony explained he was taking work around to Celia's house, his parents looked doubtful and questioned how he could possibly concentrate there. The problem for Tony was he knew his parents' concerns were well founded. Celia was demanding, she was just all consuming, the sex was just great. Just what was he to do? There was no easy answer for Tony and the pressure was mounting.

The 'A' level exams and Steve's final course exams started, and it was a strange feeling of anti-climax in a way. It was almost a relief that they just had to get on with them and do their best and yet there was a lot of anxiety. Apart from Steve, they all knew the grades they achieved would affect their University choices. The four friends didn't see each other during this exam period, there just wasn't time. They had anticipated it would be stressful and discussed the main priorities for them would be revision (often last minute cramming), eating, sleeping and last of all contact with girlfriends, but no time for the four friends to see each other.

This anticipation proved to be fairly accurate. It was certainly Tony who had the most difficult time as he felt distracted trying to keep Celia and his parents' content, yet he wanted to focus on his exams. Celia could see what he was going through, and it was then that she had what she thought was a good idea to arrange a post exam barbeque at her house. She discussed it briefly with Tony and then invited his three friends and girlfriends explaining there was a small pool at her house they could use. She also invited Tony's parents as she realised, they had not been to her house and felt it was high time they should.

The exams finished. It was a Wednesday. The barbeque was arranged for the following Saturday evening. There was a strange feeling around, sometimes called the 'post exam blues'. It was a mix of relief that the exams were over along with the boredom of having nothing to do and yet plenty of anxiety pondering whether the required grades would be achieved. So, when the four friends met on this particular Wednesday none of them really wanted to play. They stopped after a short while and just talked.

They'd not really had time together in recent weeks and although there was a lot to catch up on, the conversation quickly focused on the forthcoming barbeque and their girlfriends. They were all excited by the pool at Celia's house, Tony said it was actually quite large with a small diving board. They happily speculated on the ball games they might play and the 'ducking' and 'diving' tricks they might get up to. John was a little anxious mentioning that Susan had only just learned to swim a year ago, so he asked them all to 'go easy' on her?

They then went on to talk about their girlfriends. Initially they discussed Paul and his relationship with Jenny. None of them had met her yet and as Paul talked, they could sense he was smitten! They were certainly aware of the hotel; it was one of the biggest in town and they were impressed that Jenny's Dad owned it. It was even more interesting to hear Paul explain he'd worked there and how much he'd enjoyed it.

Steve updated them all on how much he and Jan were seeing each other and that she often stayed overnight at the farm. John's update was brief, his contented smile said it all as he explained how he and Susan had studied together leading up to the exams and how simply, they just enjoyed each other's company.

It was Tony who was least relaxed of all of them as he recounted his Mum's anxieties during the exams and how she believed he was being distracted by Celia. He smiled as he spoke about Celia and how unbelievably good the sex was. Maybe his Mum did have good reason to be anxious. Yet when Tony had worked at home it was Celia who complained that she just wasn't seeing enough of Tony! 'I just couldn't win,' Tony protested, and all four friends laughed together.

They went on to speculate about the barbeque at Celia's house on Saturday evening and the fact that Celia had wanted to invite Tony's parents too. 'It's getting serious,' quipped Steve and gave Tony a friendly 'man hug'. Tony seemed embarrassed, almost a little awkward Steve thought to himself. Perhaps the exams had highlighted some tension between Tony's parents and Celia. Perhaps the barbeque would restore the relationship. Steve thought no further about this as they went on to discuss the upcoming football season and who might do well.

Saturday was sunny and extremely warm. Tony had stayed at Celia's house on the Friday night. It was early afternoon when they started to prepare by cleaning the barbeque and collecting meat from the butchers and salad ingredients from the supermarket. Tony's Mum had phoned Celia and offered to bring the desserts, Celia had readily agreed and after the call had discussed this with Tony saying how kind she thought Tony's Mum was. She then asked Tony if he'd be 'in charge' of the barbeque. Tony visibly shrank and explained he'd never operated one before but was heartened by Celia's assurances that it was easy and that she'd be on standby to help.

It was just after three when the security buzzer sounded; Tony's parents were first to arrive. They'd not been to Celia's house before. His mum brought three desserts, a fruit salad, a lemon meringue pie (this was Tony's favourite) and a selection of cheese and biscuits. Tony helped his Mum take them into the kitchen, Celia started showing Tony's Dad around the garden; he was very impressed by the pool and admired the flower beds while Celia explained a gardener came in two mornings a week. Meanwhile indoors, Tony's Mum was admiring the house as Tony showed her around the ground floor. His Mum was really impressed calling it 'like a show home' but it was the kitchen she admired most of all.

It was around half an hour later when Paul, Steve and John arrived all together with their girlfriends. None of them had visited Celia's home either and although Tony had often described it, they were all really impressed by the house and its gardens. The thing that really blew them away though was the pool, it was bigger than they'd imagined. It was still very warm. Steve politely asked Celia if they could use it and as she said, 'Yes, of course,' there was a 'whoop' as all four friends cheered and dashed off to the small outhouse to change. Jenny, Jan and Susan walked over to the outhouse to change at a more sedate pace and were nearly knocked over as the four friends, now changed into their swimming trunks, ran out and with further 'whoops,' leapt into the pool. The three girls laughed and were soon changed and in the pool. The next hour flew by with plenty of laughter, antics and games; 'frolicking' was the word that Susan used to describe it and they all laughed and carried on using her word as they continued to play in the pool.

Celia and Tony's parents didn't go in the pool. They sat quietly in easy chairs away from the pool and watched the frolicking. They smiled politely. The conversation between the three of them wasn't easy, Tony's Mum still felt Tony may have been distracted during the exams and now she'd seen Celia's amazing house and gardens she could see why. Tony's Dad had similar thoughts to his wife, but he also could see the physical attraction in Celia; she was a really good looking woman, she was really very sexy, and he could see why Tony was so smitten, yet he was also still so young. After an hour or so, Celia called over to Tony to suggest they should light the barbeque. From the expression on Tony's face, it was clear he was reluctant to break away from his friends and yet he knew he should help Celia.

Celia noticed Tony's reluctance. Tony started the barbeque, his Mum helped and as they cooked Tony kept glancing over to his friends. There were regular shrieks of laughter and he smiled at their frolicking. Celia came over to help with the salad and brought out the desserts that Tony's parents had provided. With everything ready, Tony called his friends over to start eating. There were three circular tables on the lawn with sun umbrellas. The laughter and chattering carried on happily as they ate but Celia noticed that she was on a table with Tony's parents, whilst Tony and his friends were on the other two tables. She realised she was starting to feel isolated at her own party in her own house! Celia chose to say nothing, but she was troubled by her thoughts.

As soon as they'd finished eating the four friends ran off and dived back into the pool. The girlfriends followed shortly afterwards leaving Celia sitting at the table with Tony's parents. They decided to clean up and remove all the used plates and cutlery to the kitchen for washing up. The afternoon progressed into early evening and then dusk, the garden continued to resonate with the happy laughter around the pool. Celia continued to sit and talk politely with Tony's parents. Celia's concerns deepened; she could see how much Tony enjoyed the company of his friends and that she had no part in it. She decided to say nothing.

It was Tony's parents who decided to go first. They stood up and thanked Celia profusely, saying how much they had enjoyed the afternoon. They waved and shouted their goodbyes to Tony and his friends in the pool and they all waved back. Celia found she was relieved that Tony's parents had gone; they were a very nice couple, but she had found them boring. She busied herself clearing away and tidying up. The laughter from around the pool continued. Celia realised she still felt lonely. Whilst clearing up, she reflected on the events of the day and with much sadness, she realised she and Tony were of a different era; he was happiest in his own group of friends, there was no place for her. Why hadn't she realised this before? The sex was so good and together they got on well but maybe she fell for Tony on the rebound from her difficult divorce? It all seemed to be so obvious now.

Her thoughts were interrupted by Tony and his friends coming into the house. They were still laughing together. Celia smiled warmly as they came into the kitchen. Yes, she could see Tony was happy. They stood together and chatted about the day and thanked Celia for all her generous hospitality saying they had all really enjoyed themselves. Reference was made to the imminent arrival of the exam results and that they must all meet again to celebrate. Everyone nodded and smiled a little anxiously, that is everyone except Celia, so she felt further isolated. There were warm kisses, hugs and further expressions of gratitude as they all left together.

Finally, Tony and Celia were alone together in the house. But there was an atmosphere. Tony felt Celia was quiet and withdrawn. He was puzzled as the day had been so good and he had really enjoyed it. Why was Celia so subdued he pondered? Tony decided to tell Celia some stories from the day and the fun they had all had in the pool. But, as he spoke, he could tell Celia was not really listening. Her head was turned slightly away from him and she seemed to be staring into the middle distance and saying nothing in response.

Tony moved over to the settee where she was sitting and knelt down on the carpet in front of her. Looking directly into her eyes he was shocked to see small tears in her eyes. She looked so unhappy, whatever was the matter? Tony leaned forward and put his arms around her. Celia buried her head into Tony's shoulder and burst into tears, she was really upset. Tony was surprised and puzzled, why was Celia so upset, what had happened? Eventually the sobbing subsided, and Celia pulled back from Tony's shoulder as she explained she needed to go to the bathroom. Tony sat back and felt completely puzzled. After some minutes Celia came out of the bathroom. She was composed now but she was not smiling, she looked serious, she was still upset. Tony stood up and moved towards her, but she stepped back asking Tony to sit down and saying that she felt they needed to talk.

Tony sat down but the conversation that took place took him totally by surprise. As Celia talked, she trembled as she reflected on the day saying how much she had looked forward to it and yet now, how sad it had made her. Tony frowned and looked at her quizzically as she spoke. She realised she needed to get to the point and so she simply said, 'Tony, I've realised we can no longer see each other, we need to end this relationship.' To say Tony was stunned would be an understatement. He was certainly speechless as Celia went on to explain how in meeting all his friends and his parents, she had seen that she and Tony were from very different backgrounds in their lives, that basically she was too old for Tony, that he needed to find someone of his age and that she needed to do likewise. Tony remained speechless, he was in shock, he just could not believe what he was hearing. Celia carried on; she didn't tremble anymore and spoke with more assurance saying she was certain that parting was the best thing for both of them.

When Tony did speak his voice trembled as Celia's had done. He explained he had not seen what had happened and he was confused. The relationship with Celia had seemed so strong and the sex was tremendous. Celia smiled as he referred to the sex and she leaned forward gripping his wrist and agreeing with him. 'Let's just become good friends,' she suggested and offered to give him a lift home.

The journey home was quiet, Tony just couldn't believe what was happening. As they pulled up outside his house he leaned over, he wanted to give Celia a deep kiss, but she withdrew and suggested they spoke by phone the following day. Tony got out of the car and walked towards his house.

Tony's Dad was still up and sitting in the lounge although his Mum had gone to bed. As Tony came through the front door his Dad called out, 'Tony, is that you?' and saw immediately as Tony came through to the lounge that he was very upset, Tony slumped into an armchair and let out a deep sigh. 'Whatever is the matter?' asked Tony's Dad and was taken aback as Tony started to cry and shake. He'd not seen his son like this for years, not since he was a child. Tony's Mum had heard all the commotion and had come quickly down the stairs; the sight of her son crying made her distraught and her motherly instinct kicked in, knowing just how to hold Tony. He buried his head in her shoulder sobbing uncontrollably.

Tony's Dad turned the television off. It was some minutes before Tony calmed down and as he stopped sobbing, he became embarrassed. He just didn't want his parents to see him like this. His Dad offered him a drink, Tony nodded and whilst his Dad poured three stiff whiskies, Tony's Mum soothed him and gently asked what had happened. She wasn't surprised, in fact she was relieved when she heard Tony simply say that Celia had ended their relationship saying, 'She thought the age difference was just too much and that today's party had exposed her feelings that we're not right for each other.'

They sat talking for the next hour or so, Tony mainly to unburden his thoughts. He was completely shocked by how the day had turned out and needed to rationalise it by talking. His Mum asked a few questions to prompt him now and again, his Dad just listened. The relationship, Tony thought, had been so good, they got on so well, the sex was so good (Tony's parents quietly frowned at this), they had been on holiday together and just generally enjoyed each other's company, 'So why oh why,' he anguished, had it all gone wrong? He went on to explain she had asked him to call her tomorrow and speculated that maybe they could make it up, they could meet and talk? But Tony knew in his heart, as he spoke and mulled over the issues, that the relationship was over. He could see the look in Celia's eyes as she had spoken to him. She was a strong character and she simply wanted the relationship to finish. It was over.

Tony was talking aloud, reflecting on these matters and as he concluded that it was over, he looked up to his parents who both nodded glumly and said how sorry they were. Tony's Dad spoke at this point to suggest they could all do with a good night's sleep.

Tony was surprised when he woke up the following morning; he had been in a long deep sleep and he woke with a start. He sat bolt upright in bed, as the memory of Celia and her wish to finish their relationship hit him again. Had that really happened, or had he been dreaming? Reality kicked in; it had happened. He recalled the events of yesterday, arriving home and crying uncontrollably in front of his parents. He felt embarrassed again. However, he also thought that it had been a good thing that he had been able to talk things through with his parents, they'd been patient listeners, even though he didn't often discuss personal things with them. He then thought about the day ahead and the phone call with Celia. Would she have had second thoughts?

The call with Celia was short, almost perfunctory Tony thought. She explained she'd realised they were at different stages in their lives, that there was no future to their relationship and that she simply wanted to be free to find someone else to share her life with. There was no warmth in her voice. Tony knew the relationship was over. They discussed the few personal items of Tony's that were at Celia's house and arranged for them to be returned. Tony sat and looked at his phone for a long time after the call was over. He just couldn't believe how quickly the events had taken place and he was in a state of shock.

The rest of the day passed slowly for Tony, too slowly. His state of shock progressed into depression; his Mum could see the signs. Tony was sitting quietly in the lounge, not talking but just staring into the middle distance. She tried to talk with him, but he could only grunt a few words in response. She made him cups of tea and snacks over the next few hours, but they were hardly touched. By evening she knew something needed to be done and decided to contact Tony's friends. She used the telephone in their bedroom as this was out of hearing range for Tony. Her luck was in as the first call she made was to Paul's house and Paul answered the phone. Paul was very surprised initially to hear from Tony's Mum, but then shocked as she explained that Tony and Celia had broken off their relationship immediately after the party. He just couldn't believe it.

Paul asked Tony's Mum what he could do to help but then an idea struck him. He explained that he would be working in the bar at Jenny's hotel again that evening and he knew they were short staffed in the kitchens, so Tony could help and might this help him get out of his depression. Tony's Mum thought this would be an excellent idea. Paul explained he needed to check with Jenny first and that he would call back shortly. Tony's Mum went back downstairs and busied herself in the kitchen. The phone in the hall rang five minutes later and she was relieved to hear Paul's voice explaining that if Tony could help it would be really appreciated and asked if he could speak to Tony.

Tony glanced up as his Mum came into the lounge and passed the phone to him. He was puzzled as she explained it was Paul on the phone. She then left the room. Paul made no reference to the fact he knew Tony and Celia had broken up, he simply explained that the hotel were short staffed in the kitchens and was there any chance Tony could help. Paul could sense hesitation in Tony's voice, he seemed to stutter but then said he was free and could help. They arranged that Paul would give him a lift and would call round to collect him within an hour.

Tony got up and took the phone back to the hall. He then went into the kitchen and explained to his Mum that Paul had asked him to work in the hotel that evening. Paul's Mum smiled quietly to herself and offered to make him a snack whilst he got changed. She was so pleased to hear

Tony was talking again and had something to look forward to, she made no mention of the fact she had called Paul.

Equally Paul made no mention he had received a call from Tony's Mum as they drove to the hotel. In fact, he showed real surprise as Tony told him what had happened after the party and that he and Celia were no longer seeing each other. Tony seemed to want to talk; he was still trying to come to terms with everything that had happened. As Paul turned the car engine off on the hotel car park, they agreed to talk more later after work.

It was approaching midnight when they spoke again. Tony was exhausted. The work in the kitchens had been really demanding as he had been asked to do all the basic chores including washing up, cleaning the floors and worktops, reorganising the freezer and sorting the cleaned cutlery. He'd not stopped all evening and although he hadn't known any of the staff, he had found them to be really friendly. They had explained all the tasks to him and chatted amicably as they had all worked. There was a good team spirit which was just what Tony needed.

When he finished in the kitchens, Tony found Paul and Jenny in the front bar. They were just cashing up and restocking. Jenny looked up as Tony walked in, her face was concerned as she explained Paul had told her the news about Celia and how surprised and sorry, she was. She stepped forward to give Tony a hug. Tony found he was close to tears again but kept his composure. Jenny sensed his awkwardness and explained they had just finished, and it was time for an 'after hours tipple' and asked what Tony might like?

It was over an hour before Paul or Jenny spoke again; Tony just talked and talked. He seemed to want to explain how good his relationship with Celia had been, the fun they had, the holidays and trips they'd been on and that they'd not been aware of an age difference. It had all seemed to be going so well Tony had thought but then, on reflection, as the pressure of exams emerged, coupled with the concerns of his parents that he was distracted by Celia, maybe this was the time that things started to go downhill. Tony smiled wryly as he talked about the barbeque and how much he had looked forward to it but that he now saw how the evening had really highlighted issues between him and Celia. He mused further saying that he'd not thought about it before but that he was now starting to see what that must have been like for Celia.

It was at this point Tony paused and glanced up at Paul and Jenny. They were both looking at him and were absorbed wanting to see if there was anything they could do to help but realising Tony just needed to talk. Paul raised his glass and suggested they should get their drinks 'down the hatch' and then get some well-earned sleep. In the car Tony asked Paul if he'd talked too much. Paul just said he always talked too much and they both roared with laughter. The tension for Tony was subsiding, it was good to have friends he said, and Paul suggested they should meet with Steve and John later that week. 'Not for football' he said but, 'Let's go to the pub, to discuss and anticipate exam results!' Tony smiled in agreement; he went to sleep as soon as his head hit the pillow that night and slept heavily.

They arranged to meet in the Red Lion. None of them were at the legal age to drink but they were only a few weeks away. It was late summer, still warm and they sat in the garden. Tony appeared much older than eighteen, so he was nominated to buy the drinks and a kitty was organised. Paul had told Steve and John that Celia had broken off the relationship with Tony, that Tony was really upset. As the first round of pints arrived, Steve spoke to Tony to say he was surprised and sorry to hear about Celia, Tony smiled and held up his pint saying, 'thanks' then added, 'There are plenty more fish in the sea.' He then laughed to brush it all aside, but his friends could see he was upset.

The conversation moved swiftly on to other subjects. The football and rugby seasons were about to start but with the 'A' level exam results only a week away, where would they all be living and who would they all be playing for? Steve was the only one who was certain he would still be on the farm, playing football for his old team; it was the others who were uncertain and there was a lot of excitement in the conversation as they speculated what might happen.

There was further excitement as they discussed the upcoming eighteenth birthdays which were all happening within a few weeks of each other. Several pints had been consumed by this time and the Publican had wrung the 'last orders bell'. It was time to go home; it had been a good evening, plenty of good humour, plenty of banter which was just what Tony had needed though no one said this specifically. They were just pleased to see Tony laughing with them. In parting, they agreed to meet again in the Red Lion next week on the evening of results day to either 'celebrate or commiserate' they said with an air of nervous anticipation.

They need not have worried, well that is apart from Tony as his grades were just below the entry requirement for the University he'd applied for and he wasn't sure if his place was secured. For the others though they all passed with flying colours; John and Susan had both passed all their three 'A' levels with straight 'A' grades. This was an exceptional result; they'd worked hard together and enjoyed it and their grades exceeded the entry requirements for the Teacher training college they had applied for in Oxford.

Paul's grades were not quite so good but satisfied the entry requirements for his University Course in Business Administration in Birmingham. He'd finally made this choice after long discussions with his Dad and brothers who now appreciated that Paul wanted to develop his career outside engineering and that he may not end up in the family business. Jenny had also passed with flying colours; she had applied for a Hotel Management course in London but had now applied to Birmingham as she and Paul were planning to live together.

Steve had passed his exams and was looking forward to a further year to complete his course at Agricultural College. Jan had also passed all her exams and had secured her place on a Retail Management course in her hometown. She would still be living with her parents and working in their shop, that is when she wasn't staying with Steve and his family on their farm.

It was a good evening, time to reflect and anticipate what lay ahead for all of them. Tony mused over his parent's reaction to his grades and although no reference had been made to Celia, it was clear they felt she had distracted him. Although Tony wasn't sure where he would go and what course he might do yet, he knew it would only take a day or so to go through the 'Clearing House' system. He felt pleased and was ready to move away from home and make some changes in his life.

The four friends continued to drink, laugh and enjoy each other's company. It was another good evening, but it was when Steve suddenly commented on how things had changed since they had all met at Primary School that the conversation developed with even more vigour. All the old stories poured out with references again to Mrs Collier and 'Collywobbles', the custard sponge incident, the caning and expulsion, Steve's 'Whoopee' cushion, Tony's experiment with the salt and pepper pots and then John's experiment with tobacco and match heads.

The memories ran on and on with laughter and with more pints consumed, they started to talk about the upcoming eighteenth birthday celebrations just as the Publican rang the 'last orders bell'. The evening had all gone by too quickly; they could have carried on talking for hours!

There was just a month to go until the University courses started. It was also during this month that all their eighteenth birthday celebrations occurred; it was a hectic month! Steve and Tony's families arranged a joint party, a Barn Dance on Steve's parent's farm. John's parents arranged a party at their house and invited Susan's parents and close family too. Paul's parents arranged a disco party at the local Cricket Club. In all cases there were embarrassing speeches from adoring parents, but the message was clear from all of them. That their boys had now become men, it was official!

There was an interesting visitor to Steve's party; Uncle Frank's friend Tim came. Steve had thought about the conversation he had with Tim at Uncle Frank's wake about the Male Menopause and regretted he had no contact information for him. So, he was really pleased to see Tim and told him so. Tim responded warmly saying he had been surprised to learn Uncle Frank had shared their discussions. They quickly exchanged contact information realising they would not be able to talk long at the party amid all the music and laughter. Steve explained that he often visited Jan who lived close to Tim and they arranged that Steve would contact Tim on future visits and arrange to meet.

With the eighteenth birthday celebrations over, there was further excitement as John, Paul and Tony set off for University. Tony had successfully gone through the 'Clearing House' system and had accepted a place on a course in Newcastle in Retail Management. It was similar to the course that Jan was doing. Tony was pleased to be going to Newcastle and looked forward to the change in his life although his parents were so sad to see him go. Steve was the only one left in their hometown and he was saddened to realise he would not really have contact with his friends until Christmas which was three months away!

CHAPTER 9

DEMAND PHASE
(18+ YEARS OLD)
Men and new beginnings

STEVE NEED NOT have worried though as his relationship with Jan was growing stronger and stronger. Jan found she had a lot of time in the week for self study and course work preparation. This meant she could work from her home, or as it worked out, she could stay longer with Steve at his home.

It was then the unexpected happened; Jan found out she was pregnant. Her menstruation cycle had always been so regular, it was now a few days overdue and in her natural instinct she just knew. She felt excited, she felt anxious too. What would Steve say and what would her parents say? She decided to buy a test kit from the Chemists, just to be sure. The test was positive. Jan decided she should tell Steve first but how should she tell him and when? Would Steve be happy and supportive, were they too young? Her mind was racing.

Jan need not have worried. She was due to stay with Steve and his family overnight at the farm. When she arrived, Steve was still in the yard putting the tractors away. It was a lovely evening and as Steve came into the kitchen, he tickled his sisters who shrieked with laughter and walked over to Jan and gave her a big hug and kiss (the sisters giggled) and then asked, as it was such a nice evening, if anyone would like to go for a quick walk. Jan was pleased when the sisters explained they had homework to do, it would just be her and Steve going on a walk, an ideal opportunity to talk.

Steve and Jan walked across a field from the house holding hands. They were just chatting, but Jan could feel she was really nervous, had Steve noticed? It was when they turned to go up a lane that Jan pulled on Steve's hand and said she needed to tell him something. As Steve looked at Jan, he sensed she was anxious and looked at her quizzically. Jan couldn't wait any longer, she just blurted out, 'I'm pregnant!' To say Steve was surprised would be an understatement, he'd had no idea and was knocked off his feet but, in that moment, his true feelings were apparent. He was so excited, he laughed, he smiled, he kissed and hugged Jan. He then kissed her again and overwhelmed her with a flood of expletives saying how pleased he was and that he loved her and wanted to marry her. Jan was overwhelmed and so happy. It took them some minutes to calm down.

It was a fifteen minute walk back to the farmhouse. During this time, they didn't stop talking. Initially Steve had wanted to tell his family straight away, but they realised Jan should see her doctor first. They also realised they needed to talk to Jan's parents, Steve was insistent he wanted to ask Jan's Dad if they could get married. Where they would live, how they would manage financially, what they would call the baby? They were suddenly overrun with many more questions than answers; it was clear that they needed time to talk a lot more! It was now dusk as they approached the house and Steve drew Jan towards him. He hugged and kissed her again and then leaning back and looking at Jan with a cheeky grin he asked, 'Can I tell my Mother?'

to which Jan laughed and said, 'Of course, but only your Mother!' Jan was so pleased that Steve was clearly so happy with the news.

It was later that evening. The meal was over, and Steve and Jan were washing up when Steve's Mother came into the kitchen and started putting things away. The rest of the family were relaxing in the lounge. Steve's Mother noticed there was something different about Steve and Jan, they kept glancing at each other and laughing and so she commented, 'You two seem very happy this evening, what's going on?' to which Steve said, 'Well actually there is something we want to tell you.' It took only a minute for Steve to explain. His Mother was delighted, she liked Jan a lot and could see she was good for Steve and made him happy. She was surprised though and hadn't expected Jan to be pregnant, they both seemed so young.

They sat in the kitchen for the next half hour, the rest of the family remained in the lounge. Steve's Mother's knowledge and experience was very helpful, she agreed they should keep the news quiet generally for the next three months or so, to tell Jan's parents straight away and to see the doctor as soon as possible. All the other questions about where they should live, what Jan should do about her course and how they might manage financially would get resolved in good time. It was agreed Steve should return with Jan to her house the following day and to support her as she told her parents.

Jan's parents were shocked. Jan had decided she wanted to tell her Mum first and followed her through to the kitchen just after they arrived to make some coffee. Steve remained with her Dad in the sitting room discussing recent football results. Jan's Dad raised his eyebrows when they heard his wife calling out, 'Oh no!' and asking him to come through to the kitchen. Steve remained in the sitting room. He had heard the kitchen door close and could just hear mumbled voices. He felt a little nervous and wondered if he should go through. He didn't have to wait long, Jan appeared at the door. She was tearful but smiling saying everything was alright and asked him to come through to the kitchen as well.

They spent the next two hours in the kitchen talking. Initially the conversation had been tense; Jan's parents were concerned for her wellbeing and concerned for her career. Also, the idea they were both going to be grandparents was taking a lot of getting used to! It was the way Steve spoke that relaxed the conversation. He was just so clearly committed in the way he declared his love for Jan and that he wanted to marry her and was going to ask Jan's Dad anyway. His natural talk made Jan's parents smile. They liked him and could also see he was completely besotted and loved their daughter, that was not in question. It was just that the news was unexpected, and they then realised, happily, how their lives would change. It was exciting yet there was a lot to think about. They realised the pregnancy was at an early stage and that they needed to wait a few weeks to confirm the news. They needed to talk a lot more.

It was Steve's Mother who had commented the previous evening that she'd not met Jan's parents and would like to. She suggested Steve should invite them over to the farm next Sunday for lunch. When Steve made this invitation, Jan's parents glanced briefly at each other and then readily agreed. They had heard about the farm and Steve's large family and wanted to see for themselves.

Lunch the following Sunday was a happy occasion; Steve had told his Father the news and he had also been surprised but very pleased. He liked Jan a lot and had got to know her quite well through her recent visits. They had decided not to tell Steve's siblings yet, not for a few weeks until the news could be confirmed. As far as Steve's siblings were concerned, it was just a social lunch to meet Jan's parents. Steve's Father got on well with Jan's Dad and he showed him around the farm in his Land Rover looking at some of the crops and livestock. They then spent more time looking at the tractors and farm machinery. Meanwhile, Jan's Mum helped in the kitchen and met Steve's brother and sisters. The conversation was lively as they told stories about their schools and also about the farm animals. Steve and Jan couldn't get a word in; they just glanced at each other and smiled.

The Sunday lunch had been successful. Jan's parents were pleased to have met Steve's family and could see there was plenty of support and help for what lay ahead but were also sad to realise Steve and Jan would need to live on the farm as it was Steve's place of work. It was not clear yet what Jan might do about her college course and career.

Towards the end of the afternoon, Steve spoke quietly to Jan's Dad in the kitchen and asked if he could marry Jan, explaining that with all that had happened in the last few days, he realised he hadn't actually asked! Jan's Dad smiled and said yes without hesitation. They shook hands vigorously and then joined the others in the lounge. The children were all outside in the garden playing, Steve took the opportunity to announce he had just asked Jan's Dad if he could marry Jan and that he had said, 'Yes!' Jan quipped, 'Actually I've changed my mind!' but her beaming smile gave it away and they all laughed. Jan jumped up and gave her fiancé a huge hug, everyone laughed and relaxed, looking forward to the weeks ahead.

It was the following evening that Steve phoned Paul, John and Tony and shared the good news, Jan called her friends too. They announced they were getting engaged but didn't tell them that Jan was pregnant. That could come later. It was agreed to meet in the Red Lion the following weekend. Steve and Jan explained they didn't want a lot of fuss but just a quiet drink with their friends. Tony would be travelling back from Newcastle whilst John and Susan would be returning from Oxford, Paul and Jenny would be returning from Birmingham. It was the first time they had all met since going to University. There was a lot to catch up on, not only for the drink at the Red Lion but also to stay with their families and catch up with their news.

The evening in the Red Lion was memorable. The main focus was on Steve and Jan's engagement. There was a champagne toast early in the evening but there was just such a lot of other things to catch up on, the evening flew just by. Tony seemed happy and relaxed. The Retail Management course was better than he'd thought with a much stronger emphasis on technology than he'd anticipated. He also found his course colleagues were so interesting and came from such varied backgrounds that he was learning a lot from them as well. But the thing that Tony spoke about with most enthusiasm was the night clubs in Newcastle. They were just 'awesome' he explained and alluded to many new girlfriends he was meeting but that there had been no one 'special' yet!

Tony reflected further on his Mum and Dad, saying in many ways it felt strange coming home, it was just so quiet and calm by contrast to his new life in Newcastle. Tony spoke about his Dad and Mum's working lives and how he realised his future would be very different and certainly not like the traditional retail career his Dad had pursued. Both Paul and Jenny in Birmingham and Paul and Susan in Oxford explained their lives were dull by comparison to Tony's high life. Paul had changed such a lot, he and Jenny just seemed in tune with each other laughing readily and smiling as they pondered on their future. Would they buy and run their own hotel; would it be in the UK? John and Susan were also ideally matched. Both were quietly spoken and calm with reflections on their peaceful lives in Oxford, how enjoyable and interesting their courses were and how they were looking forward to 'teaching practice' in a few months' time.

The four friend's lives were all changing in such different ways and yet their friendship was growing stronger all the time. It was a great evening. It just flew by and when 'last orders' was announced, they realised the need to meet again at Christmas. In fact, although no one realised it at the time, the Red Lion venue was to become the meeting place for the four friends for years to come. They'd moved on from the enjoyable days of kicking the football around the recreation ground!

That Christmas would remain in their memories forever. Shortly after the first Red Lion evening Steve and Jan's wedding invitations were received. The wedding was planned to take place during the Christmas week with the reception at (as you may have guessed), the Red Lion. Jan's pregnancy tests had gone well and both Jan and Steve's parents encouraged them to get married as early as possible and before the birth. It had been decided that Jan and Steve would live in one of the farm cottages and that Jan would suspend her course for one year. It was also decided to withhold news of the pregnancy until the wedding; it was to be a double celebration!

The wedding was a fabulous occasion. Jan's white dress sparkled against the snow as she walked with her beaming Dad through the Churchyard to the Church door. The congregation all turned and smiled as she reached the start of the aisle. She looked up the aisle to Steve and saw he was dressed in a smart suit, new shoes and had even groomed his hair! As they walked slowly up the aisle, Jan was aware all eyes were upon her; they had quietly let it be known to their friends a few days before the wedding that she was pregnant. There was a glimmer of a 'bump' to be seen but it was clear to all the congregation from the exchange of smiles between the happy couple that this was truly a love child, the joy and happiness was contagious. It was a truly happy and memorable day.

David James was born in June, six months later. His weight was eight pounds and three ounces, and the birth was without any complications. Steve had never felt so proud in all his life; he was elated and found he was repeating 'Mother and baby both well' as he called all their family and friends. A couple of months earlier, just after Easter, there had been another reunion at the Red Lion, again a really enjoyable occasion but no doubt that the centre of attention had been Jan's large bump. A big debate had taken place on whether the baby would be a boy or girl. Steve and Jan had been impressed by their friends' theories which were no doubt enhanced by the beer!

Steve and Jan settled into their new lives in the cottage on the farm. Initially Jan's Mum had stayed to help; David was a hungry boy needing a feed every three hours. Steve was very busy on the farm harvesting, so Jan was really grateful for her Mum's help. After two weeks though she returned to her home and thereafter Steve and Jan drove over every Sunday for lunch with Jan's parents. It was during one of these visits that Steve and Jan arranged to call in to briefly to see Tim, Uncle Frank's friend to introduce him to David. It was mid-August and David was just three months old.

Tim was very welcoming. He and his wife happily 'cooed' over David and Tim's wife was soon into a deep conversation with Jan about her own children and grandchildren. Tim touched Steve's arm and asked if he would like a quick stroll around the garden. They told Jan and Tim's wife they would only be ten minutes.

Tim started by congratulating Steve again on the arrival of David and then made reference to how proud Uncle Frank would have been; they both smiled. They recalled how they had met at Uncle Frank's funeral and then at the barn dance. Tim said how pleased he had been to hear that Uncle Frank had discussed the Male Menopause with Steve to which Steve raised his eyebrow saying, 'There's no such thing as a Male Menopause?' and they both laughed. Steve then went on to say he had often thought of those conversations and now that he was a Father and experienced the 'procreation' part of the three 'P's' he had surprised himself how important he realised the other Ps, Provision and Protection were, and how he knew he would 'work his socks off on the farm' to buy anything Jan and David needed and equally how much he would protect his family if ever they were threatened. Tim smiled as he heard Steve talk. They could have carried on for hours, but they could hear Jan calling that David was crying and that they shouldn't overstay their welcome. Steve smiled at Tim, they agreed they should talk more again and soon.

The Christening was arranged for three months after David's birth. Steve and Jan had invited all their friends and family to the short service followed by a barbeque back at the farm. It was on the Thursday evening before the Christening that Tony phoned. Jan took the call and was surprised to hear from Tony, he didn't usually call their house. After asking how David was, Tony was brief and to the point, he asked if he could bring a new girlfriend along as well, her name was Jackie. Jan was surprised but pleased and simply said, 'Of course,' and added how much they looked forward to meeting Jackie. Steve was equally surprised when he got in later that evening, he and Jan both speculated on who this Jackie might be.

The Christening was held in the local Parish Church on Saturday afternoon. There was a happy, bubbly atmosphere as old friends and relatives met and reacquainted in stage whispers. The most contented of all was David; he gurgled in his Mum's arms looking adorable in the Christening gown that Steve's Mum had made. But then there was a distraction. Tony had just walked in and was standing at the top of the aisle looking to see where to sit. With him was Jackie! The word 'stunning' would not be adequate. She wore a simple, open necked dress in pale green with matching handbag and shoes. With long flowing blonde curly hair, a glowing smile, and an incredible figure, she certainly caught the attention of everyone.

It was Paul who caught Tony's attention and beckoned him over to the pews where he was sitting with Jenny, John and Susan. The happy, bubbly atmosphere in the church quickly resumed. Jackie felt warmly welcomed as she was introduced to Tony's friends. The service was great, a slight murmur from David as his head was doused in water by the vicar, but otherwise a very happy family service. After some family pictures outside the Church in the early autumn sunshine, they all headed off to the farm.

Steve had set up two kegs of bitter just inside the door of the main barn. Paul, John and Tony found they were on their own and together pouring some pints soon after arrival. John was in some kind of trance; he was looking over towards Jackie who was talking to Susan. He said to Tony, 'Wow, Jackie looks amazing, how on earth did you did you meet her you lucky beggar!' Tony smiled as he said he couldn't believe it himself. He went on to explain that Jackie was on his course at University in Newcastle. She was admired by all and he didn't for one moment think he had a chance. 'So, what on earth happened?!' asked Paul and was surprised when Tony said it was when he casually told her a story, apparently Jackie loved the story and they'd not stopped talking since! John and Paul were fascinated and urged Tony to tell them the story also. Tony smiled; he could see Jackie was happily talking with Susan and as he turned back to John and Paul and said, 'Well, it starts with a question,' he could tell they were fully engaged.

'What is the word. There is only one. Which is spoken in all countries throughout the world, and everyone understands it and uses it many times every day?' John and Paul looked at each other in bewilderment. Paul said 'Taxi?' and Jon said 'sex,' but then realised these words were not understood in Mongolia or by the Eskimos. They laughed and looked to Tony who raised his eyebrow and said 'OK!' and then he went on to explain, 'Although it's used and understood by everyone in the world, no one knows where it comes from. It's not in the Bible, it's not in any Dickens novels for example either, so where did it come from? Do you want to hear more?' Paul and John both eagerly nodded so Tony carried on.

'At the end of the 1800s the world was changing. Steam technology was emerging in all walks of life, particularly at sea where it was realised that if you could sail directly from one port to another in a straight line without tacking you would save loads of time! But there was a problem, a big problem, because the early steam chambers, or pressure vessels, were poorly constructed and were spectacularly blowing up at sea causing deaths. The problem was getting so bad that many sailors were deciding it was just too dangerous and opting to revert and use just sail power.'

'However, in Stettin (or Szczecin), an old Polish sea faring port on the Baltic coast, where the river Oder flows into the Baltic Sea, a young engineer found a solution to the problem. He realised that when the upper chamber of the pressure vessel was being secured to the lower chamber, not enough care was being taken to ensure the rivets on the joints were the right class of 'interference fit'. He also discovered that if he used heavily waxed hessian sack material and positioned it between the two mating surfaces it would seal the joint properly.'

'Sailors started to realise that boilers made by the methods of this young engineer were safe; they became confident in his approach as there were no further explosions. His reputation grew quickly, he was much in demand and other shipyards asked him to inspect every boiler they made and, if he was satisfied, they had adopted his methods correctly, he would use a piece of chalk and write his initials on the outer case of the boiler. His initials were 'OK' as his name was 'Otto Kleine.' Sailors asked for years afterwards if the boiler was 'OK' and of course, the use of 'OK' spread rapidly to today where it can mean so many things ie. I understand you; I agree with you, I'll do it and so on'.

At this point Tony paused, John and Paul had really enjoyed the story, but John was looking puzzled and asked, 'So you told this story and Jackie fell for you?' Tony laughed and readily agreed saying he had also been really surprised. Jackie had been so intrigued by the story and they had then just carried on chatting for hours. One thing led to another he said with a broad smile and raised eyebrow. They all laughed together. It was at this point that Jackie and Susan wandered over to join them. Paul said to Jackie, 'Are you OK?' and Jackie laughed in response knowing that Tony must have told the story. She smiled and then leant forward, and kissed Tony and they looked into each other's eyes. The relationship was clearly serious.

The Christening celebration carried on happily all afternoon. There were speeches from Steve and his Father both wanting to thank everyone for coming. The barbeque was superb. David enjoyed being cuddled and he smiled, dribbled and gurgled as all young babies do. Steve and Jan were just so proud; it was such a happy family occasion. Time flew by and it wasn't long before guests had to leave. Tony and Jackie had a long drive back up to Newcastle and in parting, a reunion of the four friends and partners was agreed at The Red Lion before Christmas.

It was just two weeks later when John and Susan popped in unexpectedly to see Steve and Jan. It was a Sunday afternoon; they'd come back from Oxford to visit Susan's parents. They were on their way back to Oxford but wanted to give David a present. They explained they had seen a red tractor in a toy shop and although they realised, he wasn't old enough yet, they just could resist buying it for him! Steve made some tea in the kitchen and chatted with John whilst Susan cuddled David and chatted with Jan in the sitting room. Susan was so taken with David and his smile, she welled up and Jan noticed a small tear and asked if she was alright.

Susan sniffed and then smiled. She then told Jan the story of when she had first met John and they slept together in her parents' house. She explained how John had crept across the landing when her parents were asleep and smiled wryly as she went on to explain the deep concern they had when she'd thought she was pregnant but then the relief when she found she wasn't. As she spoke, she looked down at David and said that now, when she saw young children like David, she often wondered what might have been and then glancing across to the kitchen door she whispered to Jan and mouthed, 'And what might yet be!' Jan was puzzled and asked, 'Whatever do you mean?' to which Susan whispered that John had asked her to marry him a few days ago and they'd visited her parents this weekend so that John could ask her Dad and he had said 'yes' too! Jan was so pleased and leant forward to hug Susan, now both of them had joyful tears.

Just at that moment, Steve came into the sitting room with the tea mugs on a tray. John was closely behind, and they could both see as the girls stepped back that something had happened. John knew straight away what might have happened and laughed whereas Steve looked puzzled. As John laughed, he said, 'You've told her, haven't you?' Both Susan and Jan smiled. Steve still looked puzzled and then Jan blurted out, 'They're getting married!' Steve looked happily stunned and putting down the tray said he felt they should be drinking Champagne, not tea! They all laughed together, there were more hugs of congratulations and then John explained in more detail how he'd only just asked Susan's parents and that they were keeping the news under wraps for a little while to plan ahead. They both wanted to complete their teacher training in Oxford. Steve suggested they should have an engagement party at the Christmas reunion at The Red Lion. John and Susan agreed that it was a really good idea!

The Christmas reunion in the Red Lion combined with John and Susan's engagement party went really well. The four friends were having an early pint together and as the evening got underway, they commented that, although they'd not seen each other for weeks, they could be immediately 'rude' to each other without causing any offence. They were fully relaxed with each other; the conversation was nonstop as they caught up with each other's news. The main topic was John and Susan's engagement. The four friends quietly raised their glasses congratulating John and there were smiles all around.

It was obvious the relationship between Tony and Jackie was stronger too. Tony was clearly and understandably smitten, Jackie was talking with Susan and Jenny across the other side of the bar and was dressed in a red, tailored trouser suit, and as they glanced across Paul said, 'Just stunning!' Everyone agreed and Tony smiled.

Steve couldn't stop talking about David and the others could see the obvious pride in his face. The stories about David's achievements were endless; David was now six months old and nearly sitting up, he slept for six hours one night last week, he might start eating solids in a couple of months and so on, Steve had clearly changed! They had been together for nearly an hour and there had not been one story about the farm, it had all been about David. It was when Steve talked about their visit to Jan's parents and the subsequent visit to see Uncle Frank's friend Tim that the focus of the conversation changed.

Steve explained that he had discussed with Tim the feelings he now felt in becoming a Father and that he and Tim had reviewed those three Ps. Steve had confessed that when Uncle Frank had initially discussed these ideas, they hadn't seemed too important, but now he was a Father, they were becoming increasingly so. 'What do you really mean?' asked Paul with a raised eyebrow. Steve said that if anyone were to attack or harm David or Jan, he would happily put his life on the line to protect them and that he really meant it! That he would 'work his socks off' to ensure they always had food on the table and a roof over their heads, that these feelings of providing for his family were so strong. He then referred to procreation and raised his pint with the others and simply said, 'You never know!' at which point they all laughed together.

The conversation flowed on to discuss David's first Christmas and the presents that Father Christmas might bring. The four friends recalled their earliest Christmas memories, and the best presents they had ever had. There was plenty of laughter, but it was when Tony said quietly, 'I've been thinking,' that they got a little more serious. Paul said, 'Oh my God!' to which they all leaned forward to hear what Tony had to say.

'You know we always say, there's no such thing as the Male Menopause?' Tony glanced around as he started, and the others all nodded. He then went on to say that he had been away from home in Newcastle for some weeks and it was just so strange bringing Jackie home and staying with his parents. 'It's been like stepping back in time,' he added, 'Mum and Dad are both working as hard as ever, but you can see they are much more ponderous now in the things they say and do.' Tony went on to say his Mum had been prescribed some medication to help her sleep at night, but she had suffered some abdominal pains and was now concerned she may have to have a Hysterectomy. The doctors had indicated some urgency was required and that both his parents were understandably anxious.

Tony then added how his Mum was in some ways accepting the inevitability of growing older and going through the Female menopause, but he had noticed that his Dad had changed markedly too, he was much quieter. Maybe in supporting his wife he was understandably anxious, but there were other things that didn't seem right. Tony could see his Dad was distracted and forgetful, he was clearly not as motivated as he used to be.

The conversation had now become more serious. It was important that the four friends could relax in each other's company so easily and share both the good and bad times. It was Steve who then spoke; he started by acknowledging what Tony was talking about and that he'd noticed changes in his family too. Steve went on to talk about his Father saying that he'd noticed was also getting slower, more ponderous. It had always been the understanding that the farm would pass over to Steve and that during the past twelve months, it was Steve who was increasingly carrying out the main tasks and making the main decisions. In some cases, Steve was introducing new ideas, new crops and thinking about the investment into more efficient farm machinery. His Father had noticed this and on the one hand he had been pleased, but on the other hand he had found he was making increasingly critical comments. Steve had found this irritating.

He had discussed his frustrations with Jan, who had noticed the issues too and they had recalled how Tony had gone with his Dad for a pint once to chat thing through. Jan suggested Steve should take his Father out for a pint and chat also. This had proved to be just the right thing to do and some weeks ago, they had been in the Red Lion early evening in a quiet corner.

The conversation had been fairly perfunctory to start with talking about the weather and football results. It was as the conversation turned towards issues on the farm that it became heated. Steve's Father didn't hold back and said clearly how he was worried the new approaches Steve was introducing would create a lot of unnecessary risks and no certainty of return.

Steve in response just felt so strongly that they needed to move the farm forward to achieve better quality and output. They had been talking for around an hour with no real progress being made. Steve was anxious that their raised voices may attract attention from other locals. It was then he noticed both their pint glasses were empty and simply said to his Father, 'Fancy another pint?'

His Father was taken aback. He had been in the middle of making a serious point about the farm baler, his face was coloured as he insisted, he was right but then he was totally deflated and laughed as he looked at his much-loved son distracting him with a query to refill his pint. It was one of those Father and Son magic moments. They both laughed out loud. Steve went to the bar.

On returning with two pints, Steve felt the whole atmosphere between them had changed; they clinked their glasses and said 'cheers'. Steve's Father spoke first, he was laughing at himself and said that whilst Steve had been at the bar, he had had a flashback to when he had taken the farm over from his Father and that they had disagreed on a number of issues and never really resolved them. He went on to say that he now knew how his Father had felt, that handing over the business was difficult, that he was no longer the 'King Pin' and needed to step back and accept he was no longer in control. Steve smiled and said he felt that wasn't exactly their situation now and that he really valued his Father's advice and help.

Steve's Father summed it all up saying he really hoped there would never ever be the bad feelings he had had with his Father. They then agreed, there and then, that if either of them felt anything needed to be discussed in future, they would arrange another pint and chat? They smiled, clinked their glasses and said 'cheers'.

Steve looked around at his friends as he told the story; they all nodded an understanding of the circumstances and changes going on in Tony and Steve's families. It was

Paul who then said, 'Maybe there is such a thing as the Male Menopause?' and they all laughed.

It was at this point that Jackie, Jenny and Susan came over to join them. Jan was settling David down to sleep in a travel cot in one of the back rooms and she joined them shortly afterwards. Many of John and Susan's friends and family had come as well. A small buffet was ready in one of the side bars and some champagne and glasses were being prepared. Neither John nor Susan's Dads wished to make a speech as they felt there were a lot of people they didn't know, so it had been agreed that Tony would say a few words of welcome and propose a toast to the happy couple.

Tony stood on a chair in the middle of the crowded bar. Some people just have the knack to say the right words at the right time and Tony was certainly gifted in this way. He carefully welcomed all Susan's family and friends, then John's and finally referred to the 'blushing couple' wishing them good luck and every success for their marriage and lives together. By this point the champagne corks had been popped, the glasses filled, and everyone toasted the happy couple and attacked the buffet. Jackie looked at Tony. She was clearly besotted, and she just hadn't appreciated how talented he was!

Later that evening, John and Susan were happily chatting with Paul and Jenny; they had been talking about the wedding. Susan had commented that they hoped to get married locally in about fifteen months' time and once they had finished their Teacher training courses in Oxford, but they had not yet thought about a church or venue. Jenny was casually talking about the wedding receptions they organised at their hotel. Susan was immediately interested, and they arranged to visit after the Christmas holiday.

Paul was in a deep conversation with John saying how much he enjoyed the Business Administration course in

Birmingham with Jenny and that they were thinking of buying a hotel business themselves in the future. John said he and Susan were similarly thinking now of which teaching posts they should apply for. They realised they were all at a crossroads in their lives and it felt exciting.

The Christmas holiday flew by. Tony took Jackie back to her parents' house just before the holidays and was made to feel really welcome. Her Mum said Jackie had never brought a boyfriend home before! Jackie felt embarrassed and frowned at her Mum. Tony returned home on Christmas Eve to be with his parents who both said how nice they thought Jackie was. Tony went for a pint with his Dad. It was a good, relaxed conversation in which the subject of Celia cropped up. His Dad referred to the previous time they'd been for a pint, when they had been so concerned that Tony was distracted by her. He should have been focused on his exams and not what a beautiful woman Celia had been.

Tony smiled broadly recalling that drink and how upset he had been soon after the exams when she suddenly broke the relationship off after the barbeque. Tony spoke about the night he broke down with his parents and how embarrassed he had been. It was good to now discuss this openly with his Dad. He then went on to reflect on going away from the area to Newcastle and that with hindsight, it had been such a good thing. Not just meeting Jackie but the whole process of meeting new friends and starting a new life. Dad and son raised their glasses to a good mutual understanding of each other and nothing further needed to be said.

Steve and Jan's Christmas was just so different. David was of course the centre of attention with both Jan's parents on Christmas Day and then with Steve's family on Boxing Day. David brought huge joy to both families. Steve and Jan felt so proud.

Paul and Jenny worked tirelessly over the Christmas holiday helping at the hotel. Paul did not mind at all, he found he was learning new things all the time and he just loved being with her. She only had to glance a quick smile at him, and he just felt tingly. He discussed this with Jenny, and she said she felt the same way as well. His parents came for lunch on Christmas Day with Paul's brothers and their girlfriends. It turned out to be a great family occasion.

John and Susan also spent Christmas together, with John's parents and his sister. During lunch on Christmas Day that his sister recounted the story of the exploding cigarette and how it had put her off smoking for life! Susan listened attentively and was horrified to hear what had happened; she kept a straight face despite knowing John was the culprit. John and Susan laughed about this later. It was just one of those things in life that needed to remain private they agreed.

The main part of the conversation was around the upcoming wedding with a lot of speculation on what the dress might look like. They wondered whether they should ask Steve and Jan if David could be a page boy, and if he would be walking by then, would he know what to do? The wedding conversations continued on Boxing Day with Susan's family; Susan explained that she and John were going to visit Jenny and Paul at the hotel managed by Jenny's parents to see if it might be a suitable venue for the reception.

A lot of discussion took place on who might be invited, menu choices, speeches, dresses, choice of bridesmaids and best man. It was all very exciting, though John mentioned to Susan on the way to the hotel early the following morning that he had found all the conversations really overwhelming. 'Let's just have a simple wedding like Steve and Jan's?' he pleaded as they drove over to the hotel.

Susan smiled and glanced at John. She could see what he meant, there really was just such a lot to think about!

It was the day after Boxing Day. Paul and Jenny met them in reception and Jenny led them on a brief tour around the hotel facilities explaining how some previous weddings had been arranged. John explained he just wanted it all to be kept as simple as possible, but he was aware of a frown from Susan and then a thumbs up and smile from Paul.

They ended up in the hotel restaurant for tea and coffee to discuss menu choices and overall pricing options. They were only planning a small wedding, but it was a lot more expensive than John and Susan had thought. Paul could see that John was anxious. It was after they had gone that he had an idea. He and Jenny had gone back into the restaurant and were alone. 'Would it save costs if it were a joint wedding?' he asked casually to which Jenny explained it would and that they had organised a joint wedding for two brothers last year.

As she explained this, she suddenly wondered what Paul was thinking and as she turned to face Paul, she could see he was grinning from ear to ear, he put his hand out and held Jenny's hand and said, 'Let's get married too!?' Jenny was taken aback; she could see Paul was serious but hadn't anticipated this. Was he just asking to then plan a joint wedding and reception with John and Susan to save money? They sat down. Paul was still holding her hand and he could see Jenny's mind was racing. Paul then knelt down in front of Jenny and said he had been meaning to ask her for a long time and that in meeting John and Susan today to talk about weddings and getting married, it had made him realise how much he loved her. He paused and then said he simply wanted to spend the rest of his life with her.

Jenny was moved to tears. Paul was now being really romantic, and she could tell he really meant it. 'I thought initially you were just trying to save money,' she said and they both laughed, and Paul then said it was only a passing thought, but that Jenny hadn't said yet if she wanted to marry him? Jenny smiled and shrieked, 'Of course!' and threw her arms around him. They kissed and then looked at each other; they both knew it was the right thing to do.

They sat in the restaurant, chatting, holding hands and kissing. The first step they agreed would be to ask Jenny's Dad and then to let Paul's family know as well. It was now mid-morning, and the restaurant was starting to get busy in preparation for fully booked Christmas buffet lunches. They were both working the lunchtime shift so decided that Paul would ask Jenny's Dad midafternoon and after lunch. They then planned to go back to Paul's house early evening to tell his family. The restaurant was getting busier, they hugged and kissed quickly again, and Jenny then said with a huge grin, 'I just can't believe this is happening!'

Lunchtime was very busy; Jenny couldn't stop smiling. Paul felt elated but then pondered on how he should ask Jenny's Dad after the shift. He needn't have worried. It turned out to be one of the easiest conversations he'd had. He got on well with her Dad anyway and found that he was initially startled but then gave Paul a firm handshake, then suggested they should find his wife with Jenny saying, 'This calls for a special 'tipple' I think!'

They went into the private lounge where Jenny was sitting with her Mum. Jenny looked up as they entered, she saw both her Dad and Paul were smiling and stood up as her Dad moved across the lounge and gave her a big hug saying, 'Congratulations!' Her Mum was startled, 'What's happened?' she asked feeling alarmed and then when Jenny blurted out, 'Paul's asked me to marry him!' she was reduced to tears of joy and gave Paul a big hug saying, 'Welcome to our family!' and then hugged Jenny saying how happy she was. Jenny's Dad then found a bottle of bubbly and some glasses. Only one of Jenny's sisters was in and she soon joined them with further exclamations of joy and a glass of bubbly too.

They sat talking for an hour. There were no wedding plans or dates discussed but at one point Jenny's Dad reflected on the University course they were both doing and pondered if one day they might end up in the Hotel business. It was discussed briefly in amongst a lot of other conversations, but none of them realised the idea would be revisited sooner than any of them realised. They discussed Paul's family and the fun they had all had at the recent Christmas lunch and how they must meet again soon. Paul and Jenny then left to see his parents.

Only Paul's Mum was in when they returned. She offered them a cup of tea as they chatted in the kitchen. She could tell something was in the air and asked, 'Is everything alright?' to which Paul simply said, 'I've asked Jenny to marry me, and she's said yes!' Paul's Mum shrieked, 'Oh! That's lovely' and stepped forward to give Jenny a big hug saying, 'Welcome to the family!' They sat down in the kitchen and the conversation flowed in the same way as it had with Jenny's family. It wasn't long before Paul's Dad and brothers came in from the workshop and then the conversations really took off, with Paul's brothers teasing their youngest brother but then realising he was the first of all of them to get married; it was an opportunity for Paul to tease them back telling them it was time they got on with it as well! They all laughed but it made his brothers think! A happy evening ensued; some bubbly wine was found, they ate together, and they had similar discussions to the ones they'd had with Jenny's family.

It was halfway through the meal when Paul had a further idea asking, 'What about an engagement party?' and added, 'How about New Year's Eve in the Red Lion?' The brothers agreed readily. Jenny and Paul's Mum were a little uncertain at first but then Paul's Mum realised all his friends would be there. Jenny felt she could ask her parents to come along early evening before it got too busy at the Hotel. They realised they would need to make a few phone calls in the morning as there were only four days to go to New Year's Eve.

The New Year's Eve party was one that they would remember forever. Jenny's Dad bought some champagne and made a really superb speech. Paul and Jenny were the centre of attention and smiled broadly at each other and kissed as everyone shouted their congratulations. The new engagement ring on Jenny's left hand glistened as she showed if off proudly.

Jenny's sisters brought their boyfriends; Paul's brothers brought their girlfriends. Steve and Jan had left David peacefully asleep with Steve's parents who were having a quiet night in. Tony arrived with Jackie, who again looked stunning in a simple blue dress catching admiring comments from the four friends when they were together, Tony again just smiled. It was whilst they were together that Tony raised his glass with Steve and John to congratulate Paul. Paul grinned and just said, 'Thanks!' At midnight the pub went wild. There was plenty of singing and further toasting. No one knew what time the party ended, they slipped away one by one and woke later that morning with heavy heads, but great memories.

It was also at this time that Tony and Jackie were offered jobs, to start their careers in retail. It had been in the final months of the course that they'd attended the Careers Fair at their University. A lot of potential employers had attended including major retail groups and a whole host of suppliers as well. Tony and Jackie had often discussed what they might do in their careers and yet neither had clarity. Should they follow their interests or seek careers where they could make the most money? The Careers Fair had all the answers!

It was during the Fair that one of those odd coincidences in life happened. Tony and Jackie had decided to go around the Fair separately; they wanted to make the best of the opportunity and not hinder each other. It was only when they met in the Pub that evening and asked which company, they preferred that they realised they had chosen the same one! It was a well-known clothing manufacturer in Yorkshire, Jackie was really interested in the design concepts and wanted to join that team whereas Tony was really keen on the marketing team. They were really motivated but relied upon the quality and designs of the creative team.

They had both arranged a follow up interview with the business; they couldn't believe they had chosen the same one! The interviews went well, and they were both offered good jobs with attractive starting salaries. They couldn't believe their luck. It meant they could buy a house together!

It was May before they all met again, to watch the FA Cup Final at the Red Lion and generally catch up. Steve and Tony had enjoyed a great season, their soccer team had won the league outright and Steve had been top goal scorer. Even little David had been along to support them! Tony had only played a few matches as he lived a long way away and couldn't get back too often. He also didn't want to leave Jackie on her own and blushed as he confessed this. They had been promoted but were anxious about the high standard of the league above them.

Paul and John talked about their rugby season explaining they'd only achieved a mid-table position in their league. Like Tony, as they lived away, they had only played a few games, but this had qualified them for the end of season club tour. They had only just got back from the tour and having been all the way to Cornwall on a bus with four barrels of beer on board, it was no surprise that they were still a little sore! They'd not won a game, but all the beer had gone with loads of new songs learned and plenty of late night curries! The way Paul and John spoke you could feel the comradeship, the teamwork and the obvious fun they'd had, even though they had not won a single game!

There was something else as well. Earlier in the season when they'd met, Paul had been chatting with John after a game and explained how he had joked with Jenny when they had got engaged, that they should arrange a joint wedding and then reception at the hotel. John had laughed with Paul but the following day he discussed it with Susan and was surprised when Susan said, 'Well, why not?' As they discussed it further, they realised both couples had many mutual friends and that they had been concerned about the costs. They only had a small family so why not join with Paul and Jenny and make a big occasion of it? It was three weeks until the next game. Rather than phoning Paul, John wanted to speak with Paul 'face to face' after a Saturday's rugby game, to see if he was really serious about a joint wedding and reception.

Susan came to the game as well as she also wanted to see Paul's response after the game. John and Paul's team won. It was a hard exhausting game but there was a good atmosphere in the clubhouse afterwards. They were standing enjoying a pint when John casually said to Paul, 'By the way, were you serious when you mentioned you thought a joint wedding and reception might be a good idea?' Paul didn't hesitate and turning to John with a big smile said, 'Of course!' and then turning to Susan said, 'What do you think?' He was pleased as he saw from Susan's expression that she was pleased also! As Jenny wasn't there, they arranged to meet the following lunchtime for a pint and chat before they travelled back to their Universities later that Sunday afternoon.

It was almost as if the idea of a joint wedding and reception had just been waiting to happen. Jenny was also very positive about the idea explaining they only had a small family and that otherwise their friends were all mutual.

'It's time for a big party' she said punching the air and leaning across to kiss Paul. They all laughed together.

The decision was made, it was now down to the detail. Jenny and Susan agreed to talk more and develop a plan, Jenny explained she thought her Dad would be more than generous on the costs of the reception at the Hotel and when the quote arrived this proved to be the case.

The joint wedding was arranged and with careful planning the timings and logistics all fell into place. The vicar had called it 'a little unusual' but he saw the strength of the friendship between the couples and the strong willingness to accommodate each other on the big day.

During the FA Cup Final in the Red Lion in May, the four friends caught up with the plans for the joint wedding. Steve and Tony were really interested to hear how it had come into being and also thought it was a great idea. The girls were talking animatedly about dresses and bridesmaids; the wedding date was arranged for July the following year. As they talked, they realised that by then they will have all completed their University studies, hopefully passing with flying colours, and would be looking forward to starting full time careers. It all seemed to be happening so quickly! The friends were so absorbed in their discussions, they hadn't noticed that the FA Cup game was over, and Liverpool had won!

They all left the Red Lion late afternoon to return to their families. It had been great to catch up with everyone's news and they laughed at themselves for not watching the FA Cup Final properly! When Tony and Jackie arrived back at Tony's parents' house his parents were relaxing in the kitchen. Tony's Mum made a cup of tea and asked if they had enjoyed the match. Tony laughed and looking at Jackie, explained they'd all been talking so much that they had missed the game!

Tony went on to explain the joint wedding and reception that was planned for next July and how much they were looking forward to it. Jackie described the wedding dresses that Jenny and Susan were thinking of and who might be the bridesmaids. Both Tony and Jackie were speaking so enthusiastically, Tony's Dad just sat and listened and then quietly said, 'Isn't it about time you two got married?'

It was one of those moments. Time stood still.

Tony's Mum glared at her husband; she could not believe her husband had been so insensitive. Jackie felt a little awkward but smiled. Tony grinned and leaned forward to hold Jackie's hand and said, 'This isn't what I'd planned but it has been on my mind a lot recently and particularly after today. What do you think, shall we get married?'

Time stood still.

Tony looked at Jackie expectantly. The atmosphere in the kitchen was electric. Tony's Mum and Dad said nothing. Jackie smiled; it was less than a second but seemed an age as her smile progressed to the broadest grin you can imagine as she responded saying, 'Of course, thought you'd never ask me!' Tony and Jackie stood up, hugged and kissed happily forgetting his parents in that moment. His parents looked at each other, Tony's Mum was so angry with his Dad but so happy too, she dissolved into tears. Tony's Dad couldn't stop smiling and gave his wife a comforting hug. Then all four of them hugged together laughing. It was a really happy moment. There was further laughter as Tony's Mum pulled herself away and looking at her husband, she reprimanded him with the sternest look saying, 'How could you?!' and they all laughed again.

The teacups were removed, a bottle of bubbly was found as they moved through to the sitting room. They sat chatting and just getting used to the idea; it had been quite a shock to all of them! They realised Tony needed to ask Jackie's Dad and that they could manage a big detour the following day on the way back to University in Newcastle. The bottle of bubbly went quickly, and another was opened as they talked about engagement rings, who should they let know, would they have a party and when might they get married.

Jackie phoned her parents and explained they were planning to call in the next day. Her Mum and Dad were really pleased as they hadn't expected a visit from their daughter. Though tempted, Jackie didn't allude to the purpose! Back in the sitting room, the conversation continued to buzz. Tony's Mum reprimanded his Dad again and they all laughed. Feeling peckish they made some sandwiches and then realised Tony and Jackie needed an early start for the long journey the following day. It was time for bed.

Tony had only met Jackie's parents briefly once before when they had come up to Newcastle. They seemed very nice, and he had got on well with her Dad. On arrival Jackie's Mum went through to the kitchen to make some drinks and Jackie went through to the toilet in the cloakroom. Jackie's Dad was talking to Tony about Liverpool's victory in the sitting room and was surprised as Tony interrupted him, 'Sorry to interrupt' he started, 'Can we discuss something else?' Jackie's Dad detected some awkwardness. His sixth sense alerted him as he then heard Tony simply say, 'I love Jackie and would really like to marry her. Would that be alright with you?'

Jackie's Dad smiled. He was more than happy, although he was surprised as he'd just not expected this question. He could see Jackie and Tony were besotted with each other, but they had only been together for a few months. He was about to respond but the door swung open, and Jackie bounced into the room and then stopped as she sensed she'd interrupted and said, 'Oh?!' Her Dad smiled and was about to say something but just then Jackie's Mum came through too with mugs of tea and coffee on a tray. Jackie's Dad looked across the room to Tony and said, 'Could you ask me that question again?' Tony glanced at Jackie and her Mum and then turning back to Jackie's Dad simply repeated his question saying, 'I love Jackie and would really like to marry her, would that be alright with you?'

Jackie's Mum couldn't help it, she let out a little 'Oh' and with Jackie, she turned to Jackie's Dad who smiled and simply said, 'Of course, we would be really pleased to have you as our son in law!' Getting out of his seat he strode over to shake Tony's hand. Jackie's Mum dissolved into tears as Jackie hugged her Dad and then Tony and finally sat down to comfort her Mum. Her Mum was overcome; she was going through fits of laughter and tears of joy and relief at the same time. Embarrassed, she stood up and gave Tony a hug saying, 'Welcome to our family, I'm so happy!' and then cried again. It was a happy occasion.

A bottle of bubbly appeared, and the conversation was again animated as Jackie told her parents what had happened the previous day and how she hoped they would meet Tony's parents soon. Over lunch the conversation was similar to the previous day with plenty of speculation on when the wedding might be but then realising, they all needed more time to think things through and plan ahead. In the end it was agreed that Jackie's parents would come up to Newcastle for the weekend in a couple of weeks' time and talk things through.

'In the meantime,' Tony said, 'We need to choose an engagement ring!' to which Jackie's Mum said another 'Oh' but this time she was plainly just full of joy. Tony and Jackie set off soon after lunch, Jackie waved to her parents as they drove away. She let out a huge sigh saying she'd not anticipated how difficult it had been for her Mum but that she was pleased to see how happy she seemed as they left.

Looking back, years later, the four friends often discussed this time in their lives and what a landmark it was, though they never really appreciated it at the time. It could certainly be described as the period at the end of their 'Formative years'. It had been significantly marked by the recent wedding of Steve and Jan, then the birth of David, then the anticipated joint weddings of Paul and Jenny with John and Susan to be followed shortly afterwards by Tony and Jackie's wedding. If that wasn't enough, there were the small matters of graduating and securing first full time jobs.

In summary, they would readily agree in years to come, that Procreation was now equally as important as Provision, though they'd not fully appreciated these priorities at the time.

CHAPTER 10

DEMAND PHASE
(25-40 YEARS OLD)
Providing, Protecting
and Procreating

JOHN'S MIND RACED as he recalled those early days of home owning, getting married and 'settling down' as it was sometimes called, along with the demands and responsibilities that came with it all, not least securing their first post-graduation jobs. The four friends had certainly progressed from boys to men!

The joint wedding worked really well. It was a warm, sunny day, clear blue skies and no wind, perfect weather for two perfect occasions. The wedding ceremony itself was held in St John's church. Paul and Jenny's family occupied the pews on the left hand side of the nave whilst John and Susan's were on the right hand side. There were only seventy people in total, a small number for a joint wedding. The Vicar spoke well and identified the strong friendships that had brought everyone together and how important it was to remain as friends in marriage too! It was of good humour and caused an exchange of knowing smiles in the congregation.

St John's Church was in the same street as the hotel which was just a short walk away. After photographs outside the church, both couples walked down the street with their guests following behind them and then walked into the walled gardens at the back of the hotel for more photographs and champagne. The brides both looked beautiful in their white dresses. The guests mixed well, there was plenty of laughter and merriment as everyone knew each other! The meal was superb, and Jenny's parents were just so proud of their daughter and wanted to give her a big 'send-off'.

The best man speeches were eagerly anticipated and lived up to their expectations. Steve was best man for John and Tony was best man for Paul. There were so many stories that Steve and Tony recalled how the four friends had met at Primary School (yes, the Mrs Collywobbles story and others!) and then grown up together. A live band performed into the small hours as all the guests celebrated a wonderful occasion.

By contrast, Tony and Jackie's wedding was a much more sombre occasion, although Tony and Jackie were not aware of the sad news that was ahead of them when they booked the wedding. They had both really enjoyed the joint wedding and had arranged their own wedding as soon as possible. It was to be a traditional wedding at a Church in Jackie's family village with a reception in the local village hall afterwards. They applied for a licence for a bar and arranged for a live country band to play some folk music. Jenny had chosen her wedding dress with her Mum and was very excited, she said Jackie looked just stunning!

Tony and Jackie had kept Tony's parents regularly informed and returned to see them one weekend to discuss the arrangements in more detail. They arrived home late Friday evening. Tony's parents eagerly greeted them as they arrived. They sat down together in the kitchen around the table for a cup of tea. Tony said later he felt there was a strange feeling as soon as soon as they opened the door, almost an atmosphere. Whilst drinking the tea and chatting through the planned arrangements, he noticed his Dad was quiet. He was not really engaged in the conversation and kept looking down to the floor. Eventually Tony simply asked his Dad, 'Are you ok?' His Dad glanced up, but he wasn't smiling, his Mum then burst into tears. Tony and Jackie were startled, whatever was the matter?

Tony's Dad leaned forward and put a comforting arm around his sobbing wife, she seemed so upset. Tony's Dad seemed upset also. Tony's Mum looked up and she could see Tony and Jackie both looked concerned and puzzled. She mopped her eyes, took a deep breath and then said, 'We're really sorry to tell you this but we've found out your Dad is really ill, he has terminal cancer.'

Tony just could not believe what his Mum had said. He was stunned. This could just not be true; his mind just would not accept what he had heard his Mum say. He looked at Jackie who also looked shocked and just didn't know what to say. Tony then just burst into tears and moved around the table to hug his Mum and Dad. Jackie also got up and hugged Tony and his parents, they all cried together. It was just awful, one of those moments in life you never want to experience and a complete contrast to the happy discussions they had just been having only a few minutes before about the wedding plans.

Eventually the sobbing calmed down and Tony and Jackie sat down again but kept looking at each other. They were all red eyed and were understandably distressed. No one knew what to say, it was just a moment to share and reflect. It was Tony's Dad who spoke first and suggested they should go through to the sitting room and get a stiff drink. The others all agreed. There was no further discussion about the wedding as Tony's Dad explained his condition in more detail and the tests he had been through. He then said he felt tired and with apologies said he wanted to go to bed. Tony's Mum went with him leaving Tony and Jackie on their own. Jackie moved over to sit by Tony. She kissed him and held his head against her shoulder. Tony sobbed uncontrollably.

Tony and Jackie went to bed, but Tony couldn't sleep. It was early morning, before dawn, when he heard some noises from the kitchen. Jackie seemed to be sleeping. Tony slipped out of bed without disturbing her and crept through to the kitchen where he found his Mum standing over the kettle and watching it come to the boil. She glanced up as Tony entered, her eyes were still red and puffy. Tony just walked over and held her; nothing was said, and nothing needed to be said. Tony would always be there for his Mum, she knew this. It was an instinctive bond, and it was there forever.

Tony sat with his Mum in the kitchen, just the two of them. They were quietly sipping tea as Tony held his Mum's hand. They were staring through the kitchen window into the dark garden but then as the early light of dawn crept over the horizon, they started talking, just in whispers. Tony's mind was swirling, he just couldn't believe what he had heard the previous evening. He needed to ask a lot of questions; when they had found out, was his Dad in any pain, what was the prognosis and how long had he got to live. How was his Mum, how did she feel?

In part, his Mum found it good to talk. She had been particularly anxious to know when and how they might discuss the news with Tony. They could see how happy he was with Jackie and all the wedding planning that was taking place. She went on to explain his Dad had felt uncomfortable some months ago and had mentioned this to his doctor during a routine check-up. Subsequent blood tests had revealed the problem although they had not initially appreciated the severity of the condition. They certainly hadn't appreciated it was terminal.

It was around this time she said, only a few weeks ago, that Tony and Jackie had called in after watching the FA Cup Final with their friends and had excitedly spoken about the planned joint wedding. She recalled how outspoken Tony's Dad had been when he suddenly asked Tony when they were going to get married. Tony interrupted saying, 'I know, it was so unlike my Dad to ask something like that.' His Mum pondered and said, 'I know, it's crossed my mind that maybe he had some sort of sixth sense and wanted to know you were going to be happy and settled.'

Tony's Mum went on to explain his Dad was on pain relieving medication, that they had no real idea how long he had to live. Tony listened as his Mum explained this and felt his tears welling up again. It was all so unfair, his Dad had worked so hard, he deserved a long and happy life. He felt so frustrated and anguished, there seemed to be nothing he could do to help, 'We'll call the wedding off, I just want to be here to help Dad in any way I can,' he said. His Mum reacted strongly as Tony said this saying, 'Oh no! You can't do that; your Dad is just so pleased to see that you are happy; he talks of nothing else and it's the only thing that makes him smile. You really must go ahead with the wedding as soon as you can!'

It was at this point that they heard some stirrings from the bedrooms and Tony's Dad called out in a drowsy voice asking if there was any tea. Tony and his Mum glanced at each other with a knowing smile. His Mum responded, 'Just coming,' and then in a whisper leant forward to Tony saying, 'Let's talk more over breakfast?'

The conversation over breakfast was difficult initially, no one wanted to say the wrong thing but then Tony's Dad spoke up and openly talked about what had happened. He seemed to want to get it all off his chest. Tony and Jackie listened. It was heart breaking to realise what Tony's parents had been through, to realise how their anxieties had escalated through various medical tests leading up to

197

the eventual meeting two weeks ago with the Consultant when they had been told the condition was terminal. They hadn't told anyone else; they had no idea how long Tony's Dad had to live nor did they know how his health might deteriorate. Tony's Dad sat back in his chair at this point. He and his wife had not cried but both had been looking down at the table whilst they had talked through the events. Tony's Dad now looked directly at Tony. His face was expressionless, he said nothing.

It was one of those moments. Tony looked back at his Dad, then his Mum and then Jackie. No one knew what to say. Tony felt so sad and completely helpless, he felt frustrated and angry that there was nothing he could do. Although it was only a few moments of silence and reflection, it seemed like an age. It was eventually broken by Tony who leaned forward and firmly held his Dad's arm saying how helpless he felt and asking what he could do to help.

Tony's Dad smiled held his hand, saying just how helpless he felt too. He then looked towards his wife and held her hand as well saying they needed to talk a lot more. He inferred that they had enough savings and pensions and that the house had been fully paid for some years ago. His wife smiled too; it was also a grimace. She said nothing.

Tony's Dad then went on to say how he needed to let his colleagues at work know. As he spoke, he was clearly troubled to know when and how he should tell them. It was then he looked towards Tony and Jackie saying, 'We're just so sorry to have to share this news with you, we didn't know how or when we were going to tell you.' He then smiled as he carried on saying, 'But the thing that has really brightened our lives is to see you both getting engaged, you are clearly so much in love with each other, and we are really looking forward to your wedding!'

Jackie and Tony looked at each other and smiled. Tony's Dad then asked if they could forget about his illness for the time being and just talk about the wedding. They all cheered up over the rest of the weekend. Jackie told Tony's Mum all about her dress and the bridesmaids. Tony and his Dad discussed the stag do. Tony's Dad recalled their wedding and how different things had been. It was early Sunday evening when Jackie and Tony drove off to get ready for work the following day. Nothing more had been said about the cancer, but it had been in the background in all their thoughts. Their lives had changed.

As Tony and Jackie drove away there were mixed feelings. Neither of them spoke for a while. Jackie moved her hand onto Tony's thigh, a simple gesture of comfort and support. It was Tony who spoke first some minutes later and asked Jackie if she thought his Dad had a long time to go. Jackie was non-committal. She said she simply didn't know but commented that although he seemed to lack energy, she had thought Tony's Dad looked quite well. Tony responded by saying he'd thought the same. He'd felt it was strange to think his Dad was going to die, he just couldn't believe it. They talked more and decided to investigate bringing the wedding forward as they didn't want to alert their families and friends to the cancer. They realised Jackie's parents needed to know though to see if the Church ceremony and Village Hall booking could be brought forward.

The following evening after work Jackie called her parents. Her Dad answered the call and was shocked and very sorry to hear the news. He realised Tony was with Jackie and asked her to pass on their very best wishes and sympathies. Jackie's Mum came onto the call at this point and as she listened to Jackie, she realised how important it was to quietly bring the ceremony forward and undertook to call the Vicar the following day.

The following evening was hectic. It started with Jackie's Mum calling to say she had spoken to the Vicar and confirmed it would be possible to bring the wedding forward and the Village Hall booking forward to a date that was only three months away. Jackie and Tony were surprised and pleased. Tony then called his Mum; she answered in a hushed tone and explained to Tony that she was on her own in the kitchen extension, as Tony's Dad was asleep in the lounge.

Tony was able to talk at length and in private with his Mum. She readily agreed to the proposed new earlier date and said how pleased she thought Tony's Dad would be also. They agreed to confirm the new date with the Church. She then asked Tony to pass on their thanks to Jackie and her parents as well. Tony went on to ask how his Dad was and wasn't surprised as his Mum explained that although he seemed well in himself, she had noticed he was getting tired. She went on to explain he was sleeping a lot more than he used to, that the clinic had informed them to expect what they called 'excessive fatigue.'

As she reflected on recent weeks, Tony's Mum indicated they had asked the Doctors how long his Dad had to live and that the answers they had received had been vague. She said, 'You can understand in part when they say everyone is different, but we'd like to know so that we can plan ahead and make the most of the time he has.' Tony nodded as his Mum spoke and said he had been thinking the same and he went on to say, 'I just feel so useless Mum, please let me know if there is anything I can do?' His Mum was silent for a while and then said, 'Let's work with you on the wedding arrangements initially and then work out how we can all support him.' It was as she said this, she added she could hear Tony's Dad and needed to end the call. Jackie looked at Tony as he put the phone down; she didn't say anything but just gave him a big hug.

Tony hugged her back. They remained silent but then he pulled back. He was still holding Jackie and looking into her eyes as he simply said, 'I love you; I love you so much!' He wasn't crying but Jackie could see he was upset and that there was a new resolve in the way he then spoke to say he realised he now needed to be so strong for his parents. Jackie could see his mind was racing. He then started talking aloud and Jackie listened.

Tony spoke about his Dad and what a proud and capable man he was, how much Tony had respected and looked up to him. Now there was an unknown path ahead in which Tony needed to work out how best to support his parents. As Tony spoke, he kept looking at Jackie. She nodded with him and occasionally added some ideas and comments. They were working together, and Tony realised and appreciated how much help and support he needed from Jackie.

It was sometime later that Jackie called her parents again to ask them to confirm the earlier date with the Vicar. Her Mum answered the phone and readily agreed she would do it the following day. Jackie kept the call short as she wanted to carry on talking with Tony.

He had poured them both a drink and they sat in their lounge, cuddled up on the sofa and talked and talked. Initially they reviewed the events that had taken place that evening and the need to support Tony's parents but in an empathetic way, quietly and without any fuss. They needed to support and respond to the unknown challenges ahead. The conversation progressed as Tony talked through some memories of his early childhood and how happy he had been. As he talked, Jackie related similar things she had been through as a young child and everything her parents had done to help her as well.

The evening had rushed by but now they both felt so tired, it was time for bed. The conversation that evening had been so important helping them to come to terms with this new situation. They'd not been sleeping well in recent days but now they felt a little better. That night they both slept heavily.

Meanwhile the other three couples were coming to terms with developments in their families. John and Susan had bought a small cottage in the town and had both secured teaching jobs in separate schools. They found working life was quite a contrast to their lives as students in Oxford; they now needed routines to accommodate the new requirements of marking students work and lesson planning. This was on top of the domestic requirements of cooking, cleaning, shopping and washing. They found that without routines, life was just too hectic.

Importantly, they both enjoyed teaching; it was what they always hoped it would be. There was real pleasure seeing their students' progress and being inspired by their subjects. Teaching practice had been an important part of their curriculum as students but now, as full time teachers, there were new skills they were learning to keep discipline and focus during classes. Although evenings were hectic, it was good to share stories of the days' activities whilst carrying out the domestic chores. Life had certainly changed for both of them and for the better. They enjoyed being married, they enjoyed being teachers but there were further positive changes awaiting them. These were changes they could not have imagined but would experience as they came to the end of their first year.

Meanwhile, like John and Susan, Paul and Jenny were also enjoying married life. After the wedding, Paul had moved into the hotel to live with Jenny in a separate annexe which gave them independence. They worked full time in the hotel and so they saw Jenny's parents and family every day, which perhaps wasn't ideal. They found they looked forward to the occasional periods of 'time off', it was a relief to visit Paul's parents and brothers, or to go out for drives and walks in the local countryside, just to escape the busy hotel routines.

After only a few weeks though, their lives changed significantly. One evening there was a knock on the annexe door. Paul glanced at Jenny with a frown on his face as he went to the door. It usually meant they needed some help in the hotel, or someone wanted to ask a question but invariably it was to provide cover when they were short staffed. Paul was really surprised therefore when he opened the door to find both Jenny's parents there asking if they could come in. This was unusual but a pleasant surprise!

Jenny made some tea and said what a lovely surprise it was that her parents had called by and that she hoped they could do this more often. It was as they sat down though that she heard her Dad clear his throat and realised there might be more to this surprise visit than just a social call. She was right.

It was a simple idea, her Dad explained. Good friends of theirs owned a hotel in the next town; they had run it successfully for over twenty years but were now planning to retire. Jenny's Dad went on to explain he was thinking of buying the hotel and he wondered if Paul and Jenny would like to run it and then over a period of years buy the business?

Jenny and Paul knew the hotel well; it had a good local reputation for its accommodation, bars and an excellent restaurant. The next town was busy and had a market, a good shopping centre and a railway station. The conversation flowed; Paul's Dad indicated he thought the asking price was good, he knew the current owner wanted to sell quickly in order to go and live near their daughter's family on the coast, as one of her children was unwell.

Paul looked at Jenny. He felt that they were still both quite young and inexperienced and asked if she thought they could cope and make a go of it. Jenny's response encouraged Paul; she was full of confidence, referring to the vast experience they had now gained and that they had both studied for this. She also indicated she had heard there was planning permission to add a fitness club and that there was ample parking in the grounds of the hotel. Her Dad then added that there could also be benefits in running the hotels as a mini 'group' to manage bookings, staffing, and get better prices from suppliers. The discussion only lasted an hour as Jenny's Dad needed to get back to the hotel, but as they closed, they agreed to look into it further, to talk more, to check at the accounts and to plan to visit the hotel in the next few days.

Paul closed the door as his in laws left. He turned towards Jenny and gave her a huge hug, 'Wow! What a great idea, you and I running and eventually owning our own hotel and we're still only in our mid-twenties!' Jenny smiled; she was so pleased to see how enthusiastic Paul was as she felt exactly the same! They carried on talking all evening about different ideas with great excitement but then found they had to remind each other to keep cool and calm, that the business would only become successful if they kept their business heads on. Neither of them slept well that night, they were just buzzing with excitement!

David James was now just over two years old. Steve and Jan were besotted; they were fascinated by his progress in sitting up, walking, talking, solid foods and now potty training, as well with the prospect of attending the local nursery school in six months' time. The weeks and months seemed to be rolling by so quickly and Jan started to ponder on her future. Should she become a full time Mum or apply to her course in Retail Management or maybe even train to be a teacher like Susan and John?

As the weeks rolled by, Steve and Jan discussed these options with increasing frequency, often when Steve got home and during the evening meal. After some weeks Steve looked at Jan one evening and said, 'I've been thinking today, should we now try for another baby, so that David has a little sister or brother? If we're lucky and you get pregnant you can always apply for a course later and if you don't get pregnant by mid-June, you could apply for a course then?' Jan smiled at Steve and said, 'I've been having similar thoughts myself!' One month later Jan missed her period and tests confirmed she was pregnant.

To say Steve and Jan were delighted would be an understatement. They decided to keep the news quiet from friends and family for three months, just to be certain. It was so difficult though as they were both so excited. In the end they decided they would tell just their parents and then plan to tell friends and family after three months. It was a few days after Steve and Jan had told his parents the news, that Steve arranged to meet his Father for a pint and lunch in the Red Lion. They had been doing this quite frequently just to chat through issues on the farm and to plan ahead.

When Steve arrived, his Father was already there and had bought the first round. He toasted the baby news with Steve and told him just how pleased he and his Mother were on the pregnancy and how difficult it was to keep the news quiet, Steve's brother and sisters would be so excited when they told them! They both laughed and clashed their beer glasses together in a toast.

It was about this time that Tony and Jackie's wedding invitations arrived; the date was much sooner than everyone had anticipated but no one knew nor thought there might be a reason. The wedding was only two months away and there was a list of local hotels and bed and breakfast accommodation which was being quickly booked up as guests made their plans. A month later the four friends had arranged to meet for a 'boy's night out' as they called it, but it was just a pint at The Red Lion on a Saturday evening after their football and rugby matches.

The evening started well; there was lots of catch up chat about the day's sporting events and recent updates on their careers and families. It was during this conversation that

Steve looked at Tony and casually said, 'Looking forward to the wedding but it's sooner than we thought.'

It was the expression on Tony's face that caught everyone's attention, he was clearly embarrassed and stuttered as he responded to say, 'Actually, we have some bad news and I didn't know when or how to tell you this, but we've heard recently my Dad has terminal cancer and we just don't know how long he has to live.' A tear rolled down his cheek as he spoke; the three friends were completely stunned. It was John who spoke first uttering, 'Oh my God, I'm so sorry,' Paul was sitting beside Tony and simply gave him a man hug and Steve added his sympathies also, but it was all too much for Tony who broke down and sobbed uncontrollably.

It was one of those moments in life the four friends would never forget. As Tony sobbed, his three friends gathered around him to conceal his despair from the other people in the bar. After some minutes, Tony's sobbing subsided, becoming embarrassed and muttering some apologies but was quickly rounded on by his friends telling him to never apologise. There were a series of muttered comments in which they all expressed their sympathies to Tony and asked what they could do to help.

More drinks were ordered, and the conversation continued though in a much more sombre tone. Tony explained everything he knew about his Dad's illness. He was clearly and understandably angry and frustrated, it helped him to share the news and discuss it with his close friends in a way that he couldn't with Jackie and his family. He explained they had noticed his Dad was getting tired and slept a lot and that he had now told his colleagues at work. He had received a huge amount of sympathy from his colleagues, and it had been agreed he would finish work the following Friday, about three weeks before the wedding.

Tony explained that he was really anxious for his Mum and had no idea how she might cope with his Dad's illness and also, how lonely she would be when he died. As Tony spoke his friends offered ideas on how they might help but they could see Tony needed to unburden his anguish and that it was helping him to share his thoughts. It was an hour later that the tone of the conversation changed suddenly in a way that further stunned the three friends.

Tony had been talking about his happy family life and how much he felt he owed his parents for all the help and security that they had provided, it had been a very happy upbringing and childhood. He paused at this time and then glanced at his friends and added, 'Actually, Jackie and I have had long conversations about things we could do,' He glanced at his friends again, 'One of the things that we discussed is that we know my Mum and Dad had wanted more children, we know that they are so looking forward to grandchildren.' Tony paused again and then added, 'So Jackie and I decided to try for a baby and we've just learned this week she is pregnant!' As Tony said these words he grinned from ear to ear. The three friends were stunned again and just couldn't believe their ears. A happy impromptu 'man hug' took place and this time they all laughed together.

The change in moods and tempo could not have been more extreme; the other people in the bar had been trying not to be nosy but couldn't fail to notice the changes that were taking place amongst the four friends who one minute had been involved in a quiet conversation (clearly one of the friends was very upset) and the next minute were all jumping around the bar, hugging each other and ordering more drinks. Very strange they thought.

The four friends settled down with their drinks. To say that the feelings were mixed would be an understatement. Laughter and tears abounded. Tony was anxious to stress though that he and Jackie had not told his parents yet,

207

understandably they wanted to find the right moment. The others nodded but the conversation was about to change again with further revelations. It was Steve who spoke first, the others would say later that as he started to speak hesitantly saying, 'Actually,' that they all guessed his news. He confirmed that Jan was also expecting but he had been told to keep the news quiet until after Tony's wedding. The friends all cheered and patted Steve on the back taking further gulps of beer.

It was then, when John also quietly said, 'Actually,' that all eyes fell on him as he added, with a huge grin on his face as well, that Susan was also pregnant and that he too was not meant to mention this until after the wedding! There were bellows of laugher as the four friends stood up and slapped each other on the back; none of them had expected this happy news as well! Eyebrows in the Red Lion that evening were raised again. Laughter abounded between the four friends. As it died down, they looked across to Paul who held his hands up and simply said, 'No, not yet!!' to which the others laughed again. A thought crossed Paul's mind that he might tell them about the hotel acquisition, but he quickly realised he should save this news for another occasion and after the transaction had been completed.

When the 'last orders' bell in the Red Lion rang, the four friends were a little tipsy to say the least. In fact, they were completely 'wasted' as the saying goes! It had been such a memorable evening and one that would be remembered for ever. They all slept solidly that night.

Over the next few days there were many domestic discussions between the four friends and their wives (or, wife to be, in Jackie's case). Central to all the conversations was the sad news about Tony's Dad but this was quickly compensated with the happy news about the three new babies and the wedding!

Tony was reprimanded by Jackie for revealing their good news but in the same moment she realised just how proud and happy he was. They realised they needed to tell his parents as soon as possible in case they heard from anyone else and then Jackie's parents too. They decided to drive over to Tony's parents the following evening. Tony's parents weren't expecting them but were so happy to see them. Tony was particularly anxious about telling his parents because he didn't know if it might create further mixed emotions.

He need not have worried. The initial conversation was understandably focussed on his Dad who explained he was feeling increasingly tired. Both Tony and Jackie thought he looked thinner, a little stooped and generally older. Tony's Dad then explained he was now in his last week at work and looking forward to a good rest before the wedding. He smiled as he referred to the wedding and the conversation quickly moved on with many updates about the wedding plans. It was only three weeks away and there was still a lot to do!

Tony then realised that nearly an hour had passed and that he'd not had the opportunity to tell his parents the special news. He cleared his throat loudly and whilst glancing at Jackie said, 'We have some other news to share with you!' Both his parents looked puzzled but then Tony simply said, 'We're pleased to tell you Jackie is pregnant!' Tony's parents both looked stunned, they couldn't believe it. They could see how happy Jackie and Tony were and how much they were looking forward to the wedding but to learn now that a baby was expected, this was beyond their wildest dreams! Tony hugged his Mum; Jackie hugged his Dad and then they all hugged together. The room was full of tears and laughter.

They then all sat down to talk, and Tony's Dad said how very happy he was. Tony said he'd been anxious about telling them but then his Dad countered saying what pleasure he now had seeing the family growing and moving on and that this was the very best news he could have hoped for! The conversation changed slightly when Tony's Mum asked how the pregnancy would affect Jackie's work and was assured when Jackie explained she could work up until eight months of her pregnancy and also, she could carry out a lot of her design activities working from home. She added that many of her colleagues had done this and it had worked well.

The following evening, they drove to Jackie's parents; they were equally pleased, in fact, completely delighted with the news. Jackie explained that they had told Tony's parents the previous evening, and they were very happy to hear how pleased his parents were as well. They fully understood how much it helped Tony's parents come to terms with the terminal cancer. It was all in all, a really happy evening, with not only the wedding to look forward to now but also a grandchild!

The next two weeks sped by. The weather on the day of the wedding was just perfect with warm, blue skies and bright sunshine. News had spread and all Tony's family had learned of his Dad's terminal illness and felt really sad. However, their spirits lifted as they realised, they were not just looking forward to a wedding but also that a grandchild was on its way too! There was a feeling of excitement, in fact the Church was buzzing as the guests gathered. Tony looked nervous. His best man was Steve, who had organised a quiet drink for the 'Stag Do' in the Red Lion the previous weekend. It had been a good occasion. There had been a lot to catch up on and Tony appreciated how important good friends were when he had really needed their support.

Tony reflected further. He'd felt the buzz in the Church had quietened when his Dad and Mum had walked in. The guests must have noticed that he walked with a slight limp and that he had become a lot thinner since they last saw him. Tony was deep in thought but jumped suddenly as the Church organ leapt into life. The bride had arrived, Jackie was here! He and Steve stood up. Everyone glanced round to the back of the Church and there was a noticeable gasp; Jackie looked absolutely stunning. She was naturally beautiful but on her wedding day, she was something else!

The wedding went well; everyone enjoyed the service and then the reception in the local village hall afterwards. Steve's best man speech was memorable and yes, 'Mrs Collywobbles' was mentioned again. The dancing went on until late and guests enjoyed catching up with each other and talked about their mixed feelings about enjoyment of Tony and Jackie's big day on the one hand, but with the news about Tony's Dad on the other.

In the post wedding period, Jackie noticed that Tony was particularly affected by these mixed feelings and that he had become increasingly quiet and subdued, almost a recluse. That wasn't the Tony she knew. Jackie tried to talk to him about this but that didn't seem to help. His mood lightened whenever they called to see Tony's parents but generally, he was very subdued.

Jackie's pregnancy went well. She and Tony made regular visits to the Ante Natal Clinic and were assured by the progress. They could have learned the sex of the baby but preferred to leave it as a surprise. Tony enjoyed updating his parents with news of the baby's progress every time they met. He could see they were excited but, it was also tinged with sadness as he could also see that his Dad was losing more weight and had become increasingly frail.

It was when the pregnancy was at about the six month stage that Steve phoned Tony and Jackie one evening on their home phone, to catch up. Jackie explained Tony wasn't in, as he had gone to do the weekly shopping. Steve then said the call wasn't important, that he was just keeping in touch and asked how she was and how the pregnancy was going. Steve wasn't prepared for her response. Jackie couldn't help herself. She just sobbed uncontrollably down the phone and couldn't talk for some minutes.

Steve was taken aback; he didn't understand what was happening but tried to offer reassuring words down the phone to Jackie. Jackie felt embarrassed, as she hadn't wanted to disclose her concerns about Tony to anyone feeling this was disloyal and something private between themselves.

That was until now. Steve's call had triggered her concerns. After some minutes she regained her composure and was able to talk and spoke for some time explaining that everything had got too much for Tony recently. The evident decline in his Dad's health had really upset him whereas by contrast, the wedding, being married and the imminent parenthood seemed to excite him, causing a real mixture of feelings. She then went on to explain how subdued and introverted his behaviour had become.

Steve listened carefully. He was shocked and had no idea Tony had been feeling this way. Trying to sympathise with Jackie he realised that it was ineffective on the phone. Jackie was also uncomfortable and started to apologise to Steve for breaking down. Steve quickly reassured her that wasn't necessary at all. He then went on to ask if they could meet on Thursday evening that week when he knew Tony would be at football training? Jackie was anxious about burdening Steve but realised she and Tony needed some help. She agreed to meet Steve; they arranged that he would come to their house shortly after Tony left for training as he was normally away for two hours.

As Steve put the phone down, he held his head in his hand. Jan was concerned to see him like this and put an arm around his shoulder. Steve explained the conversation he had just had with Jackie. Jan was shocked and surprised and had also not appreciated that Tony was feeling so bad. They made a cup of tea and chatted further. They were both troubled to learn how Tony was and wondered what they could do to help. It was Jan who then came up with an idea, 'I know,' she said suddenly to which Steve raised his eyebrow and listened.

Jan's idea was simple, a boy's weekend. Time for the four friends to get together, to go away for a long weekend, hiking, and drinking, just to talk things through and give the situation some time and space for Tony to open up. Maybe a few beers would help as well? Jan went on to say clearly that the time was now, as both she and Susan were nearly eight months pregnant leaving little time until the babies were born. Jackie felt it was important not to make Tony aware the weekend had been initiated by Jackie's concerns. 'What I mean is,' she said, 'Just indicate it's a chance for the four friends to get away before 'baby bedlam' gets underway.' Jan went on to explain that she wasn't for one moment any type of psychiatrist, but surely it would be worth attempting this simple 'remedy' which might work and was worth exploring before anything else was tried.

Steve smiled as he listened to Jan. Her idea was so simple. It might just help, and it would certainly be enjoyable! He leant over to kiss her. They then looked up potential accommodation and dates in mid Wales for the following weekend and found a couple of possible venues. Steve then called Paul and John. Paul was at work; he was concerned to hear about Tony and appreciated the need to headline the weekend as a chance to get away before the babies arrived.

Steve then asked if Paul could come with him that Thursday evening and discuss the idea with Jackie, but Paul explained he had work commitments that he couldn't change at short notice. Steve understood and then called John. He really liked the idea of a 'boy's weekend' and like Paul, he saw the need to headline the weekend as a chance to get away before the babies arrived. When Steve asked John if he could come with him to see Jackie, he readily agreed adding that they could go onto the rugby club afterwards for a drink. Steve smiled and agreed.

Jackie was surprised when she opened her front door that Thursday evening to see that John was with Steve. Tony had gone to training. Steve opened the conversation, saying how important he realised Jan's concerns were about Tony and that he had decided to privately share the information with Paul and John as they were all such close friends and that he hoped Jackie wouldn't mind? Without giving Jackie time to respond he went on to indicate they felt they could help and outlined the idea of the boy's weekend.

Jackie was initially concerned, but when she understood they were going to headline the weekend as a chance to get away before the babies arrived, with no reference to her, she relaxed. Actually, she was more than relaxed; she was so grateful for the support from Tony's friends but also for their sensitivity. It all made sense and the worst outcome was that they just had an enjoyable weekend but at best Tony may feel he can open up and talk things through with his closest friends.

Steve then said he would phone tomorrow evening to talk to Tony. As they got up to go, she hugged them both and thanked them again profusely. She felt so relieved that she had been able to share her concerns and for the help Tony's friends were offering in response. Steve and John went onto the Rugby Club for a quiet pint. John said how pleased he was to have gone with Steve as it had helped him now to understand Jackie's concerns, adding that a boy's weekend might really help and at the very worst would be just a good walk, talk and drink! They exchanged those looks that only true companions understand and clinked their glasses.

Steve called Paul the following morning to update him on the conversations with John and the meeting with Jackie. He then explained that he was going to call Tony at home that evening and would keep Paul further informed.

It was mid evening when Steve called Tony. The call was short, and Tony laughed with Steve as he suggested the four friends needed to get away for a weekend before all these babies arrived! Tony then put his hand over the mouthpiece and said to Jackie, 'Steve's suggesting that next weekend we should go away for a boy's weekend, a couple of nights in Wales. Would that be ok with you?' Jackie just smiled and said, 'Of course!' and looked back to the magazine. When the call was over Tony looked over to Jackie and said, 'What a great idea!' Jackie smiled and they chatted about the trip in more detail. Tony was certainly keen and looking forward to it!

Steve arranged to take the farm's Land Rover as there was plenty of room in the back to take the luggage and it was certainly a vehicle that could cope with the Welsh lanes and countryside terrain. The drive up was uneventful; it was just 'boy's banter' catching up on sporting events and family news. They arrived late evening at the Bed and Breakfast which was a big farmhouse. Breakfast the following morning was superb, simply ham and eggs but loads of it with tea and toast. The couple who owned it were interested to hear all about Steve's farm.

The scenery was magnificent; Steve had chosen well. They were in Snowdonia with plenty of walks over the hills, winding rivers and large flocks of sheep. They were able to start the walk outside the farmhouse and the farmer's wife had made them all a packed lunch. They also arranged for an evening meal in the 'Red Dragon' pub in the village. The weather at the start of the walk was overcast and cloudy but by mid-morning, the clouds started to break up and it became sunny with blue skies. Just perfect. The 'banter' carried on all day, plenty of laughter and leg pulling. The four friends were really enjoying themselves and kept saying they should be doing this more often.

It was when they got to the Red Dragon early evening (tired but elated), that the conversation became more serious.

The four friends had ordered their meals and they all had pints on the table. They were sitting in a quiet corner of the pub, which was very private. It was during the second pint that Steve referred to his Father, saying how he'd noticed in recent weeks he was doing less and less work. Steve laughed added that he was seemed to be enjoying his retirement! Paul then commented that he couldn't see when his Dad would finish work. The engineering business was buzzing, and his two brothers had to really force their Dad to take time off for holidays. John quietly referred to his Dad, saying he enjoyed his retirement and seemed to simply enjoy reading all day but was getting under his Mum's feet. They all laughed at this.

The conversation was very relaxed; it seemed this was just the moment Tony had needed. He started talking about his Dad and the conversation with his friends just flowed and flowed.

Initially Tony spoke about his Dad's current health. As he spoke his friends could see how anguished he was. In fact, he was angry. He reflected upon how unfair it was that his Dad had incurred this illness, why him? He then outlined how his Dad had declined, the loss of weight and that he had started to stoop. He was also limping; it was so undignified. He just didn't deserve this. He spoke about how honest and hard working his Dad had been and that now he wouldn't be able to enjoy his retirement. Tony then spoke about his Mum and how she would cope with his Dad's death? Tony cried when he spoke his future child and whether his Dad would see his grandchild, or might he have died before the birth?

The three friends listened attentively and added comments as Tony spoke. The meal was served and eaten as the conversation developed and more beers were bought. It was more than an hour later that the tone of the conversation changed as Tony started to reflect on his childhood. He had been talking of the respect he had for his Dad and Mum. He looked up to his friends at this point and said he realised how much he was going to miss his Dad, particularly as he was getting married and becoming a Dad himself! They all sympathised as these were both happy and sad reflections.

Tony carried on talking about the respect he had for his parents and the great childhood they had provided. He had wanted for nothing and he hoped he and Jackie could provide as well and become equally good parents. He then reflected on his childhood, his home life, schooling and the numerous holidays and as he reflected on these subjects his friends could see he was becoming more relaxed. He laughed as he recalled some of the stories and the friends found they could join in adding their own recollections.

Of course, the recollections of 'Mrs Collywobbles' were numerous and exaggerated, but it was she who had brought them all together. There was almost a fondness for her in the way they spoke. The sponge and custard story was particularly exaggerated, as was the humiliation Tony and Steve felt at being caned in front of the whole school and then expelled from school lunches for a week. They laughed as they recalled it was in that week that the eleven plus results were announced and how they had experienced the happy transformation from villains to heroes in a few days.

The stories just kept coming; Tony's experiment with the salt and pepper pots, the look of horror on the Police Constables' face when Paul handed him the grenade, John's experiments with cigarettes and matches and that his sister still didn't know how this had happened (but she's now given up smoking!)! It was then they started to recall stories of first girlfriends. Paul recalled his trip to America, then Trudy and the rabbit food. Steve recalled Avignon and the beautiful Camille, then they all laughed with Tony about his experiences in Port Talbot and the barbeque at Celia's swimming pool. It was then they turned on John that they all laughed again saying Susan was there from the beginning and would always be there. John agreed and was happy to acknowledge his relative lack of adventure. He and Susan were just happy!

There was a pause in the conversation at this point; it was Steve who first spoke. 'By the way,' he said, 'We often talked about the Male Menopause and we've said it didn't really exist but now I wonder? I mean when we now look back at what has happened to us and then see what's happening to our parents as well, then maybe there is such a thing?' Tony spoke up first saying he remembered Steve talking about his Uncle Frank and that he often thought about it. 'I remember he said our behaviours today were based on what I think he called 'primeval instincts' meaning when we were cavemen we had to protect, provide and procreate; it was known as the 3P's!' John then said that he remembered that too and had often wondered about it.

'Actually,' said Steve, 'since talking with Uncle Frank and then his friend Tim, I've often pondered about the things they told me. In fact, I've found out the National Health Service, have issued some information.' Steve went on to explain he was surprised to find this information because he had always thought there was 'no such thing as the Male Menopause' and his friends smiled. Steve then explained that he had brought a leaflet and that it was in his suitcase back at the Bed and Breakfast because he'd thought they might be talking about it at some point. 'Oh,' said Tony, 'Can you remember what it says?' Steve thought for a moment and then said, 'I remember it said men might get depressed, or lose their sex drive. They may experience erectile dysfunction and there were some other emotional and physical symptoms but that these generally don't occur until they are aged in their late forties to early fifties.' Steve's friends were certainly attentive. John spoke first and said to everyone's amusement that he'd not experienced any 'erectile dysfunction'.

It was at this point they had to leave the Red Dragon. The final bell had rung, and the bills had been paid. The conversations carried on as they walked back to the Bed and Breakfast but then they had to stop talking out of respect to the other guests. They crept back to their rooms but agreed to carry on discussing the Male Menopause again in the morning.

After another superb breakfast the four friends decided to go on a short walk to a nearby lake but realised, they would need to start travelling back early afternoon. It was another great day; the sun was shining, and the banter was good as they updated each other on the phone calls they'd made that morning to their wives. John, Steve and Tony had updates on the pregnancies, but attention focussed on Paul as he said he had something a 'bit confidential' to tell them.

They listened attentively as Paul said that he'd not been able to tell them before, but that Jan's Dad had now completed the purchase on another hotel and that he and Jenny were going to run it and then buy the business off her Dad over a number of years. When Paul explained which hotel it was, the three friends knew it well and were really impressed as they talked through the potential. They knew it was well located near to the town's railway station and shopping centre. Also, it had land for expansion and a health club should be very popular and should go well. Paul was pleased to hear their feedback and then laughed as John asked if they could still meet up for a drink in the Red Lion. Paul said he reckoned he would really welcome a break from his hotel life now and again!

The four friends had arrived at the lake which was stunning. There was a light wind, the clear blue water reflected the large hills that surrounded the lake. They sat down on some rocks and just took in the scenery. None of them spoke as they listened to the birds. It was one of those moments when life just felt so good!

It was John who broke the silence, referring to their conversation last evening on the Male Menopause asked Steve if he had found the leaflet. Steve smiled and said, 'I have actually,' and grabbing the small leaflet out of his backpack, he waved it in the air and asked if they'd like to hear more. The friends just nodded as Steve carried on.

It was certainly a memorable setting, beside the beautiful lakeside. Steve explained that the very term 'Male Menopause' was unhelpful (but often used in the media). He went on to read that this was because it suggested the symptoms were because of a sudden drop in testosterone in middle age, that is, similar to the changes that happen to females. Steve read on, 'But this is just not true,' and continued, 'Medical practitioners prefer to use the term 'Andropause' as although testosterone levels fall as men age, the decline is generally less than two percent a year from the age of thirty to forty, but it is unlikely to cause any of the symptoms or problems of andropause on its own.'

John interrupted asking, 'So just what are these symptoms?' Steve thumbed through the leaflet and then read on explaining that some men develop depression, loss of sex drive and erectile dysfunction generally from their late forties to early fifties. Steve paused at this point saying, 'This is what I explained to you last night in the Red Dragon?' and the friends nodded, and Paul added, 'I've been thinking about the things John said last night. We've got years to go yet and I'm certainly not experiencing that erectile dysfunction thing yet either!' They all laughed again until Steve added that there were a lot more symptoms and the friends raised their eyebrows, Steve carried on.

He read from the leaflet explaining that the symptoms were largely physical and emotional ones, apparently including mood swings and irritability and also, 'loss of muscle mass and reduced ability to exercise.' Paul interrupted at this stage and, looking at Tony said, 'You've been experiencing those for years already,' to which Tony grimaced and shook his fist. They all laughed again. Steve read on saying that men experienced fat redistribution, such as developing a large belly or even 'man boobs' which is apparently called 'gynaecomastia' and that there was also a general lack of enthusiasm or energy. It was John who then commented that he often felt tired and a lack of energy after teaching at school all day and then marking books at night and lesson planning as well! He got some mock sympathy from the others saying, 'Ahhhh!'

Steve then read on saying that further symptoms included increased tiredness and difficulty in sleeping. John interrupted here saying, 'I know, that one's called insomnia,' and the others gave him a round of applause. Then Steve added, 'And finally,' and he went on to explain that poor concentration and short term memory were symptoms as well.

The conversation turned a little more serious then as Tony commented that actually he'd seen some of those symptoms in his Dad and John agreed that he'd seen some in his Dad too. Steve then read out from another section of the leaflet explaining there was difficulty in really defining or diagnosing the Male Menopause (or Andropause) as the symptoms could also be caused by lifestyle factors or psychological problems.

He read on further, saying that for example erectile dysfunction, loss of libido and mood swings may be the result of stress, depression or anxiety and that any of these could be caused by work, relationship, money or divorce issues or through concern for aging parents. 'So, those things could really happen at any time in our lives,' said

John and the others nodded, 'But it wouldn't be the Male Menopause as such,' he added saying he could see more clearly now why it was so difficult to define medically. Again, the others nodded.

They then went quiet. No one said anything for a few minutes and instead they took in the amazing scenery and reflected on all that had been said. It was Steve who spoke first and still reading from the leaflet said, 'There is a list of possible causes of the Male Menopause, and it lists a lack of sleep, a poor diet, lack of exercise, drinking too much alcohol, smoking and having a low self-esteem.' Paul spoke up then saying, 'So all I have to do is eat well, sleep well, get loads of exercise, cut back on the beers and tell Jenny to cheer me up every day? It all seems so simple!' They all laughed with Paul but then Steve replied saying they had better head back to the Land Rover now and start the journey home to avoid the rush hour traffic.

They set off to hike back to the Bed and Breakfast, still chatting about the Male Menopause and discussing further the information Steve had read out. It was during the journey home that the conversation changed when Paul commented that the thing that he felt was missing was any real reference or understanding of the 3Ps, that surely Protection, Provision and Procreation were really what the Male Menopause was all about? They started to realise that things that had happened to them when they were younger (or in their 'formative years' as Paul called it) had actually had a huge bearing on how they behaved as adults. Conversation on the 3Ps and its bearing on the Male Menopause didn't stop until they got home.

Steve spoke about how he saw his Father had always needed to be 'King Pin' on the farm. Everything had to be run to his schedule every day to ensure the cattle were fed, the crops were tended and, in summer, that all the fruit and grain were properly harvested. 'In fact,' said Steve, 'looking back, he was clearly driven on provision but also it was protection too; if he didn't sell the crops and livestock we wouldn't have eaten! Now I can see I've been driven by protection and provision also!' The others all nodded and then Steve referred to the 'Poo poo' cushion story and that looking back, maybe that was a case of Steve testing his Father's authority and disrupting normal routine.

Paul commented on the grenade incident saying that even at a young age they realised that it was dangerous, and something needed to be done to protect everyone. 'Ok' he said, 'Perhaps it wasn't the best idea to take it to the Policeman's houses (the others laughed) but the intention was good, wasn't it?'

Tony spoke up next reflecting on his course at the National Coastal Rescue Training Centre and Commander Thompson. 'He was certainly dominant and forceful in his leadership and it was all about good protection!' John smiled at this point and asked whether the Police Sergeant who Tony kissed had felt protected? Tony smiled and then spoke about how the Police cadets had introduced him to girls and how, unwittingly, that was the time when he had become aware of the procreation instinct and those girls they had met in the evenings! Steve then added, 'Oh yes, for me that moment was meeting those girls in France. Camille was just beautiful and that was when I became really aware of procreation!'

Paul then recalled his first procreation moments, saying how much he had fancied Trudy but, he had then told that ridiculous story about Woolworths thinking he was impressing her parents. How naïve! 'But then fate was at play,' he pondered, 'First that student in America, who taught me a lot and then meeting Jenny for the first time which has led towards us to now running and eventually owning our own hotel. It's unbelievable!' Paul smiled as he pondered further and said, 'Really, Jenny has been about both procreation and provision, hasn't she?' It was John who spoke next commenting that although they'd all been unexpectedly preoccupied with procreation, they were all now going to really experience much more of the provision and protection instincts as they became parents. 'I guess you'll feel this with the new hotel Paul, but you've experienced it already as a parent Steve?'

Steve turned towards John and said, 'You're right John, parenthood completely and happily changed our lives, I'm just fully committed to Jan and our son David and will do everything I can to protect and provide for them. It's just I'd never really thought about it before or realised these instincts have been handed down the generations since time began, they originated in cavemen.'

The return journey sped by all too quickly as the four friends carried on discussing the Male Menopause and its effect on their lives and those of their parents. For Tony though, the weekend had been of enormous benefit. It was when he got home to Jackie that she noticed a complete transformation. He was happy and chatted endlessly about the various things that had happened. Above all, she noticed how much he was talking excitedly about the arrival of their baby! Her old Tony was back! The next day she called Steve on his mobile phone to thank him and asked him to pass on her thanks to Paul and John as well.

CHAPTER 11

DELIGHT PHASE
(18 – 25 YEARS OLD)
Men become parents

THREE WEEKS LATER, Susan gave birth to a healthy baby boy and they called him Michael. He was seven pounds and six ounces at birth with lots of blonde hair and blue eyes just like John. To say John and Susan were 'over the moon' would be an understatement; John just wanted to hold Michael all the time and kept looking at Susan with a huge grin on his face. The following day they were allowed to take Michael home. It was just at the start of the school summer holidays, so John had several weeks off from school. The timing was perfect! The following weekend Tony and Jackie called in briefly on their way to visit Tony's parents. Jackie was due any day. She and Tony were both apprehensive, even nervous. They took great comfort in hearing how well the birth had gone and could see the obvious delight in Michael's parents, they were so happy!

They didn't stay long, just enough time to give Michael some new sleep suits which his parents were delighted with. They then drove off to Tony's parent's house feeling very excited but were not prepared for what they found when they arrived. It was Tony's Mum who answered the door. She looked exhausted, her hair was dishevelled and there were dark shadows under her eyes.

She was clearly pleased to see them but a tear ran down her cheek as she hugged her son and then daughter in law saying how very pleased she was to see them both. With her voice lowered she explained Tony's Dad was fast asleep in the bedroom but that he had not generally been sleeping or eating well and that he had lost further weight too.

Tony helped his Mum through to the sitting room and sat her down. She put her head thankfully on Tony's shoulder and cried some more, she was just exhausted. Jackie went through to the kitchen to make some tea but on returning to the sitting room found Tony's Mum had fallen into a deep sleep. Tony had laid her on the settee and covered her with a blanket. He went through to check on his Dad in their bedroom who was also asleep and looked very peaceful.

Tony and Jackie went back into the kitchen. It was a Saturday evening. They talked in hushed voices, occasionally going through to check that both Tony's parents were comfortable; they slept well for several hours. Tony and Jackie were both shocked as although Tony had called his parents every day and mainly spoken to his Mum, she hadn't indicated how unwell his Dad had become and how exhausted she had felt. Jackie reasoned that maybe it was the case that they just wanted to cope and hadn't wanted to burden her and Tony.

It was when Jackie called her Mum that evening that they found a way forward. Jackie's Mum explained they had been through a similar situation with one of her Aunts a few years ago and had used the National Health Service help line. It was through this initial call they discovered there was a daily help service where nurses and other medical support staff would visit patients at home to provide support such as administering medicine, changing dressings and bedding and there was even a daily food service as well! When Jackie explained this to Tony, he couldn't believe it either. They called the number the following morning and although it was a Sunday, the call was answered. There were a number of options available, but it needed to start with a home visit for an assessment meeting to find out at first hand exactly what was needed. The assessment meeting could not be arranged until late afternoon the following Tuesday.

Jackie was impressed; she saw that Tony step up to the mark and that he was being strong and confident for his parents. She had heard Tony talking about the Male Menopause recently and she could see he just wanted to protect and provide for them. These instincts were strong and in obvious contrast to his behaviour before he had gone away for that weekend with his friends. Jackie was so pleased to see Tony like this, he was back to his former self. They spent the rest of the day helping with basic domestic chores and restocking the larder. Tony's Mum slept a lot. When she did wake up, she kept apologising for being a burden but both Jackie and Tony reassured her there was no problem and encouraged her to rest. Tony sat with his Dad whilst he rested in bed. Although his Dad was thin and frail and couldn't eat much, he also couldn't stop talking! He just enjoyed reminiscing with his son. It was a conversation Tony would remember always.

It was late afternoon when Jackie and Tony set off. Tony's Mum was well rested, and she looked so much better. Jackie and Tony needed to be back at work the following morning and they lived just over two hours away. Tony planned to return on Tuesday afternoon, to be present when the assessment officer arrived.

They arrived home late that night and were surprised when the phone rang soon after they had got in the house. They exchanged glances both having the same thought. Tony picked up the phone feeling anxious. Jackie looked at him earnestly and was then really surprised and puzzled when she heard Tony say, 'Oh that's great news, we're so happy for you.' He then looked really concerned saying. 'Oh no! Is everything alright now?' Jackie just couldn't understand what was going on or who Tony was talking to.

It was at this point that Tony looked up and saw her concern. He explained to the caller that he'd just like to share the news with Jackie and then turning to her said, 'It's Steve, they've just had a baby daughter called Katherine this afternoon. She was a breech so Jan needed a caesarean operation but is feeling much better now!' Jackie was excited and taking the phone from Tony, spoke to Steve to offer her love and best wishes.

Steve was so relieved and excited, he explained in some detail what had happened, but then quickly reprimanded himself as he realised Jackie was only a few weeks away from her first child. Jackie explained what had happened with Tony's parents and that it had just been one of those days of complete contrast with good and not so good news. Jackie then passed the phone back to Tony and left them to finish the call. She sat down and rested, listening to Tony saying he thought they would be visiting a lot in weeks to come and how much they looked forward to meeting Katherine!

Tuesday afternoon's meeting with the assessment officer was encouraging. Tony's Mum looked much better, though she felt guilty in realising she needed help. Tony's Dad was the same, they felt they had always coped and that now they couldn't. As the discussions went on Tony thought back to the Male Menopause discussions he'd been having with his friends and that here, with his own family, he could now understand. He could see that his Dad felt his protection and provision instincts were being eroded; it was obviously uncomfortable for him. It was agreed that daily support visits would take place to assist with household chores and that a nurse would visit once a week to monitor his Dad's medication.

It was early evening when Tony was preparing to leave. Both his parents seemed relieved and much more relaxed. Tony implored them to be fully open when he phoned them and not to conceal any difficulties! They both smiled and appreciated his care; he was protecting them.

It was then that Tony told them about the arrival of Katherine. They were really pleased to hear that Mum and baby were now well and then with broad smiles said, 'Not long for you now!' and Tony grinned from ear to ear as he hugged them and said goodbye. It was a long journey back but it passed by quickly as Tony's mind was racing through all the recent events that had happened. They were mixed feelings; he felt sad and anguished about his Dad wishing he could do more, yet he felt so happy about the births and looked forward so much to their own.

Andrew was born two weeks later; he weighed six pounds and twelve ounces. He was a healthy baby with brown hair and brown eyes. The birth was straightforward and there were no complications. Jackie and Tony were 'over the moon' telling family and friends that he was the 'best looking baby ever.' However, it had been a long birth and they were both completely exhausted. They were released from hospital the next morning and went straight home for more rest and what the midwife had explained would be a period of acclimatisation.

When they got back to their house, Jackie's parents were there to greet them, and to help with all the domestic chores. They were really excited to meet Andrew as he was their first grandchild. Jackie knew what was on Tony's mind, that he was anxious to take Andrew as soon as possible to meet his other grandparents. She explained this to her parents, and they slipped away early that evening leaving the new family to enjoy their first night together at home.

Their sleep was disrupted that night with regular feeding. The following morning Tony woke up and got out of bed to make a cup of tea. He stopped by the small crib in their room and just stared down and then smiled at Andrew who was so peacefully asleep. It was at that moment that Jackie stirred, her eyes fluttered, and she saw the loving smile on Tony's face. It was a perfect moment. Jackie propped herself up on her elbows and saying a cheery, 'Good morning!' to Tony, asked if he would like to take Andrew to see his other Grandparents. The broad smile on Tony's face said it all; he sat on the bed beside Jackie and kissed her. They then looked into the crib to see their son remained peacefully asleep, they both felt so proud. 'Would you like a cup of tea?' asked Tony.

They spoke in whispers whilst drinking their tea as Andrew was still asleep. Tony had booked a full week's paternity leave off work and it was Jackie who said, 'Do you think your parents would mind if we stayed with them all this week?' Tony hadn't considered this, but he was so pleased to hear Jackie suggest it and imagined his parents would be really pleased. They would have to take it 'day by day' in case his Dad's health deteriorated. He called his Mum who was so pleased to hear Andrew and Jackie were well and then really delighted when Tony explained they were planning to visit later that afternoon and then stay for 'just a few days.'

The decision to visit Tony's parents as soon as possible and stay for up to a week proved to be the right thing to do. It was mid-September, the weather was good, and it was such a happy week in which Tony's parents both enjoyed holding Andrew and making strange 'googling' noises. It was even possible to arrange a post natal midwife visit to check on Jackie and Andrew. Although unusual, it was when Tony phoned and explained the circumstances that the local midwives were more than helpful. As Tony put the phone down though he paused as he realised, he was being protective.

Many photographs were taken, some indoors and some in the garden. The week was relaxed as Jackie started to establish a more regular feeding routine and Tony became skilled at nappy changing. Steve, Paul and John realised Tony and Jackie were back and arrangements were made to meet at the Red Lion early Saturday evening after Paul and John's rugby match. It would be the first time the babies had all met each other!

The reunion in the garden of the Red Lion that September evening would be one the friends would remember for ever. It was such a happy occasion. The new babies, Katherine, Andrew and Michael were admired, photographs were taken, a bottle of champagne was bought to toast the 'newcomers' and a fuss was made of David who had grown so much and was now walking and talking! Paul and Jenny spoke enthusiastically about their first month running the hotel. They'd experienced over eighty percent occupancy, the takings in the restaurant and bars had been good too. It was clear they had made a good start.

They had agreed to meet for just two hours as young children needed their sleep! After the first hour the four friends migrated towards each other, initially to hear Paul and John talk about the rugby match which they had won; John had scored a try! But the conversation then changed direction when Steve said, 'You know what, I sometimes think about that journey home from Wales and the conversation we had about the Male Menopause.' The other three all exclaimed, almost in the same breath, 'So have I!' and then laughed at themselves. It was Tony who spoke first to say that only that week he recognised how protective he had been arranging a local midwife for Jackie and Andrew.

John then spoke about the massive change he had felt becoming a parent and that he hadn't really thought before about the responsibilities it brought to provide and protect, 'Don't get me wrong,' he added, 'The daily pleasures in having Michael in our lives far outweighs the feelings of responsibility.' Steve smiled saying, 'Wait until you get your second ones!' and added that he had often thought that if there was a graph of chaos on the one axis against the number of children on the other, that the plotted line would be exponential!

Paul then said he had thought about their Male Menopause discussion as he and Jenny had taken responsibility for the hotel. 'I've heard people talk before about the burden of responsibility,' he said, 'But this is the first time I've experienced it at first hand.' He went on to recall that they'd discussed the primeval instincts and how they could see examples of it in their everyday lives. Steve then said, 'One of the things I've been thinking about,' he then paused and glanced around, 'is that this so called Menopause apparently doesn't exist for males, yet it does for females?'

The others looked on. They weren't really used to Steve being profound or serious but right now, he was being both! He continued to say his thinking was that all humans, male and female, go through their lives with a mix of physiological and psychological feelings and developments, 'Blimey, you're getting serious!' said Paul but Steve just carried on. The others listened attentively as Steve explained that said he thought women had a higher mix of physiological feelings whereas men experience a higher mix of psychological feelings.

'I look at my parents,' he went on. 'My Father can no longer carry out all the physical tasks he used to do on the farm and he gets very frustrated. You can see how he gets so angry with himself,' Steve went on to explain how he went to the Red Lion with his father now with increasing regularity just to talk things through. 'After a couple of pints away from the farm in the Red Lion, I can see my Father relaxes, he laughs and chats about what might have happened, and the issue just goes away.'

The others nodded heads in agreement, but it was Tony who then spoke about his Dad and in particular the recent conversations they had been having whilst his Dad was unwell and so weakened by the cancer. 'I see frustrations in my Dad too,' he said, 'My Dad just feels so useless at the moment. He spends most of his time in bed and tells me how weak he feels. You can see how it affects him; he is often tearful with frustration.'

The others could tell how upset Tony was in talking about it. Paul put his arm around him and picked up the conversation referring again to their journey back from Wales saying, 'So all our behaviours today relate back to the instincts of our primeval forefathers; that to survive we had to be providers, protectors and procreators? Is it really that simple?' The others paused and it was John who, in his usual quiet voice said, 'I'm starting to think there might be such a thing as the Male Menopause?' and raised his glass. The others nodded and raised their glasses too.

It was at this point that Jan interrupted them saying they'd now been together for the agreed two hours and it was time to drink up and get the tired youngsters to their beds for much needed rest. Paul and Jenny waved them off and then stopped behind, for them it was relaxing to spend time together away from their hotel and just chat.

Initially they talked about their friends and their children; they spoke about how much the arrival of David, Katherine, Andrew and Michael had changed the conversations. The children were now the focus of their conversations and how happy everyone was. Paul then reflected that their focus had changed too, and that the hotel was now in a way 'their baby' as they thought about it with every waking moment. Jenny nodded in agreement, saying how much she realised their lives had changed too and how much she was enjoying it. They clinked their glasses together, but then found during the next half an hour or so they chatted through current issues at the hotel, mainly staffing issues.

It was Paul who suddenly said 'Hey!' and smiling at Jenny, said they shouldn't be talking about the hotel, that time away was precious and they needed to talk about other things. Jenny said that she had overheard Paul and his friends discussing the Male Menopause and asked what that had been all about. Paul summarised the conversation and then said that he had not really thought about it too much before but that it had made him think about his Dad and his brothers.

'What do you mean?' asked Jenny and was surprised when Paul said that it was only little things, but that he had noticed that his brothers were increasingly making suggestions on how the engineering business should be run and that his Dad had been dismissive, often saying he had tried the ideas in the past and that they hadn't worked. Paul then spoke at some length about recent discussions about a new machine tool the brothers had wanted to buy, yet his Dad couldn't see that it would bring in enough new work to justify the expenditure.

'What do you think will happen?' asked Jenny and she could see Paul was troubled as he spoke, saying he hoped they would find a way forward but that it was possible that one or both of his brothers might break away and form a new business. 'They've seen you and I are running a hotel Jenny, so why can't they set up and run their own engineering business too?' They paused together in thought; Jenny could tell Paul was anxious. He pondered on the notion of some sort of power struggle taking place in his family. Did this relate at all to the conversations he'd been having with his friends earlier about the Male Menopause? The

'Last Orders' bell rang and there was no time to discuss it further. It was time to get back to their hotel and check there were no problems.

The following Saturday morning the sun shone brightly into Tony and Jackie's bedroom window. Andrew had just woken and Tony picked him up. He made it known he was thirsty, that he wanted his Mum! He suckled eagerly on his Mum's breast; it was all so natural. Tony and Jackie looked at each other and nothing needed to be said; their love for each other and their new child was just so obvious.

Tony went through to the kitchen and put the kettle on. The phone rang and Tony picked it up. He could tell it was his Mum, but she couldn't speak. She was sobbing uncontrollably down the phone. Tony froze; he knew instantly what had happened. He tried to talk to his Mum and eventually she confirmed that his Dad had died peacefully that morning.

Although Tony had often anticipated this moment over recent weeks, he still wasn't prepared for it. His Dad was dead. He just couldn't believe it.

Jackie overheard the conversation and came through to the kitchen holding Andrew. Tony had ended the call with his Mum explaining he would call her back. He sat at the kitchen table sobbing and shaking. Jackie put her arm around his neck and just held him. He sobbed more. Nothing was said. Nothing needed to be said. Jackie passed Andrew into Tony's arms and then made the tea. Tony held Andrew carefully but closely and calming down he sipped the tea. It was Jackie who spoke first saying, 'Let's pack the car and go to your Mum's as soon as possible' Tony nodded his head in agreement. He also agreed that Jackie should call his Mum to explain they were coming. Jackie was pleasantly surprised that when she called Tony's Mum, she was quiet but not distraught;

she seemed really relieved to know that they were on their way.

The car journey was quiet. Jackie drove and Tony sat in the back to keep an eye on Andrew who slept most of the way. Jackie pondered on her telephone call with Tony's Mum. Just what had she been through in the last few hours and on top of everything else, having to phone their only son that morning to say his Dad had died. How awful that must have been for her and what could Jackie do best to help? Jackie glanced in the rear view mirror and saw that Tony was just staring out of the side window into the middle distance. What could she do also to support and help Tony?

It was Andrew who provided the answers. They were only around twenty minutes from arrival when he suddenly bawled out as babies do. It certainly drew Tony out of his trance as Jackie pulled over into the next layby. After a quick feed they drove on, this time with Tony driving and Jackie in the back with Andrew. Tony became a lot more vocal as he drove. As they got closer to his Mum's house, he relayed a whole host of questions and ideas and shared them with Jackie to discuss what they should do to help his Mum. All these questions had clearly been playing on his mind and he now wanted to help his Mum and ensure they carried out his Dad's wishes.

It was Andrew again who helped when they arrived; he was the focus of attention. Tony's Mum was overjoyed to see them all, but as she held Andrew she laughed and then just cried. After around half an hour and a cup of tea, Tony and his Mum went through to see his Dad. He looked so peaceful; he was at rest. Tony held his Mum and they both cried together. Nothing was said. They were interrupted when the front doorbell rang, it was their family Doctor. Tony's Mum had called the surgery earlier to notify them of the death. The Doctor didn't stay long and didn't say too much either, he left the 'Medical Certificate on Cause of Death' on the kitchen table. Tony shook his hand as he showed him out through the front door.

Returning to the kitchen he found his Mum with Jackie just staring at the Certificate on the table. It seemed unreal, had this really happened? The moment was broken as Andrew awoke in his cot in the next room. He cried out as he needed a feed. Tony put his arm around his Mum and simply asked, 'Time to call the Funeral Director?' His Mum looked at him; her eyes were glazed as she asked Tony if he could do that.

The call with the Funeral Director was also short, almost perfunctory Tony thought. Just people going through their regular day to day jobs and yet in a sombre, quiet way out of respect for the deceased and their family. It was a Saturday and the Funeral Director arranged to collect Tony's Dad that evening. A meeting was arranged with Tony's Mum at home the following Tuesday afternoon. Tony explained he would be joining the meeting by phone to support his Mum.

Tony explained these arrangements to his Mum who was sitting in the kitchen with Jackie who was feeding Andrew. His Mum nodded to acknowledge what Tony had said. Her face was sad, but as she turned to Andrew her eyes lit up. Tony left the kitchen and went back into see his Dad in the bedroom. He just looked so peaceful.

Tony just sat quietly for over an hour; he recalled so many memories. Firstly, the busy daily routines with his Dad working at the clothing shop whilst his Mum worked at the newsagents. Then he frowned as he remembered the salt and pepper incident, the caning and expulsion from Primary School, and then the pride on his parents faces when he gained entrance to the Grammar School. Tony frowned as he recalled their concern at his relationship with Celia, the barbeque at Celia's house and how supportive they had been when the relationship finished. Then as he remembered the first time that they had met Jackie, and now how much happiness the safe arrival of Andrew had given them all.

Tony was lost in his thoughts; it was good to sit with his Dad and just quietly recollect. Jackie came in with a cup of tea and sat with him for a few minutes. They just held hands until they heard Andrew crying out, it was feeding time. Tony followed Jackie out. The Funeral Director arrived an hour later. They were quietly efficient, full of respect as they moved the body onto a trolley, then down the hall and loaded him into their hearse. Tony held his Mum as they watched, and she sobbed quietly. Then they waved as the hearse pulled away.

They went back into the kitchen. They'd not eaten and busied themselves making a meal. Andrew was then fed and bathed and asleep when they sat down to eat their meal. It was then that the conversation really started. Tony's Mum explained that she felt she'd known for some months that Tony's Dad would die but still wasn't prepared for it. Tony said he had felt exactly the same and how difficult it was just coming to terms with it. But his Dad in a better place now; he'd been so weak in recent weeks.

The conversation unravelled. Tony and his Mum were able to just simply talk and share their memories and their feelings too, both the good and the bad ones. Tony explained he'd been quietly reminiscing about his Dad before the Funeral Director had arrived. It was all part of coming to terms with what had happened. It was so good to talk. Andrew woke up again just before midnight and they realised they were all tired. Tony and his Mum cleared up whilst Jackie fed Andrew. That night they all slept soundly.

The conversation carried on through breakfast the following morning. Jackie thought Tony's Mum looked quite well and that she and Tony were both in better spirits than yesterday. They talked about the upcoming meeting with the Funeral Director, which Tony was planning to join in by phone from work. His Mum was quite relaxed about this and explained that she and his Dad had often discussed his funeral in recent weeks and that she felt confident she knew what he wanted. They realised they needed to let other people know and drew up a list of friends, relatives and work colleagues.

It was a sunny day and they decided to go for a walk and took turns pushing Andrew's pram. They started to feel more relaxed as everything that needed to be done had been done. It was late afternoon when Tony asked if they should stay over and travel back on Monday morning. His Mum insisted they should travel back that afternoon. She fully understood they had work and domestic commitments and that she now needed to get used to her new way of life without her husband. She didn't cry when she said this. Tony could see his Mum was full of resolve and felt proud of her.

It was on the journey home that Tony reflected further. He thought back to the conversations he had had with his friends recently about the Male Menopause on the journey back from Wales and when the protection instinct was discussed. He could see how much he had felt this in the last few hours, towards his Mum and also to Jackie and Andrew.

The funeral took place two weeks later. It was a typical Autumnal day, dry with the sun shining brightly and a strong breeze blowing with leaves swirling. Tony, Jackie and Andrew had stayed overnight. It had been a quiet night and getting up that morning had felt strange. Today was the day for Tony to say goodbye to his Dad. In his mind he still couldn't believe it. It was when they were all quietly assembled in the front room though, that he felt the impact of this occasion. Tony was dressed in his black suit, tie and shoes. He felt strange. It was when he saw his Mum in all black with Jackie and Andrew too that he realised today was the day to celebrate his Dad's life. He had a strange feeling of strength and resolve in memory of his Dad, but he realised it was also all about supporting those closest to him.

Tony felt strong, he hadn't expected to.

The funeral cortege arrived. As they glanced through the front room window, they saw two black hearses pulling slowly onto their front drive. Somehow, Tony thought, they looked almost graceful. He could see his Dad's coffin in the first hearse; it had the white garland of lilies on top that they had ordered. Tony's Mum linked her arm through Tony's as they slowly followed the coffin through the Church Lychgate. Jackie walked on the other side holding Andrew who was peacefully asleep.

The Church was full. There were old friends, neighbours, work colleagues and noticeably Paul, John and Steve with their families. Tony was so pleased see his close friends; their support meant such a lot to him. The service was beautiful. The choir sang so well and the vicar conducted the service quietly and with real dignity. The eulogy was delivered by one of his Dad's work colleagues. The words meant such a lot to Tony and he glanced at his Mum to see her eyes were full of tears as she reflected also. Tony felt the presence of Jackie and Andrew as he reflected further. He realised he was now taking on his Dad's role in the family. It was a special moment in a special service.

Tony's Dad had wished to be buried, not cremated. They stood around the grave in the Churchyard as the coffin was lowered slowly and carefully. They then stood over it for some moments to bid a final farewell. Tony stood beside his Mum; tears ran down her face. After a few minutes she threw the lilies onto the coffin and then moved away holding onto Tony's arm for support. The Vicar accompanied them back to the Lychgate. It was at this time that Andrew woke up and grizzled quietly seeking a feed. Everyone smiled as it was such a happy contrast to the sadness, they had all felt. They drove away in the hearse to the reception at the Red Lion.

It was a further act of thoughtfulness and kindness from Tony's Dad. He knew Tony and his friends enjoyed the Red Lion and specifically requested in his 'wish list' that the reception should be held there. A buffet and open bar had been arranged and during the first hour Tony, Jackie and his Mum were fully occupied thanking friends and relatives for attending. Many happy memories were shared. It was after an hour or so that Tony managed to work his way over to join his friends. Steve handed Tony a fresh pint of his favourite bitter and the four friends clinked their glasses and simply said, 'Tony's Dad.' It was Steve who spoke first and said what a good service he thought it had been and then asked how Tony felt. Tony didn't answer straight away. He just looked at his pint and then said, 'Actually, it was a good service yes, but it all felt a bit strange.'

The others listened attentively as Tony carried on saying how much the service had brought home to him the fact his Dad had died and that he would no longer be around for chats or advice. Also, at the same time he had looked around to his Mum, Jackie and Andrew and realised how much they meant to him and how much it was now down to him to protect and look after them.

Paul, Steve and John could see Tony was in deep thought. It was Steve who commented first, saying he'd been thinking too and that his mind had gone back to their return journey from Wales a few months ago. 'This might be a bit off the rails,' he said. 'But I saw a wildlife documentary on television a couple of days ago. It was all about animal behaviour and how they behave in groups or packs.' He carried on explaining it included elephants, lions, wolves, even bees and ants! He then added, 'All these animal groups needed a leader and protector, often the strongest male.' Steve looked around him and then carried on, 'The programme suggested there are analogies between human and animal behaviour, and it made me think about our trip to Wales?'

John asked what Steve meant exactly. 'Well,' said Steve, 'I was listening to Tony just now and that moment in Church when he realised, he needed to act as his Dad had, and become the provider and protector to his immediate family. That's what we discussed in the car back from Wales isn't it?' Paul then said he understood what Steve had meant adding that a male's instinct is still to protect and provide, but we live in a so called modern world now and women thankfully carry out their fair share of responsibilities, don't they? 'Yes,' said Steve, 'But the point is that if we accept the Male Menopause exists, then as a male declines in old age, these basic instincts we're discussing still kick in.' He glanced around and added, 'Males still try to be protective and provide, even if they are not as able as when they were younger.'

Steve carried on. 'In fact, when I look back in our family, at when my Father passed the Farm responsibilities over to me, there have been awkward times as you all know.' It was then John who added, 'Yes, and we know that you and your Father have had to drink gallons of beer to put things right!' With this comment the others all laughed and raised their glasses. They agreed that humour is a good release when conversations start to get too serious.

It was at this moment that Jackie glanced across the pub and saw how Tony was laughing and enjoying himself with his friends. She was so pleased to see him smiling again as the last few days had just been so difficult. Then, in that instance, Tony glanced over to Jackie, their eyes met, and she blew him a kiss. Though nothing was said they both shared a feeling that life must simply just move on.

Tony moved away from his friends to check his Mum was alright. He needn't have worried as he found her in a quiet corner at a table with a friend from the village. The friend was an old neighbour and was inviting his Mum along to the local Women's Institute or 'WI' as they called it. They were both sipping sherry. Tony smiled as his Mum explained she'd not been able to join the WI before as she had always wanted to be at home with 'tea on the table' for his father. Tony kissed his Mum on the cheek and said he would come back in a few minutes after catching up with Jackie and Andrew.

Andrew was only ten weeks old. Jackie was holding him in her arms as Tony approached. It was a further memory Tony would keep forever from that day because as he walked over Andrew seemed to recognise him and gave a broad grin. It was the first time Tony had actually seen his son smile in recognition, it was a magical moment! Jackie caught sight of that moment too and she laughed with Tony as he took Andrew from her arms and held him aloft.

Andrew grinned again and his eyes sparkled. All their friends looked on and cheered as well. This wasn't how Tony or Jackie had thought that the day would end. They had not expected to feel any happiness. They discussed their mixed feelings with Tony's Mum when they got back to her house and had settled Andrew down to sleep. It was Tony's Mum who then said, 'Life I find is always full of surprises, your Dad would want you all to move on now and enjoy every day to the full!' Tony and Jackie nodded their heads as she spoke. They were pleased to see Tony's Mum was in relatively good spirits and seemed to be dealing with her emotions.

The conversations carried on over breakfast the following morning. Tony's mum explained to Jackie that she was thinking of joining the WI and told her about the old neighbour she had met in the Red Lion. They enjoyed a long breakfast discussing all the events of yesterday and the people they had met. They then decided they should take Andrew for a walk in the push chair. They hadn't planned it, but in walking into the village they were drawn to the Churchyard and to the graveside of Tony's Dad. It was no longer a hole in the ground, it was now covered over with fresh soil. A new headstone would be installed by the stone masons in the next week or so.

They stood by the graveside for a few minutes in silence. Tony looked around him; there were green fields alongside the graveyard with sheep and cattle grazing. He then looked up into the trees. They were bending in the wind and leaves were still fluttering down in the autumn sunshine. Tony was thinking to himself what a perfect resting place this was for his Dad and with that thought he glanced at his Mum. He was pleased to see she was smiling in her thoughts as she looked down fondly at the freshly dug soil.

Tony carried these memories home as he drove Jackie and Andrew back that evening. His Mum had been quite insistent that they should get on with their daily lives and that they were only a phone call away from each other. She assured them she would be alright.

Steve, John and Paul had often talked amongst themselves about Tony and his family during the period leading up to the funeral. They had been concerned to see how troubled he had been, yet how a couple of days in Wales had helped. After Wales they'd noticed he had changed, much for the better and was almost back to his former self! He was noticeably less quiet, and he now clearly realised the role he needed to fulfil to support not just Jackie and Andrew, but his Mum also. He was much more focussed and positive.

It was Andrew's arrival that had really transformed Tony. Steve often thought about it as he drove his tractor up and down the fields every day. He reflected on Tony's situation and compared it to his own experiences with Jan and bringing up David (who was now a lively toddler) along with the arrival of Katherine. Children he thought, just changed your life and so much for the better. Was this something connected to our basic instincts? He'd read about something called our 'raison d'etre' and that it meant the most important reason or purpose for someone or something's existence. Steve felt his raison d'etre was to be with his children so what had been his Uncle Frank's, who sadly hadn't had children?

There were no conclusive answers as Steve asked himself these questions though he realised and appreciated how lucky he and Jan were. They were happy with their lot. Might they have more children? This thought often crossed his mind and he would then smile again.

Meanwhile, Paul and Jenny were completely focused on running and developing the hotel. The day to day trade was building nicely. There was generally good client feedback and their accountant told them they were making profits each month. They realised this was largely down to their committed staff who seemed to be working well together. There was a good team spirit.

The confidence was such that they had started to think about the future development of the hotel. Plans had been prepared to extend the hotel to provide a new gymnasium and fitness room off the main lobby and six extra bedrooms above it. They had found there was a lot of interest locally in a fitness club. They would need to take out a large loan with personal guarantees, would they be able to afford it? How certain were they that they could maintain and grow the overnight hotel occupancy? Would the increased footfall create a higher demand for lunches and evening meals from the restaurant? What should they be doing to market the new facility? Paul and Jenny seemed discuss these questions with every waking moment they had. They were concerned, they were anxious, they were stressed.

Meanwhile John and Susan were experiencing big changes in their lives too. As new parents they were completely besotted with their son, Michael. He had dark hair with big brown eyes and now, at six months old, he had developed the most engaging smile you could ever have imagined as John would often boast proudly whenever someone would listen! Susan was on maternity leave from school. She had adjusted to a whole new way of life. She often wondered if she would miss marking and lesson planning but soon realised she didn't. Changing nappies, feeding, playing with Michael and household chores were now the happy order of each day.

John's school workload had changed. It was a big school and he had been promoted to head of the History department with four other teachers in his team. He enjoyed the planning and day to day management issues but really disliked the senior management meetings he now had to attend. They were held every two weeks and John found that they were tedious and time consuming. He was increasingly stressed by the expectations of the management team on class attendance, performance and results. He just didn't appreciate stress. It wasn't what he had gone into teaching for. He sat in those meetings, longing to be back at home and playing with Michael.

Tony was surprised one day when he was called into the Sales Directors office at work and told he was to be promoted to an Area Sales Manager. His salary was increased; he would have a better company car and some expenses allowances as well. Tony was delighted and Jackie could see how thrilled he was when he came home that evening. As he talked through the promotion with her, he expressed his surprise that it had happened. He thought he was too young to have been considered for this role and was flattered. However, he also realised the enormity of the task as he would be responsible for six sales agents to deliver an annual sales target. Could he achieve that target and how would the Sales Agents (they were all older than Tony) respond to his promotion? Had they hoped to have been offered this promotion and would they be envious?

Jackie listened carefully. Andrew was fast asleep upstairs. She could tell Tony was excited but also anxious and stressed. Maybe though, she thought, that wasn't such a bad thing? She noted how he'd referred to how proud his Dad would have been had he known he had been promoted and perhaps the pressure and stress of this role would further help Tony in dealing with his Dad's death. Jackie could see that in overall terms the promotion was a really good thing to have happened. She was relaxed about Tony's concerns as she was sure his personality and drive would carry the day. Furthermore, as she was still working part time with the design team, she had an insight to the business. Without soliciting any comments, she had been pleased to hear on the grapevine how well his promotion had been received generally. She realised Tony was respected at work; she was really impressed and proud of him.

The next six months passed by quickly. It was late Spring when the four friends and families arranged to meet at the Red Lion for Sunday lunch. The reunion was long overdue. It was a warm, sunny day and they sat in the garden at the Red Lion catching up with each other's news and making a fuss of the children who were all growing so quickly! It wasn't long though before the four friends sat together and had a 'mutual rollicking' concerning that fact they'd not met for over six months. The conversation just flowed as always, the familiarity and friendship as strong as ever.

The strange thing was though that none of them had expected to be discussing stress! Yet it kept coming up. John talked about his extra responsibilities at school and his 'love' for management meetings while Steve explained he had now taken on full day to day responsibility on the farm as his Father spent an increasing amount of time away travelling. Paul was stressed by the hotel extension and the loans they had now secured whereas Tony was stressed by his promotion and the performance expectations of his Sales Director.

Several times they heard themselves saying there just weren't enough hours in each day and it wasn't until John rounded on them saying, 'Just a minute!' that they all paused and looking at John he smiled as he repeated some of the conversations back to them and asked if any of them felt stressed. They all laughed at themselves realising John had highlighted the issue of stress was afoot in all their lives and then readily agreed with John when he suggested another pint was needed!

As the new pints went down, they reflected further. They laughed at themselves and the conversations they'd just been having discussing about stress issues. 'Really, just how lucky are we really?' asked John. 'We can surely cope with a bit of stress in our lives. After all, we have beautiful wives, lovely families, nice homes, great jobs and amazing kids.' He then paused and added, 'And what's more we're all great sportsmen, aren't we?' With that last comment he glanced around his friends and with his eyebrow cocked knowing it would inspire some heated discussions. He wasn't wrong.

Steve spoke first and told them he was feeling indignant, and he was really upset. He'd been dropped from the Rugby first team to the second team as there was a younger, fitter colt player. The Coach had wanted to try him out three weeks ago as they were close to the end of the season. The first team won that match and the colt had played well. Steve had therefore remained in the second team for the last two games as well. The first team had won both their last two games and in the last one the colt had won the 'Man of the Match' award presented by the Coach. 'After all my years of loyal service for the club,' Steve protested, 'And that's how you get treated, it's not fair is it?'

He looked towards his friends for moral support. It was John who spoke first. He played for the same club and he knew all the background. 'I know,' he started, 'I've been playing second team rugby all season and seen these Colts coming through. The bottom line is they are keen, fit, fast and strong and have very good skills after all their years training in the Colts. I suppose it's good for the future of the Club, after all it's only a game isn't it and so long as we enjoy our rugby and a good pint or two afterwards, then that's all we want isn't it?'

Paul could see Steve was upset as he listened to John's reasoning and decided to distract the conversation by talking about the younger players emerging at his football club. Tony joined in to say he was finding the same at his football club too, yet he felt he was still in his prime and reckoned he'd still be playing in ten years' time!

It was John who then referred to his injuries. He explained that on some Saturday afternoons, when getting his kit on in the changing rooms he found his bruises from last week were still there! Paul laughed at this saying he was finding the same thing too and now thought that maybe they were all getting too old for active sport.

The others nodded. They were in their late twenties now, but it just seemed too early to consider that they were getting older. They just felt they were fighting fit and 'full of beans'. The conversation moved on the summer sports. They enjoyed sports that, like Rugby, were really competitive and needed good teamwork. Their main interests were in Cricket and Tennis though with increasing family responsibilities, they were finding that Cricket took all day whereas Tennis was usually just a couple of hours.

Jan caught Steve's eye at this stage and indicated that both David and Katherine were getting restless. He nodded back to say they'd leave shortly. He realised that time had flown by again; it was just so good meeting and talking with his old friends. 'I have to go soon,' Steve said to the other three and they all suddenly realised it was now late afternoon and time to get the young children home. Steve added that they must get together again soon and suggested a date for a late summer barbeque at the farm in September. The others all readily agreed.

It was later that evening, after the children had been fed, bathed and put to bed (David had needed a story about tractors) that Jan and Steve were able to have a quiet evening to themselves. Steve poured two glasses of white wine and they sat watching the sunset on the back patio. Jan asked Steve if he'd enjoyed the day and he reflected for a moment and said that although they'd not met together for some time, it was so nice to see how old friends could slip back into conversations so easily. They could tease and be rude to each other without any risk of offence and yet, their lives were changing so much. Jan raised her eyebrow and simply said, 'What do you mean?'

Steve chuckled to himself and went on to explain how they had all discussed the increased stress in their lives with responsibilities in their careers. He described John and Tony's promotions and Paul's plans to extend the hotel. Steve added that they'd laughed amongst themselves but at the end of the day there were the bills to be paid, plus loans and mortgages along with the day to day living costs. 'On top of all that,' he added, 'we also realised we're getting older. We're not as fit and fast as we used to be, younger lads are coming through not just in our Rugby Club but in Tony and Paul's football clubs too!'

Jan laughed with Steve as he recounted their conversation, but she could tell there was a serious undercurrent too. Steve went on to add that they'd realised what a change children had made to their lives in a way they just could not have imagined.

He then related John's stories about sitting in boring management meetings at school longing to be home with young Michael, and just playing with him. Jan smiled. Steve then asked Jan if she had enjoyed the afternoon as well and they carried on happily talking about their friends and how all the children were growing up so quickly.

The sun went down as the temperature dropped. Steve and Jan stepped back into their lounge. As Jan turned on the television, Steve sat down and started thinking about the barbeque in September and wondered what new developments might have occurred by then.

CHAPTER 12

DELIGHT PHASE
(25 – 40 YEARS OLD)
Men building family lives

THE BARBEQUE AT Steve's Farm that September was great fun. Steve was pleased his Father really took control of the occasion, his vitality and enthusiasm were clear to see as he organised Steve's younger sisters and brother during the morning. They helped him prepare the food and to set up the tables and chairs on the farmhouse lawn. Steve's Mother asked them to help her prepare the salads and puddings in the kitchen. There was already a buzz before the first guests arrived.

Steve's main task was to set up a barrel of beer in the barn door. He felt he had to test it several times just to ensure it was good enough for his friends. Jan observed his interest and with a 'tut tut,' she suggested he should be careful. Steve chuckled but knew she was right! Jan helped him set up a table alongside the barrel with soft drinks and glasses for the children and some chilled white wine for anyone who didn't like the beer. Finally, they found the rounders bat, balls and some posts and set up the rounders pitch in the field beside the garden lawn. The rounders match was to be 'boys versus girls'; the girls could see the boys were confident, perhaps a little too confident they wondered?

When Steve had made the invitation, he'd mentioned that there was no 'special occasion' to celebrate, it was just to get everyone together. The sun shone, it was warm, and they couldn't have hoped for a more pleasant afternoon. It was only Steve's immediate family and friends, a small group, but there was such a lot to catch up on.

For the first couple of hours the talking, drinking and eating was incessant, the laughter and exclamations were a joy to hear. Steve's Mother and Father stood back at one point and commented on what a happy occasion it was, how good it was to see the farm being used in this way and how important Steve's friends were to him and Jan.

The main focus of conversation between the friends were the children and how much they had developed. David, Steve and Jan's eldest was now five years old and had just started Primary School. The school uniform hadn't changed, it was still green and yellow in colour, but it was no longer necessary to wear caps. David was puzzled as he listened to his Father's friends discussing someone called 'Mrs Collier' and then he heard words like 'Collywobbles' and 'Wobblycolly'. He was puzzled as he saw his Father roar with laughter with his friends at the mention of these names, but he couldn't understand what was so funny!

Katherine, David's sister, was dressed in a beautiful pink dress and shoes. Jan explained to the other Mums how much time they'd taken preparing her hair and how the bow had to be positioned properly. The others all smiled and laughed that Katherine should be so self conscious at such a young age. Michael, John and Susan's son, and Andrew, Tony and Jackie's son, were about the same age as Katherine. At roughly three years old, they were at various stages of potty training and they only needed nappies at night.

These developments caused a lot of discussion. Notes were compared on the relative progress initially but then their attention was drawn by something else; there was a box of toys on a rug and Katherine, Michael and Andrew had started playing with them. The parents were watching and commented on how Katherine naturally picked up and played with the dolls from the box, whereas Michael and Andrew were playing with the tractors and cars? Why was it that boys were drawn to 'boys' toys' and girls to 'girls' toys?' A few glasses of wine and beer were drunk whilst the theories tumbled out. The amount of drink consumed ensured no obvious conclusion was reached but there was plenty of laughter as the theories evolved!

About an hour after everyone had arrived, Jenny was talking to Susan and discussing how she and John had changed their domestic routines since Michael had been born. Susan raised her eyebrows and laughed to explain it had completely transformed their lives but then hesitated as her sixth sense told her there may be a purpose behind Jenny's question. She looked directly at Jenny and just raised her eyebrow, Jenny blushed and looking back at Susan said, 'Don't tell anyone yet, we've only known ourselves earlier this week!' Susan leaned over and hugged Jenny saying how delighted she was. There were tears of joy in both their eyes.

It was Steve who was standing nearby at the time and leaned over to casually ask what Jenny and Susan were celebrating. It was just one of those moments; Susan and Jenny both looked at each other not knowing what to say. Jenny realised she had to reveal her news and standing up to clutch Paul's hand who was standing nearby she said, 'I'm afraid I've let the cat out of the bag!' Paul looked at Jenny and then glanced around as he realised everyone else had stopped talking and were looking at him. 'Errrr,' he stuttered, and then with a broad, proud smile explained he and Jenny had only found out earlier this week, that they weren't meant to tell anyone until three months, but he was delighted to say Jenny was pregnant! There were hugs of joy, and happy chaos for the next ten minutes.

Everyone was so pleased as up to that time, Paul and Jenny were the only one of the four couples who'd not had children. They had been so busy with the Hotel. But now their lives were about to change! As the chaos settled down, the four friends found they naturally congregated by the barrel to freshen up their pints and the conversation flowed with the beer. Paul commented that they really shouldn't have told anyone yet, it was just too early, and they hadn't even told their own families yet! He implored his friends to keep the news to themselves but realistically he realised he and Jenny had better tell their families pronto!

Paul went on to say that the Hotel extension had now been completed along with the extra rooms. He explained that he and Jenny had been happily surprised to see how much the Fitness Club membership had mushroomed and in turn, this had led to increased occupancy of the rooms and the restaurant in the hotel. Paul then added how anxious they had been in the last few months as a lot of money had been invested but that now, in recent weeks, he and Jenny had started to see the effects of all their hard work and had felt much more relaxed, 'So much so,' laughed Paul, 'that we invested in a bottle of wine a few weeks ago and had a romantic night!'

The three friends laughed with Paul and patted him on the back. Life was just so good! As they reflected and sipped their beer Paul noticed Tony glancing across to Jackie who seemed to gesticulate, 'Come on!' As Tony glanced away, Paul caught his eye and asked, 'Everything alright Tony? Tony hesitated, smiled and at that moment John and Steve also looked at him quizzically. It was almost exactly as Paul had done; Tony stuttered. 'Errrr,' and before he could say anything John blurted out, in more than a stage whisper, 'Is Jackie pregnant too?!' Tony's face said it all.

The party erupted again, no one could believe there were two items of such good news in one day. As everyone quietened down, Tony explained that they had been waiting for three months to let everyone know their news also but that today seemed the perfect opportunity to let all their friends know and, like Paul and Jenny had requested, if everyone could keep the news under wraps for the next few weeks. More beer and wine was consumed, the party had buzzed to start with but was now on 'full throttle' Steve said.

It was around half past three when Steve looked at his watch and realised that they needed to get the rounders match underway. He tapped his beer glass to announce the match was on! There were more cheers and then Steve was pleased as he heard both Jackie and Jenny volunteering to look after the children on the garden lawn. That meant the boys and girls teams were evenly matched, six players a piece, well, evenly matched by numbers at any rate. They tossed a coin and the boys decided to bat first, they also decided that there would be two innings. It was the boys over confidence that would be remembered for years afterwards. Was it the combination of high spirits, warm sunshine and excessive beer people would ask? Yet the real answers lay in the makeup of the girls' team. Susan had taught rounders at school and loved the game, Jan was sporty too, she not only liked sailing but loved all games and had good hand and eye coordination. But it was Steve's three sisters who were the real 'secret weapons' as they all loved the game having played regularly at school and were determined to win!

Little did the boys team know what they were up against. With great confidence they assumed they would win easily. There's a saying, 'How the mighty have fallen,' and this was just one of those occasions. It was almost embarrassing to see by how many times the boys missed the ball when batting! Jenny and Jackie were cheering on from the garden and when the boys missed the ball, they laughed and cheered even more which caused more distraction. Try as they might and although the boys were concentrating as hard as they could, it seemed to be getting worse and worse for them. Even Steve's Father, who could normally hold his drink, explained that the ball just seemed to be travelling in a blur! Everyone laughed as he said this and shortly afterwards the boys' team were all out and had only succeeded in scoring three rounders!

The girls' innings was a complete contrast, they hit the ball well and it went a long distance. Within a short time, they had scored ten rounders and exposed the boys' ball handling skills, even simple throwing and catching seemed to be a problem! They quickly scored two further rounders and put the boys in to bat again for their second innings. The boys realised they were in trouble! Steve gathered the team into a huddle on the batting crease and urged his team on. 'Come on!' he said, 'We can't be beaten, I'll never live this down with my sisters!' Steve's urging and encouragement didn't help, the boys continued to lack any coordinated approach. The beer had been good, too good, and they realised an historic defeat was a few minutes away. They were right; the boys could only manage five rounders in their second innings so they had been beaten by an innings and four rounders!

Before the rounders match the party had been buzzing. They were all now in a period of shock; it was only a game of course but the girls just couldn't believe they had won so well! They hugged each other and spoke animatedly, recalling various shots and catches. By contrast the boys were, to say the least, a little subdued. As they heard the girls celebrating, they just couldn't believe it. How could they have lost so badly? They found they naturally congregated by the barrel again to pour more pints and to commiserate with each other. Would they ever hear the last of this they asked?

The grimaces were in abundance and it was John who commented that the beer was really nice but that maybe they shouldn't have drunk so much before the game. The other boys all acknowledged him; this had clearly been their undoing they said. It was at this time that one of Steve's sisters casually asked Steve if they'd be up for a return match next year? There was a tease in her tone, Steve bit and without consulting with his team said, 'Of course, game on!' It was to be the start of an annual barbeque and rounders match that would go on for many years.

It was later that evening, when Steve and Jan were going to bed that Jan commented to Steve that she had not heard anyone mention the Male Menopause? Steve chuckled with her saying he thought the men (or boys' team) were still in a state of shock. He agreed what a great occasion it had been and that everyone had seemed to enjoy themselves. He then reflected further and agreed with Jan that it was strange the Male Menopause had not been mentioned, 'After all,' he pondered, 'when Uncle Frank argued that our instincts today are based on those three P's of our forefathers, he would have expected us modern day males to be good at the 'Provision' and 'Protection' skills and that we surely couldn't lose to a team of girls could we?' As he said this, he raised his eyebrow whilst looking at Jan and they both laughed and hugged each other. Jan smiled at Steve and asked if he was still any good at the other 'P?'. They both laughed and turned the lights off.

The next few weeks and months rolled by quickly. John and Steve found they were now regular second team players at the rugby club. Those colts had become men in their early twenties and were basically fitter and faster than John and Steve were, as they approached their mid-thirties. It took a few post-match discussions and reflections over a pint or two to come to terms with this. They were really playing for fun, the exercise was good, but they still felt very competitive and really wanted to win every game!

Similarly, Tony and Paul found they were not playing first team football. In Tony's case he was finding his work commitments were increasingly demanding but also, realising the second baby was due towards the end of the season, he agreed with his coach to play less often. There were plenty of younger players coming through. Tony often laughed with Jackie as the pregnancy progressed when they recalled Steve's comments that if there was a graph of chaos on the one axis against the number of children on the other that the plotted line would be exponential!

Tony also felt additional responsibilities for his Mum since his Dad had died. He made sure he contacted her regularly and was pleased how things were going so far; in particular she had become an active member of the Women's Institute and was really enjoying their meetings and outings.

Paul had reduced his commitment to football over a year ago. At the time it was to ensure he was 'on site' at the hotel as much as he could be to manage the contractors as they finished the new fitness club and room extension. As the building was being completed, he and Jenny had to launch a marketing campaign to offer fitness club memberships and to market the increased bedroom capacity.

Looking back though, Paul and Jackie felt their time had been well invested; they now had a very capable team running and promoting the facility. There was a very good feeling of 'team spirit.'

The two new babies arrived in early summer. Tony and Jackie's arrived first; it was a boy and they called him Thomas, a brother for Andrew. The birth though had been difficult. Thomas was a breech and needed to be delivered by caesarean section. Jackie had to stay in hospital for two nights for medical observation and monitoring. When they learned Jackie could go home, there was great excitement, mixed with concern for her health and comfort. Initially,

Jackie's Mum drove over and stayed for three nights when Jackie got home. Tony's Mum then came up on the train and stayed for the following three nights. Tony and Jackie really appreciated the help; Jackie was exhausted and needed the rest.

Meanwhile, Tony hadn't been able to keep up with his obligations at work and had needed to attend some meetings and make a lot of phone calls. After a week Jackie felt much better. Thomas was such a good looking little boy. Jackie couldn't believe how lucky she and Tony were.

Two weeks later, Jenny gave birth to a little girl. They called her Emily. The birth was thankfully quite straightforward, no complications. Paul and Jenny had been very concerned leading up to Emily's birth as they heard of the problems and discomfort Jackie had suffered. It was a huge relief that everything went so well and Emily was soon home with her parents. It was in the months to come though that Paul would joke with Tony about Steve's exponential graph theory when discussing the happy chaos that came with a new baby. Paul would say he just couldn't have imagined how someone so small could cause so much disruption. As he said this you could see how happy and proud, he was.

It would be some years later that the boys would reflect on their mid-thirties (or 'going on forties' as it was sometimes called) and smile; without fully realising it, they were at the zenith of their lives.

Everything was happening in terms of building their lives, their families, and supporting their careers. The children were developing their characters and personalities and it was during these formative years that the four friends had to provide support and guidance. Tony and Jackie would often laugh in the evenings after Andrew and Thomas were tucked up in bed. So many things were happening every day with things that had been said and the endless questions. There was certainly the need for firm direction when they played with balls near windows or crossing roads for example. It was exhausting but so rewarding to see them growing up into such fine young characters.

Steve and Jan were equally besotted with David and Katherine. Every day was different with hectic schedules getting the children to and from school. Mealtimes had to be fitted around the day to day activities of running a busy farm. Years later Steve would often say to Jan that they were hectic but happy days.

Paul and Jenny were just enchanted with Emily. Although the hotel was running very well maintaining high room bookings and fitness club membership, it was Emily that drew their attention first and foremost. The hotel was always of secondary importance they found. Jenny used to find Emily the prettiest dresses and Paul would spend hours playing with her in their own private quarters or in the local park.

John and Susan found their lives were equally busy. Susan returned to teaching on a part time basis, and this worked out well as their son, Michael went initially to nursery and then junior school. Susan organised her schedule so that she could take him in the mornings and John was then able to collect him late afternoon.

Yet alongside all the positive aspects of growing and developing families there was a downside too, stress. The four friends were finding that with the increased responsibilities in their careers there were a whole host of new challenges. John was initially promoted to head of his department at school and then, as he approached his forties, he was promoted to Deputy Head Teacher. Although he was flattered to be offered these roles, there were so many new tasks to undertake, mainly with staffing and administration duties. His actual teaching time was reduced, and he often reflected with Susan in the evenings that he really missed teaching.

Paul was stressed by the financial commitment he and Jenny had taken to finance the extension to the hotel. Although things were going very well, he felt he just couldn't relax, that he had to keep working with the marketing team to create more membership offers and boost numbers.

Steve found his Dad now had virtually no involvement in the day to day running of the farm. He preferred going out with his wife to the shops or meeting friends or going on holidays and day trips. Steve often heard his Father say, 'You work all your life to make money, it's important you find time at the end of your life to spend it!' Steve was happy to see how relaxed his Father had become and yet, on the other hand realised he now carried all the responsibilities. It was this burden of responsibility that Steve found stressful, and he was relieved he could discuss it with Jan in the evenings.

At one point there was a sad development on a neighbouring farm; the farmer committed suicide. He lived on his own with no family, his parents had died some years before. Jan and Steve realised he must have become lonely and how important family was.

Tony's career in the retail group really took off, mainly through hard work but he had some good luck on the way too. He had been appointed Area Sales Manager at a young age and was happily surprised that in the first two years his area achieved the highest sales with best growth. Jackie was still working as a member of the design team and often heard mention of Tony in the offices and how well he was doing. She felt immensely proud.

There was an annual sales conference to review progress and also to plan for the next year ahead. All the Directors attended this conference. They were impressed with

Tony, he was clearly someone who achieved results and he was also so enthusiastic about the company and its products. Tony hadn't appreciated the reviews the Board were undertaking at that time in which they were concerned about their age profile of the Board and that a lot of them were from an accounting background. They felt they needed to be making more informed decisions as they planned ahead. The general feeling was that it was time for change and to appoint new, younger blood, by appointing Directors who were closer to the markets they were trying to reach.

Tony hadn't been aware of the Board's thinking. He did know however, that many of the current Board were accountants as it was often referred to in humorous conversation when comments were often exchanged wondering if accountants really understood the business?

It was a two day conference; everyone was staying overnight. There was a real buzz in the bar that evening during pre-dinner drinks. The conversation focused in part on the discussions and ideas that had taken place that day. It was also a good opportunity to develop relationships as many of the delegates were from different locations and whereas they spoke almost daily on business matters there was rarely time to talk socially. Therefore, when they moved through to the dining room the four circular tables were laid out with named places to ensure everyone mixed and could get to know each other.

Towards the end of the dinner the company Chairman spoke and provided a broad overview of where he thought the business had progressed to and where it might go to in the future. The Managing Director responded to thank the Chairman saying that the formalities were now over (everyone cheered) but that he was looking forward to including the Chairman's thoughts when developing the new plans and ideas tomorrow. He then added that to lighten to occasion they had planned a games evening (eyebrows were raised) and passed over to the Personnel Manager.

The Personnel Manager was handed the microphone and explained the arrangements. There would be four teams, lined up as they were seated. There would be three events and the winning team would receive a 'mystery prize'. The last event was to be the 'best story', each table was asked to nominate someone on their table to tell a story.

There was a lot of concern as they learned of this last event. Tony looked around at his colleagues, but in that moment, he had an idea and before he knew it, he heard himself saying, 'I might know one!' The concerned looks of his colleagues were transformed to broad and relieved smiles and, 'Thanks Tony,' was muttered around the table.

The games evening proved to be just the right thing to do as it involved everyone. The laughter and leg pulling relaxed everyone, the drink helped too. They were all enjoying themselves, but it was also good for team building!

It was then the last event. Tony's table would be the last one to go. Tony listened to the other three stories which were good and created a lot more laughter. It was then Tony's turn; the microphone was passed to him.

'Have you heard the story about the blind snake and blind rabbit?' he began. All faces turned to Tony wondering what this story might be about. Tony took a deep breath and began. 'Well,' he started, 'One bright summer's morning, in the jungle, a blind rabbit was running down one path and a blind snake down another path. The paths intercepted and, sure enough, the two animals didn't see each other and collided, fell over and lay sprawling out at the intersection.'

Tony glanced around him. All eyes were in his direction, looking a little quizzical, 'As you may know,' he continued, 'animals in the jungle are always polite to each other and it was the blind rabbit who spoke first saying he was terribly sorry, that he was blind and just couldn't see where he was going. The blind snake was surprised to hear the blind rabbit say this and explained that he was blind also. The blind snake then asked if he could feel the blind rabbit all over to see what sort of a creature he was. The blind rabbit said, 'Go ahead' and the blind snake felt him all over saying, 'Ah, furry skin, long ears, bushy tail, goodness me you're a rabbit!'

The rabbit was very impressed, he smiled saying, 'Yes, that's amazing!' and then asked if he could feel the snake all over. The snake said, 'Yes', and the blind rabbit then felt him all over saying, 'Ah, slimy skin, forked tongue, no balls, goodness me you're an accountant!

There was an audible gasp and then a moment of stunned silence. People just could not believe the punch line Tony had just said! But then there were uncontrollable roars of laughter, tears rolled, backs were slapped, glasses were raised. There was certainly no question as to who had told the best story but equally how really close to home it was! The Chairman walked over to Tony's table and handed out the 'mystery prizes', they were pint beer pots in really nice cut glass. The Chairman shook everyone's hand and winked as he handed one to Tony saying, 'Us accountants have a lot to learn you know!' and laughed. Tony laughed with him.

The conversation at the bar that evening buzzed. Everyone enjoyed themselves but when referring to Tony's story it was in hushed laughter acknowledging how apt it was to their business but also speculating and asking whether any offence had been caused. The following day went well, and a lot of good ideas emerged on the future development of the business. Jan was impressed with the beer glass Tony brought home that evening but then horrified when she learned about the story Tony had told. She just couldn't believe he had the nerve to tell it and also queried whether any offence had been caused.

It was a month later that Tony was appointed Sales Director. He was the youngest Director the business had ever had.

Jan couldn't believe it. She had been anxious ever since Tony had returned from the conference and had worried that he might have caused offence. It was a popular appointment within the business and the Board. Tony was widely respected, but it was also generally acknowledged that with his relative youth and non accounting background, that he could provide new ideas. He was part of the 'new blood' that was required, and that new direction was now needed.

Tony's friends were amazed. They were in the Red Lion, on a Friday evening, a week after his appointment had been announced. Tony and Jan had brought Andrew and Thomas to see their Grandma. The children had been fed, bathed and were now tucked up, fast asleep in bed. Grandma was babysitting, she was happy, and Tony and Jan had an evening to themselves to spend with their friends. They were happy too. Likewise, Paul, John and Steve had made similar arrangements. It had been some time since the eight of them had been able to get together without worrying about their children. The Red Lion was the venue of choice as there were so many memories there for all of them. The evening had started with Tony's good news. Initially they just heard the news at face value, and it wasn't until Jan told them about the 'Blind Rabbit, blind Snake' story that their jaws dropped, they were aghast. There was plenty of laughter as they all realised how precarious the outcome was and what might have happened if Tony had caused offence.

It was a great evening, just so good to catch up with everyone's news. Particularly the children but also the future school and holiday plans. It was interesting that the boys tended to congregate at one end of the table as the evening progressed with their conversation focused on work and sport while the girls at the other end of the table focused on children and family issues. Jenny was saying how much she and Paul were hoping to have another baby, a sister or brother for Emily who was just the prettiest, sweetest little girl ever she said. The others smiled understanding how Jenny felt. Susan added how she and John hoped for another also. Jan explained Steve was keen on more children, possibly two more as he had loved being part of a large family. She speculated she might become a 'professional' farmer's wife and that she might never get to University!

Jackie then spoke but it was in a quieter tone and caught the other's attention. She explained how difficult the breech birth of Thomas had been and that she doubted whether she and Tony would have more children. There was a small tear in her eye as she reflected. The boys at the other end of the table were too involved in their conversation to hear what Jackie had said.

The boys had initially spoken about Tony's success and they congratulated him again. They then discussed their careers realising they had all made good progress and were enjoying themselves. It was when they discussed the increased responsibilities though that they started to talk again about stress; it was good to share their thoughts and experiences. It was John who lightened the conversation when he said he'd realised there was really only one advantage to becoming older. As the others raised their eyebrows he said, 'As men get older a greater number of women seem attractive' The others all thought for a moment and then burst out laughing. They then tried to think of other benefits to getting older and then realised there weren't any!

It was Paul who then said, 'Actually, I've been thinking!' The others all looked at him, feigned a grimace of anticipation, as he went on to say how he'd realised they were now going through their mid thirties and that forty was just around the corner. 'Why don't we plan a boys long weekend walking in Wales like we did some time ago to celebrate our forties?' The others all whooped and Steve said, 'Great idea!' in a loud voice. It caught the girl's attention and when they learned of Paul's idea, they all agreed. Jackie in particular remembered how that break had helped Tony and she teased the boys saying she realised that men had something called a 'Mid Life Crisis' ahead of them and that they would need all the breaks they could get to rest and relax and cope with life!

Although she was teasing them, and they all laughed, the expression 'Many a true word spoken in jest' went through Steve's mind at that moment. He wasn't the only one to have that thought!

It was a couple of years later, when John was thirty eight that he suffered a setback and his rugby playing career came to a sudden end. John had broken clear with the ball as they attacked the opponent's line. He was about to dive for the line but was heavily tackled from the side. He felt a weird sensation in his lower leg and heard a strange sound. He learned later that it was a spiral fracture of the left tibia, the fibula had snapped as well. An ambulance took him to the local hospital and that evening the bone was reconfigured, and metal plates and some pins were installed under a general anaesthetic. He came to and found his left leg was encased in a heavy plaster cast. He stayed in hospital for three days for post operation 'observation', but he was also helped by the Physios who showed him how to use crutches, particularly up and down the stairs.

Susan was devastated; not only was she rushing around to look after Michael, run the house and work part time at the local school but she now had the prospect of John needing her help whilst hobbling around the house! However, within a few days she realised her anxieties had been a little exaggerated as they came to terms with the situation. John had stayed for few days resting at home but had become bored. This coincided with the conclusion of the daily physio visits to supervise his post operation recovery. The physio was really pleased with John's progress to the extent that they suggested he could return to school. John was pleased with this; he had been in regular contact with his colleagues but really needed to be there in person.

New routines came into effect quickly. A colleague who lived nearby was able to give John a lift to and from school. John found ways to teach and participate in the school meetings and the administration staff were very helpful with lesson planning and preparation. The prognosis was that the plaster could come off in six weeks' time, but an unforeseen problem arose after four weeks. John felt something was wrong, his leg felt tight and a lot warmer than it had done initially. He telephoned the hospital and booked an appointment with the surgeon. Over the next two days the leg became more uncomfortable. On the third day, the day of the appointment, John booked a taxi to take him to the hospital as Jan was working. The surgeon listened to John's concerns and then opened the plaster. He then stood back as a great deal of thick, yellow puss emerged, the smell was certainly unpleasant.

Even the surgeon called it 'pungent!' He then added, 'We have a problem here. The wound is infected, you have a case of Osteomyelitis.' He went on to explain they would need to operate straight away to remove all the infection. John had no choice; he left a voice message on the house phone for Jan and within half an hour, he was in the operating theatre.

The next thing John knew he was looking at Susan. She was sat at the bedside reading a book with Michael on her lap. John couldn't understand what was happening, Susan looked a little fuzzy and out of focus. He murmured and Susan swung round, smiled at him and then John heard her calling out for the nurse. John started to recall all that had happened, his vision improved, he felt down to his left leg and realised a new plaster had been fitted, it felt lighter.

It wasn't long before the surgeon came to the bedside. He explained that they had cleaned the wound thoroughly and removed the plates and pins. John was surprised at this, it seemed too early. But the surgeon explained that actually, the bones had already started to re fuse, that being a spiral fracture there had been a lot of bone surfaces to 'mate' as he put it. His primary concern was to ensure all the infection had been removed. He felt they had been very thorough and that it had been necessary to remove all the pins and plates to ensure every area and each crevice in the bone had been cleansed thoroughly.

John glanced at Susan and realised how anxious she was as well. 'What should we do now?' John asked and was pleasantly surprised as the surgeon explained they should carry on life 'as normal' but that he would like to organise a schedule of regular inspections over the next twelve months. Susan was relieved to hear this. John returned home the next day and daily routines were established.

After six months the leg plaster was removed. John had returned to the hospital every month and was so relieved that no further infection had been found. John could now drive a car and push the lawn mower again! He and Jan were so relieved. The surgeon was also pleased as now that the plaster had been removed, he could ask the physiotherapists to work on the muscle structure in the leg. It had diminished a lot and needed rebuilding. The next six months were hard work but worth it; John's mobility felt fully restored and at the end of twelve months the inspection routine was reduced to an annual check up. That was unless John felt any discomfort and in which case, he was asked to return to the hospital immediately.

Steve, Tony and Paul had kept in regular contact with John during this recovery period and had often taken him for a drink at the Red Lion to assist with the recovery. Sometimes all four of them went but more often it was one or two of them as they were all leading such busy lives with work and family commitments. Sport, politics and family matters were commonly discussed but often they would chat about the upcoming trip to Wales again to celebrate being forty.

It was also during this period that more babies were conceived! Paul and Jenny had another daughter, Jane, a sister for Emily. Jenny had been really concerned about 'breech' births but found her conversations with Jackie very helpful to understand what should be done in that event. The arrival of Jane turned out to be straightforward and she was beautiful, 'Just like mother and sister!' proclaimed Paul as he raised his glass in the Red Lion.

Jackie and Tony explained they had decided not to have anymore, there was just no time. It was not just Tony's work commitments but looking after his Mum and all the activities they took Andrew and Thomas to; they were such energetic boys who never sat still!

John and Susan hadn't planned anymore either and were therefore really surprised to find she was pregnant. They then recalled the bottle of wine they'd drunk to celebrate the removal of the leg plaster! Peter arrived a few months later. Michael took his favourite toy, a model train to the hospital to give to his new brother for the first time he met him. John and Susan were so touched by his kindness.

It was Steve and Jan who surprised everyone with the birth of twins; a boy they called Ian and a girl called Helen. Steve was so surprised! He asked his Mother and there was no history of twins on their side of the family. Jan asked her Mum who recalled there had been twins, one of her Mum's Aunties but that they had lost contact over the years. Steve and Jan were so excited. The birth went well with Ian arriving ten minutes before Helen.

It was then, over the next few weeks, that the chaos truly set in and Steve's theory about the graph of chaos was highlighted again but now with a knowing grimace. It was so fortunate that Steve's Mother lived a short distance away and often popped in to help with the chores. David and Katherine enjoyed stopping over at their Grandparents house now and again. Jan's parents also drove over to help frequently, they had now both retired. Somehow, they coped and happy chaos abounded!

The four friends became forty! It was agreed to hold a joint party and barbeque at Steve's farm. In part, this was a practical decision, it was cost effective, parking was easy, and they all had young children to look after but also, it was a good opportunity to involve some of their friends in the annual 'girls versus boys' rounders match. Yes, the boys were embarrassed as since the match in the first year, they had only managed to win once, the girls had won all the other years! This year's barbeque was to involve more of their friends and relatives, and it was hoped some of the new boy players would make a difference. Despite that, the girls won again! Afterwards one of Steve's sisters commiserated with him. She could see Steve was trying to alter the format of the event and with a 'wink' in her eye, said how much she looked forward to next year's match. Steve smiled and then laughed with her.

A huge birthday cake had been made by Steve's Mother. The four friends gathered around the cake and the 'Happy Birthday' song was sung by all. When they finished, they heard some cows 'mooing' in a nearby field and everyone laughed. Disco music was then played and both young and old people danced. Some of the dancing was politely described as 'interesting' and various comments were made about whether the drink had any effect.

All good things come to an end and it was late afternoon when some parents started to leave as there were a lot of young children to be bathed and put to bed. The four friends had really enjoyed the occasion and gathered with Steve and Jan to thank them for the party. The farewell conversations though were dominated by the prospect of the following weekend. They were setting off for the return walking and drinking trip to Wales. This time though they were staying for two nights.

Tony arrived at Steve's farm early the following Friday morning and parked his car. It was a beautiful sunny morning with blue, cloudless skies and the birds were chirping. Tony felt good. Steve and Tony drove over to Paul and John's houses to collect them. The four friends were in high spirits. It would be good to get away from their normal routines for a few days.

Whilst driving, Steve reflected on their previous short break in Wales and how careful they had been with Tony fearing he might have been close to a breakdown following the death of his Dad. What a contrast now, Steve thought, Tony was the most outgoing of all of them and talked with such enthusiasm.

Unbeknown to Steve, John and Paul were having similar reflections, it was just so good to see the changes in Tony. It wasn't long before Tony referred back to when they had decided to take this break and how Jackie had spoken about how men suffer the 'Mid Life Crisis' He recalled she had said that they would all need a break to get away from the stresses and strains of life.

As they talked more, they referred to the Male Menopause and realised they had not discussed that either for some time. Where had their lives got to, where were they now and where were they going to? The scene was set, just the four friends on their own, in the middle of their lives and with plenty of time to talk.

It was John who then spoke saying he thought this so called 'Mid Life Crisis' was when men realised, they had gone through the peak of their lives and that they needed to cope, to come to terms with the fact they weren't as fit and strong as they used to be. Steve chipped in agreeing with John and adding that really the Mid Life Crisis was the start of the Male Menopause and those 3Ps. He chuckled and went on to say that in terms of the modern day 'provision' front they were now all in stable careers earning decent incomes but realised how hard they had all worked and that in terms of 'protection' they were all moving away from active sports and look at the recent injury to John? 'Finally,' Steve said, 'On the 'procreation' front our children are all evidence to how active we've been in the past!' They all laughed.

It was Paul who then spoke saying, 'You know what?' and the others all glanced over, 'The thing that got to me in recent years has been the number of times we've lost to the girls at rounders!' The others all nodded as Paul carried on saying, 'The thing is, us blokes, we just don't like losing, do we? It's in our blood to be competitive and those girls have shown we're not what we thought we were!'

Tony groaned at this saying, 'Blimey Paul, what you're saying is that we are now in a Mid Life Crisis and have been in the last few years and just not recognised it?' He then added, 'Or maybe we just couldn't or didn't want to accept we are getting older and getting less able? The weird thing is that the evidence is in front of our noses every day. What I mean is just look at the best sporting teams in the world, most of the players range in age from late teens to early thirties. Once we have got over that age in our lives, we've found it difficult to come to terms with losing.'

Tony then turned to Steve and added how he remembered when he had been dropped from the Rugby first team and hadn't found that easy to come to terms with. Steve nodded and smiled. It was true he said, in fact he still found it difficult to come to terms with he added and they all laughed with him.

They had booked the same farmhouse Bed and Breakfast they had stayed at before. The owners remembered the four friends and Steve in particular, as he ran a farm like they did. A packed lunch had been prepared; the four friends set off soon after arrival although Steve had to be dragged away from an involved discussion about a new form of cattle feed!

The walk that afternoon was glorious. A winding trail alongside a rocky stream, then rising through woods and open fields which led along a ridge of hills. They ate the packed lunch on some large rocks on top of the hills. The views were just magnificent. Some miles away, a long way down in the valley, they could just see the Red Dragon pub, their destination that evening and with a few pints in prospect, they were working up a thirst!

It was John who took went back to talking about the Male Menopause. 'You know what?' he began, 'That conversation we had in the car about men getting older and becoming less able?' The others all nodded, 'Well, it's reminded me of something someone said about one of the benefits of getting older. 'Ah, you mean there are some after all?' said Tony. John went on to say that they had discussed it briefly, and recently, when Tony had advised them of his promotion to becoming a Director. Steve recalled and said, 'Ah yes, I remember, it went along the lines that the older we get then there are more attractive women in the world?' John was pleased Steve recalled this and said he had been considering if there had been any other benefits? The four friends started the long descent down the valley to the Red Dragon.

The conversation was disjointed as they walked but they carried on discussing the benefits and their experiences of getting older. John added that although there were more attractive women as you got older, there was another saying; 'It's alright getting your appetite away from home, so long as you eat at home!' The others all laughed at this but then took interest in Paul as he explained there were several regular bookings by couples at the hotel, particularly at lunch times. He'd often discussed this with Jenny. It was none of their business (of course, he added) but it was interesting that most of these couples were middle aged. 'Maybe men going through their midlife crisis?' said Paul and then added, 'Maybe it's in response to this Mid Life Crisis, and then the Male Menopause, that men just need affairs to prove they are still attractive, that they are still capable of making love?' The others nodded, maybe Paul was right.

It was Steve who then spoke saying that John's expression. 'It's alright getting your appetite away from home, so long as you eat at home!' had stuck a cord with him as over the years they had many part time, seasonal female workers on the farm helping with various harvests. They always enjoyed some banter, often with a 'suggestive overtone' as he put it, but that there was 'no way on this earth' that he could imagine anything serious developing. 'Actually,' Tony added, 'We've got a problem at work now. One of our Area Sales managers has recruited a very attractive sales representative. We're sure they are having an affair.' Steve asked why this was a problem and Tony explained that when it came to bonus allocations for the area, he was certain the Area Manager was allocating a higher proportion to her than was fair. Tony went on to add that the Area Sales Manager was in his early forties. A family man with children and Tony wondered if he was going through some sort of a midlife crisis as well, maybe leading to his male menopause?

The conversation developed further as they came down the hills and into the woods. John spoke about money, that he and Susan weren't rich by any stretch of the imagination but as they had got older they were more 'comfortable' as he put it and could now plan ahead to pay off the mortgage, also to fund Michael and Peter if they wished to go to university. They were also contributing to 'final salary' pensions as a part of their pay arrangements as teachers. 'I guess,' added John, 'That when we go back to your caveman instincts Steve, that this is all to do with the 'provision' instinct and how it occurs in our lives today?'

Steve said he thought John was right, that it did relate to the 'provision' instinct. He then added that in his case they had some wealth on paper being farmland, buildings and equipment but added the problem he and Jan would have would be to convert this to cash. Particularly in future, he added, as the children grew up and there might be four lots of School fees, University fees and weddings to fund!

Paul then said he and Jenny were in a similar position to Steve, that all their wealth (such as it was, he added) was tied up in the business. He was happy they were servicing the Bank debts they had undertaken to fund the fitness club and accommodation expansion but had only recently looked into Pensions. 'I guess it's been the arrival of Emily and Jane that's made us think about the future,' he said.

They had now come down through the woodland and were walking alongside another rocky stream. There was only another two or three miles to the Red Dragon. As they sat down on the rocks for some refreshment, it was Tony who then said, 'I've just been thinking, looking back at the conversations we've had coming down these hills. First of all, about men and affairs, all driven by the Steve's caveman's instincts of 'procreation' apparently, and then all the 'provision' instincts to fund our growing families.' John was puzzled and couldn't see what had made Tony was thinking of until he then added, 'Maybe after all, there is such a thing as the Male Menopause. Maybe we're all going through this Mid Life Crisis and the Male Menopause is kicking in for all of us from here on?'

Everyone went silent for a while; the sound of the trickling stream was soothing. They were thinking through the conversations they had been having. Tony then spoke to say he and Jackie had been also talking a lot recently about this 'provision stuff', as he put it adding they had not thought of it in that way but that it had just seemed sensible to plan ahead for their boys, Andrew and Thomas. He and Jackie both had pensions, the mortgage would be paid off on the house by the time they were in their fifties which would be when they might also need cash to fund University education. 'It's all very stressful, this provision stuff,' Tony added. 'On top of everything else, Jackie wants us to take the kids on regular holidays, to show them the world she says, and then adds that we can't spend the money when we're dead!'

At this point Steve thought they should change the subject and said, 'Come on, I'm gasping for a pint!' They all agreed and set off alongside the stream towards the Red Dragon. The conversations continued with more stories about provision and procreation, but also questioning whether they were really going through a Mid Life Crisis, and had they started the Male Menopause? The first pint went down 'without hitting the sides', a second round was quickly ordered. It was some pints later, and after a good meal, that John suddenly said, 'You know what?' As the others glanced over, he said, 'We've spoken a lot about Steve's thoughts on provision and protection caveman instincts today but none of us have mentioned the other instinct, you know, protection?'

There was a pause as the others realised that John was right. Then Tony spoke, saying that obviously cavemen had spears and clubs which is clearly not what modern day man would carry around with him. He then added that modern day man would clearly defend their families 'to the hilt' and went on to explain he meant they would defend to the death as caveman would have done. The others all nodded. Tony then said that maybe modern day man's protection instincts were surely evident in the way they craved to be good at sport and to be competitive? This thought inspired a lot of conversation as the four friends recalled their limited sports careers and then compared themselves with football, rugby and tennis stars.

Breakfast the following morning was great. Bacon and eggs but again, with all the trimmings. There were lashings of coffee and toast, as much as they could manage. The four friends set off, again with a packed lunch, but in a different direction. This time to an old mining railway that was still operational but now just for tourists. The train would take them off to the old slate quarries high up in the mountains. It was again a sunny, dry day, just perfect weather for walking and the views from the Slate Quarry were just magnificent. John had checked out a route for them, following old sheep trails along the mountain tops. There was a strong breeze which in part was welcome, as it was cooling on what was a sunny, warm day, but on the other hand conversations were difficult.

Clearly all four friends were thinking and reflecting as they walked. Whenever they stopped for refreshment beaks and also lunch, the conversations quickly swung into Mid Life Crisis and Male Menopause thoughts. The same topics were covered but many more anecdotes were recalled, and ideas emerged.

John was talking to Steve about the protection instinct at one point and referring to the rugby club. He speculated that neither of them would play rugby again, so should they take up tennis. John was very enthusiastic and explained that now his left tibia and fibula had fully recovered he definitely wanted to get back into competitive sport. They agreed to visit the local tennis club together when they got back. Paul overheard and said he felt he could no longer commit to the football club as there wouldn't be time away from the hotel. He went on to explain that Jenny's parents were looking to retire from their hotel and to plan some holidays whilst they still had relatively good health. The idea was that Paul would step in as a relief manager initially but that maybe, in years to come, he might run both hotels as a small group.

With that thought in mind Paul asked if John and Steve could find out if there were any social membership options as he would like to play with them now and again. Tony was listening too; tennis wasn't for him he said but that he was thinking of training to be a soccer coach and then support Andrew and Thomas as they grew older. The train took them back down that evening, the views were again magnificent.

When they arrived at the station at the bottom of the mountain they were still talking and set off towards the Red Dragon without discussing where they should go that evening. It was when they were about ten minutes away that Paul suddenly said, 'Just a minute, where are we going?' The others all stopped and looked at him and realised they had headed off without discussing or thinking where they were going. It was John who simply said, 'You know what, the Red Dragon has become our second home, just like the Red Lion!' It was Paul who mimicked Steve and said, 'Come on, I'm gasping for a pint!'. They all laughed together.

Breakfast again the following morning was a 'complete treat' as Steve put it. The landlady heard him say this as she brought more toast in and she beamed with pride. After breakfast they paid their bills and were given another packed lunch. It was Paul who said how much he'd enjoyed it and that they must do it again. The landlady waved as they drove off. Paul said to the others how much he thought they should all do it again and they all agreed with him.

Steve had planned something different for the final day. It was a bit of a dog leg, but he drove off to the coast explaining to the others that it was for 'sun, sand, vanilla ice cream and fish and chips'. They all laughed but that is exactly as the day turned out. There was good sunshine, Tony bought a beach ball and they played football on the sandy beach. Tony and Steve claimed they beat John and Paul and an energetic conversation took place with no resolution. They laughed at themselves realising their competitive (or protection) instincts were still as strong as ever!

They ate the fish and chips on a sea wall at lunchtime, realising they would have to head off after lunch to get home and help with bath time routines. They had missed their families. The break had been very good for all of them, and they reflected during the home journey on their Mid Life Crisis with good humour and wondered how they might cope with the upcoming Male Menopause.

CHAPTER 13

DELIGHT PHASE
(40 – 60 YEARS OLD)
Men supporting family lives

♂ **THE FOUR FRIENDS** were now in their early forties, life sped by, largely driven by the demands of their growing families. Their careers had also become more demanding with increased responsibilities and stress. They were also starting to change physically, even Tony's magnificent moustache had some grey hairs. The banter between the four friends often highlighted their changes; Tony would respond to comments from Steve that his greying moustache was in preference to Steve's greying head of hair and the emerging bald patch!

But the banter was never serious, it was just part of 'our coping mechanism' John said, who rarely made any personal comments. Paul was conscious though that he was putting on weight and decided it was time to take an active interest in the hotel's fitness club. It wasn't long before he started to 'shape up' as he put it. John noticed and he then joined the fitness club too but Steve didn't as he was physically active every day on the farm. Tony was too far away to join but he started to focus on fitness training with his local soccer club.

They still met in the Red Lion and this was often when Tony let the others know he was visiting his Mum. Occasionally, just the four of them met and the subjects of Mid Life Crisis and the Male Menopause would come up. It was on one of these occasions that Paul said something that none of them would forget; he was referring to the Male Menopause and simply said he had read recently what an irony life was for men who came out of a Vagina and that they then spend the rest of their lives trying to get back in!

The others all rolled about laughing at this and often referred to it in future conversations. It touched their consciousnesses as they questioned just what this procreation drive or instinct was all about but, on the other hand, thank goodness as the future of the human race depended on it!

Over the ensuing years the boys versus girls' rounders match was held annually. The girls made sure they continued to win, even though the boys tried to alter the arrangements, but with no success. Steve's sisters kept a close eye on things as they really enjoyed the event.

The four friends walking breaks tended to take place every two years; it wasn't possible every year they found, due to other family commitments. They didn't go back to Wales for a long time, as they realised there were other parts of the country to visit and over the next few years, they went to the Lake District, the Yorkshire Dales, the Scottish Lowlands, the west coast of Ireland and Dartmoor as well. In fact, the walks encouraged all four friends to maintain their fitness and they would often say that they wanted to walk as much as they could, whilst they could!

It was during these discussions in the Red Lion and also on the walks that the conversations about their children arose with increasing frequency. The Male Menopause discussions almost took a back seat as the four friends shared stories about how their children were developing and what they needed to do to support them. They were all learning how to be parents!

Steve's son, David, was the eldest and he had now entered his teenage years. The expression 'typical teenager' often came into play but it was interesting to hear Steve's frustrations as on the one hand David tested his Father's patience yet on the other hand Steve was just so proud of him. On one occasion Steve found that David had been sampling some of his whiskeys in the drink's cabinet, on another he had driven the farm van around the farmyard. Steve would share his anguish with his friends over a pint and seek some moral support whilst also regaling his friends with stories of David's accomplishments on the school's rugby and cricket teams as he apparently scored a try after a thirty yard solo dash or batted for the school first team scoring over fifty runs.

Tony and John were very interested in David's development as they both had boys and although a lot younger than David, they could see what might lie ahead and what they could learn from Steve's experiences. Paul was interested in the development of Steve's daughter, Katherine. She was a lot older than their two daughters, Emily and Jane. It was interesting, when Steve spoke about Katherine, to realise how sensitive she was to people's feelings. This was particularly noticeable when she came home in the evenings with stories about her friends at school but also, in the privacy of their home, how very moody she might become, particularly if she was tired or hungry.

'It's a funny old life,' said John one day and when Tony asked what he meant, John explained he'd been thinking about their recent discussions and the emerging parenting skills but that actually it's just the 'cycle of life' as he put it. Tony raised his eyebrow and John carried on explaining that he suspected their parents would have had similar anxieties to the ones they had been discussing and that there was no 'Parents Handbook' to help. 'In fact,' John continued, explaining that parenting was all about discovery by chance or 'serendipity' as he believed it was called.

The conversations continued to develop every time they met to include sport, careers, Male Menopause, wives, families and parenting but increasingly, and sadly, as they progressed through their forties and into their fifties, they found they were discussing death with increasing regularity.

Of the four friends, it was Tony who had the sad experience of losing his Dad. At the time many people had said, intending to be kind and supportive, that you never get over a death. Tony had found this was true, but he also recalled the state of depression he had gone through, then the help and support he had received from Jackie and his close friends. He would never forget that. He realised support was so important but also, that he hadn't appreciated how much self-discipline had been needed to come to terms with it. No, he would never forget his Dad.

Steve's Father then died suddenly. It was a complete shock. He died peacefully in his bed. It was very early one morning when the phone rang on Steve's bedside table. Steve could hear it was his Mother, but she was distraught. She kept saying that she, 'Couldn't believe it,' she was just inconsolable and couldn't stop crying. Through her sobbing she explained they had gone to bed the previous night and kissed as they had done for years to say 'goodnight' and put the lights out. In the morning she found him just lying there. She had shaken him several times and called his name with no response. The awful truth then dawned on Steve.

It was only a few minutes later when Steve arrived at the house. He was half dressed and so shocked by the telephone call from his Mother. He hadn't understood her at first as she was sobbing so much but then, he too realised the awful truth. As Steve came into the kitchen, he found his Mother sat at the kitchen table, sobbing. Steve bent down on one knee and put his arms around her shoulders protectively and they both sobbed together. After some time, Steve stood up without saying anything, and made a cup of tea. His Mother looked up as he handed her the tea. They both calmed a little and started to come to terms with the situation. Steve asked his Mother if he could go upstairs to see him. She nodded. As Steve entered the room, he just couldn't believe what he saw. It was perhaps the realisation, the realisation that this wasn't a bad dream, it was real. His Father looked so peaceful, yet so lifeless.

Steve found his Mother's dressing gown on the back of the bedroom door and took it back downstairs with him. She was still sobbing; Steve wrapped the dressing gown around her and then sat her in a more comfortable chair explaining he needed to let people know. His Mother nodded but was still sobbing. Steve then phoned Jan; she was still half asleep but also shocked and she asked how Steve was.

They realised they needed to let the children know. Jan agreed she would wake them up and that it was probably best to get them into their normal routines for school. Steve's brother and three sisters all lived away in different towns. They were completely shocked; they just couldn't believe what had happened. It was still early morning, and they were just waking up. They all indicated they would come straight over to the farm to support their Mother.

Steve then contacted the family Doctor to arrange a death certificate. He quickly realised though, that they may need to report it to the Coroner. This was because the death had been unexpected and that an autopsy may be required to discover the cause of death. Steve's Mother found all this unsettling, so it was good that Steve's sisters had arrived to calm her, to get her dressed and make more tea. It was a very difficult situation. Steve contacted the Funeral Directors and arranged for his Father's body to be collected. When they arrived Steve and his brother helped to move some furniture on the landing and in the hallway to allow the trolley with their Father's body on to get by. The trolley was loaded into the Funeral Directors collection vehicle and driven away. Everyone cried.

A rota was agreed. That night Steve's brother would stay with his Mother for company and then Steve and his sisters arranged to stay over on other nights. Steve would be popping in regularly every day anyway as he moved around the farm. After a few days they heard the Death Certificate had been issued with the cause shown as 'natural'. The funeral arrangements could now be made. It was during this time that one of the sisters found an 'Expression of Wishes' form relating to one of the Steve's Father's pensions. It was a recent document in which Steve's Father had asked to be cremated but that his ashes should be buried under a tree on the edge of the farmyard. In his own hand her Father had written, 'So that anyone can come over and talk to me whenever they wish!' Steve's sister burst into tears when she read this. When she showed it to the rest of the family, they all cried and smiled too, realising he had anticipated his death and yet wanted to find some way of maintaining contact.

The funeral was arranged. Initially, close family and friends were invited to the local Crematorium, a short service was held with readings and a hymn. More tears were then shed as the curtains closed as they said goodbye.

A few days later a service was organised at the local Church to celebrate his life. The Church was packed, Steve's Father was a well-known member of the local community and highly respected. Steve did one of the bible readings. He felt he might get too upset to do the eulogy and so that was provided by an old farming friend. Steve's Mother had chosen two of her husband's favourite hymns. Everyone said it was a such lovely service and a fitting tribute to a truly great man. It was only a short distance from the

Church to the farm. Everyone was invited back afterwards for some refreshments. The funeral cortege was long as the cars and pedestrians streamed from the Church to the farm. There was plenty to drink and a large buffet had been prepared. It was just so nice to 'relax, mix and chat' and to celebrate his life with so many friends.

During the afternoon it was quietly explained to the guests that Steve's Father's ashes had been buried under a tree in the farmyard in line with his wishes. Everyone was touched by his invitation that should anyone wish to discuss anything with him they should stand under the tree and just talk. It caused some happy smiles as they realised the kind thoughts he must have had.

Steve and his brother got into a conversation with the farming friend who had provided the eulogy. They wanted to express their thanks; the farmer had no way of knowing though what an effect the eulogy had on Steve. It was just one of those coincidences in life, that over the last few months Steve and his friends had been talking about generally on walks and in the Red Lion. They had discussed the male 'cycle of life,' all about their development as men, going from formative years, then parenthood leading towards the 'Midlife Crisis' then alongside that the emergence of the Male Menopause until ultimate death.

The farming friend had certainly not spoken in those specific terms but the way he outlined Steve's Father's life had caused Steve to reflect and to think about his Father in ways he hadn't before. When the farming friend had talked through his memories chronologically, starting from when they had been at school together, then as a sportsman, Steve found he was nodding his head recognising what his Father had worked through and realising it was so similar in so many ways to his own. Indeed, it was the Cycle of Life! The eulogy then continued describing his early working years on the farm and then getting married, learning how to be a parent and then retiring; it all rang so many bells. But it was then that Steve's attention was really gripped as he spoke about the difficulty Steve's Father had retiring and initially handing over to Steve but then recognising what a good job Steve was doing and learning how to step away, to fully relax and enjoy his retirement.

Steve didn't share his thoughts with his brother or the farming friend. He just wanted to express his thanks without revealing the effect the eulogy had on him. There were still plenty of guests in the farmyard, but it was Tony who sidled over to Steve and whispering in his ear said. 'Wow, that eulogy, so many parallels to things we've discussed?' Steve looked at Tony and smiled saying it really had made him think too but they both realised they couldn't develop the discussion further and agreed they should meet soon in the Red Lion.

It was two weeks later, and Tony was back visiting his Mum with Jackie and the children. It had been arranged that just the four friends would meet in the Red Lion. Steve welcomed the opportunity to talk with them. He still just couldn't believe his Father had died; it was still a shock. Steve spoke for some time explaining that every day as he worked around the farm, he was reminded of conversations or things they had done together. He then spoke about the number of times he had stood under the tree in the farmyard and spoken to his Father. It was comforting to feel close to him.

It was Tony who first referred to the eulogy saying how much it had made him think, as the farming friend had taken them through Steve's Father's life chronologically. There were clearly so many parallels to their lives. Paul and John nodded in agreement as Tony spoke and over the next hour or so they reflected on the eulogy and made comparisons with things happening in their own lives.

At one stage, when talking about the Male Menopause, John spoke about Susan and said she was clearly going through the female menopause now as she had started to miss her periods. She was also feeling tired, not sleeping as well as she used to and was putting on weight as well. The conversation opened then up as the other three spoke about the symptoms they had noticed in their wives also. There was clearly physical evidence in what was happening to them and this was having psychological effects also making them moodier and more tearful than usual. It was Tony who said that he spoke quite a lot with Jackie about her experience, to give her any help and support but they would never talk about the Male Menopause. Then with a smile and a wink in his eye added, 'Because there's no such thing as the Male Menopause!' The others all laughed with him.

It was Paul who then spoke saying that just listening to John there were very similar things happening with Jenny and him and that Jenny wouldn't ask about Paul's ageing issues. 'Maybe,' he continued, 'it's because men are just meant to cope and get on with our lives?' and then added, 'It's all connected with that protection instinct?'

The others all nodded wryly as Paul said this and then Steve added, 'You know what?' The others listened as Steve said, 'The real problem is us, Paul's right you know. We are expected to cope, it's just not in our basic instinct to admit to any weakness or frailty. We don't readily talk about these things amongst ourselves, we certainly don't discuss them with our wives, do we?' The others looked on but no one said anything. There was silence. It was one of those moments of realisation, one they would remember.

John broke the silence asking, 'Does anyone want another pint?' It was a simple question and a much welcomed break to the almost 'trance like' mood they had got themselves into, thinking about what Steve had said. The smiles broke back on their faces as the pints were ordered, but there was a feeling of 'unfinished business' amongst them. They had got to a stage of realising, ironically, that the problem, the recognition of the Male Menopause and male ageing issues was theirs. Yes, as Steve had simply said, males are expected to cope, but should they actually be talking more readily about these so called 'ageing issues' amongst themselves and with their wives?

'If you identify a problem, you're halfway to sorting it,' John said and added that he thought that was an old Chinese saying but relevant. He carried on and asked, 'So, what are our ageing issues?' The four friends looked at each other, they realised time was moving on, that they only had around an hour before reporting back for 'Domestic Duties'! Tony then said, 'Let's brainstorm them. We do this at work, let's just list what we think our ageing issues are, here and now, and then we can talk in more detail about them over future pints?'

The others nodded in agreement and Tony said, 'I'll start!' The conversation over the next hour was certainly energetic, such was the long term friendship amongst the four friends. It was open and honest too. Many topics cropped up and included stress, greying hair, baldness, dementia, physical fitness, sporting ability, weight gain, depression, suicide and midlife crisis. As every topic was mentioned they started to discuss it in some detail but then realised that they didn't have time. They found they had to nudge each other and move on. It was when Tony said 'Erectile dysfunction' though that there was an initial hush and then laughter; it was really nervous laughter and they realised they would need a lot of time to talk about that one as Tony added, 'It's really all to do with our procreation instinct'.

The hour slid quickly by. It was Tony who had a particularly close eye on the time as he knew Jackie was anxious about being on her own with his Mum and looking after the boys as well. He explained to the others that he would have to go and fended off the allegations about being 'hen pecked' with a smile and some gesticulation as the others laughed. He then added that there were just two other items he wanted to mention before dashing off.

The others then listened attentively as Tony said he thought there might be a trick that they had all missed, that it was right under their noses and something they could learn from women. The others were now fully engaged with Tony and wondered just what he was about to say. 'Just think about this for now,' said Tony, 'What we men need is a 'Men's Institute' just like the 'Women's Institute or WI.' Tony could tell from the expression on his friends faces that they weren't initially impressed, time would be needed to discuss the idea further!

Tony, wisely, didn't try to explain the idea there and then. He realised time was needed for them to all ponder on this conversation and then, the next time they met, he would raise the idea of a 'Men's Institute' again. It was Paul who then asked if Tony had something else? Tony explained it was only a small thought, but he had been thinking back to some years ago, when Steve had spoken about his Male Menopause discussions with his Uncle Frank and the idea that everyone has a purpose in life. Tony continued to say that it had made him wonder just what was the male role and purpose in life was? Tony then asked, 'Just what precisely is my 'Raison d'etre as the French call it'? He glanced around at the others quizzically.

As Tony looked around him Paul said 'Oh!' He explained he could see what Tony was thinking, it was all getting a bit deep but very interesting, he added that he could see that they would need loads of pints to talk these items through! At this point the glasses were clinked as they said goodbye to Tony, but it was as he was leaving Paul added, 'There's something else you know, we should also start these discussions about male ageing with our wives, shouldn't we?' Thumbs went up in agreement as they finally said goodbye.

Over the next few years, as the four friends progressed through their fifties, they regularly discussed examples of the ageing process and with their wives also. It became a natural, open and relaxed topic of conversation. They agreed it shouldn't dominate their conversations as they feared they might all become depressing hypochondriacs but on the other hand they wanted to be able to talk about it whenever the mood took them.

It was the subject of 'erectile dysfunction' that they were most sensitive about. Initially, in their early fifties they would only talk about it in a passing reference and indicate they had heard there was medication available. The notion they should cope was strong, they couldn't easily acknowledge their sexual appetite was slowing. By the time they got towards their late fifties though the subject occurred more regularly, sometimes with some humour making a connection to the amount of beer they had drunk! It was in their own privacy, and talking with their wives, they realised their sexual lives were slowing down and that medication did have a role to play!

Every time they met there were numerous discussions about the male ageing process as the four friends sought to understand more about the Male Menopause and look back at the so called Midlife Crisis that they had been through. The most common subject they discussed was stress. They were all in demanding roles and working hard.

In Tony's case he was now responsible for all the commercial teams; these included the field sales teams, the overseas agents, the central marketing team, and the telesales operation. There was a huge expectation of Tony as every team needed to be well led and motivated, targets had to be achieved, monthly reports were required.

The Board expected Tony to report on time, every month. Underperformance was scrutinised.

Time was always a precious commodity. He realised he often missed being with his children as they grew up. Jackie was immensely proud of Tony and he was often referred to when she was talking to her colleagues in the design team. On the other hand, and in the privacy of their family, she worked hard to give Tony space to relax but also spend good time together as a family. Jackie often reflected and realised how important it was that Tony could talk openly with her about stress. There was no recurrence, thank goodness, of the way Tony had felt and behaved as his Dad had died.

In Paul's case, as they progressed through their fifties, he found he was increasingly required to manage Jenny's parents' hotel as well as their own. Like Tony, this took a lot of time when he would have preferred to be with his young daughters as they grew up. Jenny could see Paul's mix of responsibilities caused him a lot of stress, but she was really impressed to see how cordial and calm he seemed to be on the exterior. He never overreacted or became angry. He patiently dealt with situations as they occurred and worked to find the best solutions. In fact, she thought proudly to herself, he had become a true hotelier!

John was perhaps the least stressed of the four friends. He had remained at the same school all his working life. Yes, in his role as Deputy Head, there was plenty of stress as he dealt with day to day issues. But, on the other hand, he was working in a structured environment where situations could be often processed quickly and effectively dealt with. He gave positive encouragement and direction to those involved. In fact, he quite enjoyed it. There were two other aspects he realised that helped him to cope; one being that Susan was a part time teacher and fully understood the stresses. This was really important as John often felt completely exhausted when he got home and needed a good sleep.

The other positive aspect was the retirement arrangements. John could look forward to retiring at an early age with a final salary pension. They knew they wouldn't be rich, but the security of the guaranteed pension gave them a lot to look forward to as they planned to travel and 'see the world.'

In Steve's case, the stress was closer to home. His eldest son David was just graduating from Agricultural College and Steve was in his mid-fifties. In some ways the situation that was emerging was really amusing, it was so similar to the situation Steve had been in with his Father. David was developing opinions on how the farm was run, he was increasingly making suggestions to Steve and getting frustrated when he didn't get his own way. Steve laughed out loud one morning when shaving. Jan could hear him from the bedroom and asked what was so funny. When Steve came out of the bathroom, he explained that he had only just realised how similar his situation with David was with his own Father. He smiled as he said it was time to take David for a pint at the Red Lion! Jan laughed with him; it was another example of that so called 'cycle of life' she said, how funny that situations recur.

And so, the subject of stress came up in conversation time and time again as the four friends progressed through their fifties. But there was another form of stress that came up, infrequent and unwelcomed, it was the emotional stress of death. In particular, it was the way the four friends coped with the demise of their parents. It had started first with Tony's Dad and then Steve's Father; in both those cases the four friends had realised how important it was to be able to open up and talk to each other about it.

The death of Paul's Dad was sudden, a short illness. He was taken to hospital but died suddenly of heart failure.

It was a big shock to Paul's Mum and of course to Paul and his brothers. The service at the Crematorium had gone well, the reception afterwards was held in Paul and Jenny's hotel and there was plenty to drink and an excellent buffet. Although sudden and also a big shock as his death was there was, strangely, a positive outcome.

It was some days after the death when Paul met with his brothers for a pint in the Red Lion, not Paul's hotel. Paul and his brothers could relax. The subject of Paul's Dad's engineering business soon arose and Paul quickly expressed his thoughts that the business ownership should now be shared equally between his two brothers. The look on the brother's faces were of complete relief as Paul spoke. They explained to Paul that their Mum had been anxious that Paul should have a share. Paul said he thought that was a complete nonsense, that not only had he done nothing towards the business over the years and knew nothing about it but also, his hands were now completely tied up in the hotels. He just didn't have any time to help them even if it was needed!

It was an open and frank discussion; the air had been cleared between the brothers. It turned out that Paul's Dad had not made a specific provision for the business transfer in his Will. Although it took some months, the business was eventually, legally transferred to the two brothers. Paul's Mum was so relieved that a solution had been found amicably. It helped the family cope with the death of their Dad.

John's Mum and Dad died suddenly and tragically in a car accident. It was mid evening but dark. The car had been approaching a small river bridge down a country lane and had apparently collided with an oncoming lorry as it came over the bridge. The car had then careered out of control into one of the bridge walls and then spun down the bank and into the river below. The Police arrived very early the next morning at John's house, John was in an understandable state of complete shock. He was told that his parents just had no chance. The vehicle had been recovered from the river with his parents still inside. Their bodies were at rest in a local morgue, until the postmortem.

John broke down as the Police left and they closed the door. Susan held him. Their two teenage sons, Michael and Peter hugged their parents too. They all sobbed together. It wasn't just the shock of John's parents dying so suddenly, but it was just so tragic as well. It was in the Red Lion the following evening that John sat at a table in a corner with his three friends. It was one of the more macabre discussions they had ever had, John just needed to talk. He was still in a state of complete shock, he just couldn't come to terms with it. It would take a long time, but he really appreciated that he was able to express himself completely with his friends and discuss his feelings with them openly. When he got home, Susan sat up with him until the early hours. She could tell John's drink in the Red Lion had helped him. He could never come to terms with the shock but was now able to rationalise things more clearly.

Tony's Mum started to suffer from Dementia when Tony was in his mid-fifties. Initially it was just losing things, no real problem. Tony made sure a spare set of keys had been hidden in the garden. She had started to build quite a social life, not only the Women's Institute, but through her increasing network of friends found she was invited to coffee mornings and evening games of cards which involved supper and wine as well. Tony and Jackie were so pleased to see how her life had opened up as she developed her independence following the death of Tony's Dad.

It was as Tony was approaching sixty though that they noticed her dementia was getting worse, that they would need to visit and stay with her more often. When discussing this with his friends in the Red Lion they responded positively in part, commenting that Tony would be visiting them more frequently. Whilst he was discussing his Mum with his friends Tony told them how much benefit she got from the Women's Institute and tried to work up the idea with them, that there was a need for a Men's Institute too? The reaction he got to the idea was at best cool with often short thrift replies saying, 'Us men just go to a Pub, don't we?' Tony could see the idea wasn't going to catch on readily, but his instinct told him not to give up, yet!

With the sixtieth birthday on the horizon, the four friends increasingly discussed the outward signs of getting older. The greying hair, the baldness, the wrinkles, the increased waistlines. These all came up for passing comment regularly, but in the form of friendly banter. There was never any serious criticism as they were all in the same boat! It was in those private moments, often in their bathrooms on their own, that they would look at themselves and sigh. Steve said that many times he had to look twice as he thought he saw his Father in the mirror.

Alongside the apparent deterioration in physical appearance the four friends realised their fitness and sporting abilities were deteriorating. It wasn't an easy thing to admit to. In fact, in one conversation, when Paul had been explaining the increased fitness programme he was planning, Tony just asked, 'Why don't you just grow old gracefully?' This prompted a wide ranging discussion. Why couldn't they all just accept the fact that they were growing older and less able? John and Steve spoke about the enjoyment they were getting from regular tennis, but Paul wondered if that pushed them enough physically. It was John who suggested it was the basic male instincts of provision and protection that were driving the need to remain fit and to be competitive. The others all agreed.

In other discussions the tone became even more serious. They had been talking about how the ageing process made them often feel fed up and maybe even depressed. They'd talked about the Mid Life Crisis being the time in their lives when they had finally realised they were ageing, that thereafter they were in the Male Menopause, a long process in which each of them were trying to recognise their physical and consequent mental deterioration and how each of them were finding ways to cope. It was at this point they recalled the expression, 'There's no such thing as the Male Menopause,' and smiled in reflection.

A longer discussion took place when Steve recalled his farming friend who had died by suicide after a long period of increasing depression. 'It's often made me think,' said Steve, 'that our friendship is so important, the fact that we can discuss anything amongst ourselves at any time and just get it off our chests, way before it builds up into something serious.' The others all quietly nodded. Tony added how lucky he thought they were, but for those men who didn't have the friendships they had, then surely Men's Institutes would be a good idea. The others groaned quietly to themselves but were starting to see where Tony was coming from.

There was a further ageing condition, dementia. Initially it was Tony who had spoken about the concerns for his Mum and her increasing forgetfulness and misunderstanding things. Over a period of time, Steve realised his Mother was getting more forgetful as well, he was having to repeat conversations to ensure she had understood. Both ladies were elderly, in their mid-eighties but physically well. One day, to lighten the discussion about dementia, Steve asked the others if they had heard the story about the Battle of Waterloo?

The responses from the others were wary, they realised one of Steve's dodgy stories was coming up and resigned themselves to the fact they would have to listen. 'Well,' began Steve, 'As you probably all know, it was Sunday the 18 June 1815, the Duke of Wellington was in command.'

Steve went on the explain that as the Duke of Wellington saw the enemy ranks split and retreat, he sent the order, 'Send reinforcements, we're going to advance!' The Duke's order was passed back through various levels of command until it got to the Captain of the reinforcements but by then the order came over as, 'Send three and fourpence, we're going to a dance!'

The story itself wasn't that good, but it was the way Steve told it with such enthusiasm that made them all laugh. The main outcome though was that in any future discussions about dementia and the elderly ladies, they would refer to it as a 'Battle of Waterloo' moment. What the four friends didn't appreciate though was that there would soon be a few 'Battle' moments for themselves!

It was twelve months before their sixtieth birthday that the four friends started to talk about how they might celebrate. After several pints and with various options discussed, they agreed on two things. One was a long weekend away or the 'boys hiking, walking, drinking trip'. There was an overwhelming feeling they should return to Wales. The breakfasts were fondly remembered alongside the Red Dragon pub which remained as their second favourite pub.

The second thing was to arrange a joint party. Steve readily offered the use of one of the barns. They agreed to rent caterers to provide all the food and a late bar which was to run through to the early hours and when the disco closed. The caterers would erect a catering tent alongside the barn. There was plenty of parking in the fields alongside the barns and farmyard. They anticipated a large number of guests!

The walk was arranged first, for late July and the party to be held nearly three months later, in mid-September, to avoid the peak harvesting times on the farm. The walk proved to be a big disappointment for the four friends. When they arrived at the Bed and Breakfast, they were initially all taken away by the views again and said that nothing seemed to have changed in the fifteen years since they were last there. But when they walked through the front door, they realised the couple who used to run it had retired, there were now new owners. They weren't greeted in the same friendly way that they had by the previous owners and also there was no packed lunch. The new owners suggested they might try the convenience store in the village.

The walk that day was superb though, a sunny day, warm with a strong breeze. It completely met their expectations. But the Red Dragon that evening was very disappointing. The pub was not busy, the beer and food were really 'second rate' as Paul described it. It was John that night who made them all think when he asked if they saw things through 'Rose tinted glasses'.

His question caused all the others to think and to wonder if that applied to a lot of the other memories they discussed. They then really enjoyed going down 'memory lane' to question whether their recollections on all sorts of stories and memories were misplaced. Tony and John relived the moment Mrs Collier had caught them making up derivatives of her name. Even after all these years they still felt her anger, they were still frightened of her! They laughed and then Steve relived the Whoopee cushion moment with his Grandmother and that moment when he laughed out, but thankfully his Grandmother had laughed out as well, what a relief! With every story they recollected they assured themselves their memories weren't misplaced, that all these events had really happened and, as they had remembered them.

The memory lane conversations carried on with plenty of laughter the following day as they revisited the old slate quarries on the train. This cheered them up as the breakfast that morning had been nothing like the ones they had remembered. The walk around the quarry matched their expectations. They then felt they needed to revisit the Red Dragon that evening through some kind of loyalty, they supposed but sadly, found little change to the previous evening.

The final day, the detour to the beach, thankfully did meet their expectations. It was sunny and warm, they played football on the beach, ate some delicious vanilla ice cream and for lunch the fish and chips were just as good as they had remembered. Thank goodness! Yes, the final day made up a lot for their disappointments.

Whereas the trip to Wales had been largely disappointing to celebrate their sixtieth birthdays, the party at Steve's farm in mid September was in complete contrast. John said it was one of the best evenings of their lives. They had all invited their families and friends. Over the years the four friends had become well known in the area, there were lots of members of the rugby, football and tennis clubs along with most of the regulars from the Red Lion. Everyone turned up in a good party spirit and were looking forward to enjoying themselves. They weren't disappointed!

Looking back, there was no single event that caused the party to be so successful. It was just one of those evenings where everything seemed to happen with plenty of 'buzz' and there was a very happy atmosphere. Everyone mixed well, many knew each other and were catching up with each other's news, the food and drink (supplied by the Red Lion) was superb, the music and dancing went on all night, the speeches were short, another large birthday cake appeared and the four friends blew out all the candles.

It was two o'clock in the morning before they knew it. It was Tony who spoke to Steve at around that time, his voice loud and raised above the music. 'Great party!' he said and looking at Steve said, 'We've made it, we're actually sixty!' Steve laughed with him and they clinked their glasses but then Tony looked at him and in a more serious tone he said that he had been thinking. Steve frowned as Tony continued and said, 'It's nearly time for us to retire, what shall we do?' The question was then lost in the happy melee of the party, the question would recur however in a few days' time.

The four friends had been photographed together with pints in hand just after midnight. The photo showed four beaming smiles and due to the drink, they clearly needed to hold onto each other for support!

The photograph caught the moment and would be circulated widely after the party; four friends, more than happy in each other's company and always there to support each other. True friendship!

CHAPTER 14

DETACHMENT PHASE
(60 – 80+ YEARS OLD)
Men reflecting

IT WAS THE following Friday afternoon; Tony was driving to visit his Mum again with Jackie. They were on their own in the car as their boys were both away, studying at University. Tony felt good, just so relaxed and happy.

He had been thinking. His mind went back to that moment at the party when he had celebrated with Steve, the moment of realisation that they were actually sixty! It hadn't really occurred to him before, he had always thought of himself as young and fit. Now it dawned on him that he wasn't so young anymore!

Since that moment he had thought regularly about retirement. It had only been a passing thought in his mind before as he had always been so focussed on his work and his family. He hadn't discussed retirement with Jackie, they had just been getting on with their lives. As they drove along that morning Tony suddenly had an idea and turning towards Jackie he said, 'Have I told you about Project Tanzania?' Jackie was surprised and puzzled; the question had come out of the blue. Just what was Tony talking about? She cautiously said, 'No,' Tony smiled and then carried on and explained that Project Tanzania was a plan for them to sell up their house and all their investments, to retire from the retail business and to buy a farm in Tanzania and spend the rest of their lives there.

Jackie was shocked. She had never heard Tony talk about this before, what on earth had caused him to come up with this idea? It was just so wrong; they would be miles away from their boys and their friends. Also, what was it like to live in Tanzania, in fact where was it? And also, why run a farm. They had no experience of farming, it would be so physically demanding when they should really be retiring. The more she thought about what Tony had said the more alarmed she became. Her response was therefore somewhat agitated, she could not disguise her concerns as she said, 'What on earth are you talking about?!' She then set out her immediate thoughts about why it was a bad idea and felt herself feeling almost angry. But it was in that moment, as she glanced at Tony she realised he was smiling. Had Tony been teasing her?

Jackie still felt agitated and a little angry when Tony said he was teasing her but then added there was a serious intent. He certainly had Jackie's full attention as he started to explain.

First, Tony set out to assure Jackie there was no way he would really wish to buy a farm in Tanzania and spend the rest of his life there, away from his friends and family and working hard. He then explained that 'Project Tanzania' was just a concept, an idea for them to work on. Jackie still looked puzzled, though a little less concerned. Tony continued and said, 'Ok, if we're not going to buy a farm and live in Tanzania what are we going to do?' Jackie started then to understand and as Steve added that they had no plans for their retirement, that reaching sixty had made him think and that they should surely start to make some plans? At this point Jackie laughed, it was mainly relief but also the realisation that Tony was right. In fact, this was something to look forward to!

They carried on talking in the car. 'Project Tanzania' started to take shape. It was in part contingent upon what they thought their two sons might do with their lives and where they might live. Alongside that, they discussed Tony's Mum and Jackie's parents. The other part of their conversation dwelled on things they wanted to do, where they might live, would they travel? Also, would they take more interest in walking, reading, gardening and as they spoke the list of activities grew causing them to think they had better start to take this Project Tanzania more seriously. They realised that they needed a plan but the plan, as such, would change over time as their unknown circumstances became known. Before they knew it, they had arrived at Tony's Mum's house. Tony leant over towards Jackie, kissed her and simply asked, 'To be continued?' Jackie smiled and just said 'Project Tanzania!'

The rest of the day was spent with Tony's Mum. It was clear the dementia was getting worse; she could not hear very well and kept either forgetting things or misunderstanding conversations. She was getting thinner and quite frail and no longer walked with confidence. Tony was upset to see the deterioration in his Mum as she was fiercely independent and proud and had coped so well after the death of Tony's Dad. It was Jackie who really caught Tony's concern and quietly said she thought they should think carefully about her safety, that there was increasing danger she might fall or burn herself on the cooker or one of the fires.

Tony and Jackie helped with a lot of domestic chores and then, early evening, they prepared and ate a meal with his Mum and settled her in the lounge watching the television. She was happy. Tony and Jackie set off to the Red Lion.

Their friends were in a buoyant mood. It was only a week after the successful sixtieth birthday party and there were plenty of happy memories to recall. It had been a great party! The stories continued happily until Paul said, 'We're now sixty!' and they all raised their glasses saying, 'Cheers!' As they put their glasses down, Paul simply added, 'What next?' They were all surprised when Jackie blurted out, 'Project Tanzania!' What on earth was she talking about they all wondered?

With all eyes upon her Jackie realised she needed to explain. She outlined the conversation that she and Tony had shared that morning in the car and how Tony had shocked and teased her. She then went on to say that actually Tony was right, they didn't have any plans for retirement, but they realised it would be a good idea to start talking about them.

The others all readily agreed. Tony was frowned upon for teasing Jackie, but the term 'Project Tanzania' stuck as they all started to talk about their ideas and plans for retirement. Tony said, 'It's all about adventure before dementia.' He didn't for one moment know how prophetic that was.

John and Susan had the most developed plans. It was because they were both teachers and could retire on a final salary scheme, which provided a guaranteed income after their retirement. John and Susan explained they had discussed retirement a lot recently. With both their sons now living away from home in fulltime careers and with partners, they now wanted to focus on travel whilst they were still healthy enough to do so. It was clear when Susan started to list New Zealand, Australia, Thailand, Vietnam, India and South America that it was more than just a 'pipe dream'. They were actively planning.

Steve and Paul were in similar situations. They both wanted to hand over their businesses to their children and then make sure they put their 'retirement funds to good use'. Steve laughed at himself saying that he really realised now how his Father must have felt, it was so difficult to let go! He and David, his eldest son, went regularly to the Red Lion just to talk and clear the air. Steve laughed at himself saying that he should really stop worrying and just let go. Jan nodded and smiled. Paul and Jenny had taken steps to appoint both their daughters, Emily and Jane, as 'Senior House Managers' at each hotel. They had been surprised how much both daughters seemed to enjoy the responsibility and had almost got to a stage of telling Paul and Jenny to back off and leave them to run the day to day activities.

As Tony and Jackie listened to the others, they realised they had probably been the least diligent in planning for retirement. The conversations with their friends had certainly been revealing and useful. It was time to reflect and make some plans they said. Tony raised his glass and said, 'To Project Tanzania,' The others all smiled and clinked their glasses. It was then Paul who asked, 'How does all this retirement planning fit into our discussions about the Male Menopause then?'

His question sparked a good discussion. Tony responded to Paul saying, 'It's back to those basic instincts of us males.' The others listened as Tony carried on, 'You know, protection and provision. In the case of retirement, us males can see the end of the cycle of life ahead of us, so we are trying to protect ourselves and our wives. We are trying to provide safety and comfort when we realise, we are getting weaker and more susceptible to dangerous occurrences. We are just working with our basic instinct to survive for as long as we can'.

Steve shook his head in disagreement and said, 'No, all these conversations about the theory of the Male Menopause just get too complex. All it's about really, is to have some blooming good holidays!' The others all laughed with Steve but then he added, 'Anyway, the Male Menopause just doesn't exist you know? Even our National Health Service, the NHS, doesn't recognise it!'

John then commented quietly saying Steve wasn't quite right and explained that the NHS had come up with a new name. 'Do you remember that NHS leaflet I read out to you beside that lake in Wales? The NHS now call it the 'Andropause,' he said. He then went on to say that as far as he could see the NHS just wanted to distinguish that the male ageing process was different to the female one, that the female process was primarily physical whereas the male process was more psychological. 'That's an oversimplification,' John added, but then commented that at least the NHS were starting to recognise ageing in males and there were even signs of medication emerging to ease the process he said and smiled.

Steve then huffed saying that this so called 'Andropause' was just a play on words, 'It's time society recognised we males get older. In fact, we should be able to look forward to more benefits and support as we get older!' he added.

It was at this stage that the girls started talking about the female menopause. They had all started to be aware of their physical changes and reflected on stories about some of their friends and the difficult times had been through and some were still experiencing. As they spoke, they compared the female and male experiences. Should the male condition be called the 'Male Menopause?'. There was no real conclusion as they all realised it was a discussion that was likely to recur in the years ahead.

The discussions about the Male Menopause carried on as they progressed through their sixties. Their lives were changing in so many ways. Of particular interest to all of them was the progress all their children were making in their lives. There were so many things happening to them in their careers and also in their social and domestic lives.

After schooling and then further education they had been getting into serious relationships with partners and then some were getting married.

After that grandchildren were arriving! The four friends now found they were being called up for babysitting duties again. This was so enjoyable! The grandchildren were great fun, they developed so quickly and in so many ways. It was strange as they found they felt even more responsibility for their grandchildren than they had for their children! Through discussion they realised this was because the grandchildren weren't their children, they were someone else's and extra care needed to be taken! In turn this discussion caused them to reflect on their protection and provision instincts and to ponder that these instincts were even stronger now in their roles as grandparents!

Whilst the grandchildren were developing, their great grandparents were deteriorating. Tony and Jackie realised his Mum was increasingly at risk and getting lonely at home on her own. They realised she should go to an old people's rest home where she would be safer and perhaps happier in the daily company of other, older people.

Tony's Mum was initially resistant, but after they visited some homes with her, she saw the benefits and a move was eventually arranged. Soon after moving, Tony's Mum deteriorated further. The dementia seemed to get worse. Tony was concerned the move to a new environment may have accelerated this. She also became thinner and frailer. This was a surprise because the meals at the rest home were regular and she ate well but she just seemed to be getting weaker. She initially used a stick for walking assistance and then found a frame helped her as it gave her more stability and confidence.

Tony was really concerned when, after about twelve months, he visited her. They were drinking tea and talking. As the conversation progressed, Tony realised his Mum was talking in an abstract way and not really recognising him. He spoke to the staff at the rest home who told him this was a common occurrence in the ageing process. Tony just couldn't believe that his own Mum could not recognise him and was very upset. Jackie tried to console him when they met later that day. The deterioration continued over the next few months.

Around twelve months later she died. Tony had mixed feelings; he was very sad she had died and yet, on the other hand, he felt it was the right time for her.

Tony discussed his feelings with his three friends in the Red Lion. They were very sympathetic as they had experienced similar feelings and situations in their own families. It wasn't easy, the long process of deterioration and slowly slipping into death somehow seemed undignified. As they talked more, they discussed the male instincts to protect and provide. They realised that in the case of death that sometimes, you just have to accept that nothing can be done; it is frustrating. It was so good to talk, Tony realised again as they spoke how much he welcomed the support of his friends.

Within a month of Tony's Mum's death, Steve's Mother died also. She died in her sleep in her bed, similar to the way Steve's Father had died. Steve was again shocked as his Mother had appeared so well just the day before and there was no sign of any problem. Jan consoled Steve but he just sat in their kitchen looking at the floor, unable to accept the news. Time was needed. Steve was normally so outgoing, sociable, and even extrovert. Not now. He was a complete contrast and felt so depressed. He hadn't expected it and was in shock.

Tony's Mum's funeral took place a few days before Steve's Mother's. Steve went to Tony's Mum's funeral to support Tony and it was this that strangely lifted him. It was when he realised and reconciled the long and difficult illness of Tony's Mum in contrast to the shock of his Mother's

311

sudden death. With these comparisons in Steve's mind, he realised both situations were hard to deal with, but it really brought home the need to ensure that the most was made of every living day and then at death, it was so important to celebrate life. Steve smiled as he thought these things through and realised that over the last few days, he had felt depressed.

Jan noticed the change in Steve after the service. She was relieved to see he seemed more alert; she sensed the 'sparkle' in him was starting to return. As they stood at the church doorway she looked up to Steve and smiled. He smiled back and bent down to kiss her. Later Steve found he could talk to Jan and he simply apologised. He then spoke about the last few days, how shocked he'd been with his Mother's sudden death. He realised he had been depressed and down in spirits, but he now realised he needed to celebrate his Mother's life, as life is a gift. Jan smiled and hugged his arm. She didn't say anything, nothing needed to be said.

In the Red Lion later, Tony spoke again about the anguish he had been through with his Mum's long illness. His friends listened and commiserated. They then offered sympathies and best wishes to Steve for his Mother's funeral in a few days' time. Steve smiled in acknowledgement but chose to say little. He felt much better now. He didn't want to distract the discussion away from Tony's Mum and he was pleased as the conversation focused back onto Tony and his family. There were a lot of happy memories and a lot of Tony's family and friends had joined them to celebrate and share those memories. Tony's Mum, they said, would have enjoyed the day, it was a happy occasion.

Steve's Mother's funeral was a few days later. Steve found he was composed and although he realised, he would never get over the shock of her sudden death he wanted now to celebrate her life. The service was good, David did the eulogy and Steve was so proud. As his son spoke, he captured Steve's Mother's life in such a way that they could all reflect and recall what a great life she had led, a wife, mother, grandmother and more recently a great grandmother.

Steve's Mother had asked to be cremated and her ashes to be buried under the tree in the farmyard where Steve's Father's had been buried some years before. After the church service everyone was invited back to the farm to celebrate as they had after Steve's Father's service. It was a happy occasion. Steve looked around him and reflected, he was so lucky to be alive, to enjoy celebrating with all his friends and family. He found comfort in just celebrating quietly and catching up with everyone's news and future plans.

As he and Jan chatted that evening in the privacy of their lounge, he spoke about the day and the various conversations he'd had. It was so good he said, to see how the cycle of life just keeps going. They were enjoying a late evening drink; they clinked their glasses and Steve leant forward to kiss Jan.

The two funerals affected the four friends as it really brought home their discussions and that they should now make the most of their retirements and that every day was special! Project Tanzania (as they now referred to it) cropped up in discussion often. They would plan to visit many exotic places, but also realised that satisfaction and enjoyment could equally be found in the simple things in life, appreciating and enjoying their family and friends.

It was John and Susan who had started to travel first. They focused on the Far East and then Australia and New Zealand. The pictures and stories they brought back certainly inspired the others. Steve felt he had not travelled at all as running the farm had been a seven day a week operation, but now all the responsibilities had been happily passed over to David who was doing a good job.

Steve and Susan had initially booked several long weekend visits to capital cities in Europe. Paul and Jenny joined them on some as they had also passed all their day to day business responsibilities to their daughters. They really felt they could relax! They had a particularly great time in Paris. Paul and Steve had retold the Charles de Gaulle story about happiness that Paul's Rugby coach had told him all those years ago. It still caused them to laugh. Jan and Susan had heard it so many times, it just made their eyes roll and they smiled. Happy days indeed.

Tony and Jackie also travelled. Tony had successful retired from the retail business and received a lot of money for his shares. Jackie had retired at the same time. They chose initially to go on expensive cruising holidays in the Mediterranean, the Canaries and then in the Baltic sea. They had enjoyed the luxury, the meals and the entertainment. There was plenty of time to rest and reflect.

And so all four friends were now fully retired and recalling Tony's advice, 'Adventure before Dementia,' they made sure they followed it! However, the process of retirement had not been easy for any of them. They had often discussed the strange experience of not feeling responsible, not having to do anything. Just sitting, relaxing, chatting made them feel almost guilty! New hobbies emerged, all four of them had joined the local golf club together but none of them did very well. They realised they still needed sport, to remain competitive.

John and Steve continued to play tennis until they were nearly seventy. They played at a reasonable Club standard but also enjoyed a good beer in the Clubhouse afterwards. The post competition banter with their tennis companions was always good. Tony bought an open top red sports car. His friends teased him suggesting he was trying to recover his youth. Tony realised they might be right, but he just enjoyed the thrill of open top driving so much. He also thought there was good practical justification as they needed to travel regularly to see their friends. Jackie had smiled wryly as she heard his justification and suggested he could have bought a standard saloon car. Tony frowned; he knew she was right.

All four couples enjoyed walking and went on regular hikes often involving a pub for lunch. It was something they could all do together, and they also realised there were so many nice places to visit locally with no extensive travel involved. Gardening was popular and they would often discuss their most recent gardening projects when they met. The girls also developed other interests; they all joined 'keep fit' classes and Jenny and Susan joined the local choir.

As they progressed through their late sixties and realising, they were approaching their seventies, the four friends found they were becoming both physically and mentally less able and were generally less active, they were more ponderous. The great thing was that they could talk about it and even make fun of each other.

On one occasion in the Red Lion, whilst the four friends were enjoying a quiet pint, John laughed at himself and started talking about his weekly routines. Every Saturday morning at nine o'clock precisely he had to wind up their five clocks, two were grandfather clocks. John reflected with his friends, asking if it was because he just needed a regular routine, a purpose in life? The others smiled and then admitted they too have developed regular routines. Paul confessed he cleaned their two cars every Sunday morning and that he and Jenny went shopping every Friday morning. They just felt they needed some structure in their lives and it was becoming almost imperative that these jobs were completed on a certain day, at a certain time each week.

Steve and Tony also had regular routines and laughed as they too 'confessed'. Tony asked if this behaviour was part of the Male Menopause and in the discussion that followed, they generally realised that it was, that it went back to those basic provision and protection instincts and that they all needed routine and structure to give some purpose and direction to their lives. Tony smiled as he said, 'Relaxing all day is just fine but it can be a tad boring too can't it?' The others all agreed.

It was at this point Tony that raised his idea again that there should be Men's Institutes, a place where men could mix and integrate, share ideas on new hobbies and interests. 'As I've said before,' he said, 'Men are just expected to cope and get on with things. The problem is that many men just isolate themselves when actually they need to mix more and exchange ideas!'

Over the years when Tony had raised this subject, the others just raised their eyebrows and hoped he would change the subject. Now, with the experiences of retiring, of changing from active working to a period of relaxation, they could see Tony might have a point, it might be a good idea.

As they talked more, they referred to the discussion about the Male Menopause. They felt it was more of a mental ageing process and that closer integration and contact with other males might help. The thread of the conversation was lost again at that point as they realised, they needed to order another pint.

The discussions about ageing and the Male Menopause continued as they progressed into their early seventies. Significantly dementia started to occur more frequently along with increasing hearing difficulties. The four friends continued to enjoy each other's company and realised humour was vital. The ability to laugh at each other without causing offence was key. Tony's sons started to give him a lift to the Red Lion, even though it was a fairly long drive, they realised how important it was that their Dad should still meet his friends.

It was when they reached their mid-seventies that something unexpected happened. For some reason it had not cropped up in their conversations, nor had it not been anticipated.

Paul died.

THE FINALE

Review life

The rain was falling, it was cold. John was wearing a large blue overcoat. He was standing beside his lifelong friends, Tony and Steve. They were both feeling cold too, and sad. All three men were standing in the church graveyard beside the freshly dug grave of their lifelong friend Paul.

The service had been good; the vicar had not rushed the proceedings. The chapel had been packed with Paul's family and friends. Tony had given an excellent eulogy causing John to think a lot about Paul and how much they would miss him.

There were just so many memories. They had first met at Primary School. Paul had always advocated you should live life to the full and, 'Make the most of every day' was something he was renowned for saying. John hadn't agreed with everything Paul had said, but that's what good friends are for. The ability to discuss and argue things that we believe in is so important in any good friendship.

John smiled as he reflected further and thought more about Paul; he particularly recalled Paul's interest in the 'Male Menopause.' All four friends had discussed and debated the issue so often. It was not medically recognised, yet it was a condition that so obviously needed to be acknowledged. 'There is no such thing as the Male Menopause' was one of the main things Paul often said and would be remembered for; they certainly knew and understood much more than when they had all been younger.

John smiled to himself as he recalled those early years and everything that had happened since to all four of them.

The reception was arranged back at Paul's hotel. Jenny and her two daughters welcomed everyone. They were clearly and understandably upset. Paul had died so suddenly; it was a complete shock. It was not surprising that the reception was packed. He was well known locally as a successful hotelier and a business leader in the community. Everyone was shocked.

Food and drink were available in abundance and the room was full of laughter and conversation as guests recalled their happy memories of Paul. Steve, Tony and John were sat at a table on one side of the room and beers had been brought over for them. The problem was they just couldn't hear each other. Steve managed to find David and suggested they should slip away to the quietness of the Red Lion. Tony and John readily agreed.

Fifteen minutes later the three friends were sat at a table in the bar in the Red Lion with pints. The pub was quiet so they could now hear each other! David returned to the hotel and said he would let their wives know where they were and would come back anyway in two hours to give them a lift home.

The conversation started. They had all been shocked by Paul's sudden death, none of them had seen it coming and had thought Paul looked so fit and well. They all said that they still couldn't believe he had died. It was strange and almost as if they expected him to walk into the room at any moment.

The conversation flowed. There were so many memories to recall and they could hear each other clearly. The barmaid kept coming over to ask if they wanted their pints refilling. They smiled as they recalled the first day they met at school, then Mrs Collier and the 'Collywobbles' stories tumbled out, particularly the sponge cake and caning incidents. Then the progression through senior school to Universities, working lives, meeting wives, children and then grandchildren. There were so many happy memories and the three friends laughed so much as the conversation developed and they enjoyed each other's company.

They then recalled their discussions about the Male Menopause. They believed it occurred at and around the so called Mid Life Crisis, at the start of the ageing process, and developed from there. They further discussed the idea that the Male Menopause was linked to the basic instincts of their forefathers or cave men, the need to Protect, Provide and Procreate.

They believed that all modern day men's behaviours can be traced back or associated with those origins. There was just one serious moment, it was Tony who recalled that one of the things he remembered about Paul was when he said that although the Male Menopause was not exactly 'medically recognised' it should be at least 'socially recognised'. Tony raised his glass saying that Paul had really made him think when he had said this. As the glasses clinked, they all said 'Paul.'

A few minutes later David arrived and gave Tony and Steve a lift back to the hotel. John said he would prefer to walk home as it wasn't far. They shook hands and wished each other well. None of them knew that would be the last time they would meet.

It was only a few weeks late that Tony's dementia became much worse. Jackie found she couldn't cope with him at home, and he ended up living in a care home, just like his mother had done. He died two years after moving to the care home. Steve died at the same time. His death was sudden, just like his Mother's. There had been no sign of ill health the night before he died, and his family were all deeply shocked.

John didn't know that he wouldn't be meeting his friends again. He finished his pint in the Red Lion and as he put the glass down, he simply smiled and said to himself, 'There's no such thing as the Male Menopause.'

But …

… but that's not true. Is it? (see below!) …

… your thoughts and ideas are much welcomed! Please visit https://www.parkhousepublishing.co.uk

And let us know your thoughts? Thank you!

Printed in Great Britain
by Amazon